FACTORY PHYSICS FOR MANAGERS

FACTORY PHYSICS FOR MANAGERS

How Leaders Improve Performance in a Post–Lean Six Sigma World

Edward S. Pound • Jeffrey H. Bell • Mark L. Spearman

New York   Chicago   San Francisco   Athens   London   Madrid
Mexico City   Milan   New Delhi   Singapore   Sydney   Toronto

3 4 5 6 7 8 9 10   LCR   21 20 19 18 17 16

ISBN: 978-0-07-182250-3
MHID: 0-07-182250-X

e-ISBN: 978-0-07-182261-9
e-MHID: 0-07-182261-5

Factory Physics® and LeanPhysics® are registered trademarks of Factory Physics Inc.

Library of Congress Cataloging-in-Publication Data

Pound, Edward S.
  Factory physics for managers : how leaders improve performance in a post-lean six sigma world / by Edward S. Pound and Jeffrey H. Bell, Mark L. Spearman.
     pages cm
  ISBN-13: 978-0-07-182250-3 (hardback)
  ISBN-10: 0-07-182250-X
  1. Production management. 2. Factory management. I. Bell, Jeffrey H. II. Spearman, Mark L. III. Title.
  TS155.P59 2014
  658.5—dc23

                                                                    2013046378

McGraw-Hill Education books are available at special quantity discounts to use as premiums and sales promotions, or for use in corporate training programs. To contact a representative, please visit the Contact Us page at www.mhprofessional.com.

To Meg, my one and only, Zachary, Madeline,
and Audrey—epiphanies to me. Every breath is a blessing.
May the Peace of Christ that passes all understanding keep your hearts
and minds in the knowledge and love of God.
—Edward S. Pound

To my wife, Julia; my parents; and the team at Arc Precision.
—Jeffrey H. Bell

To my wife, Blair, who for thirty years now has picked me up when I was
low, has kept me humble when I was haughty, and has loved me always.
And to my children, who have blessed me and taught me more than I have
taught them: Jacob, William, and Rebekah; and to my grandchildren, a
wonderful blessing, Alana, and Jake. And to the only wise God be glory
forevermore through Jesus Christ! Amen.
—Mark L. Spearman

Contents

FACTORY PHYSICS FOR MANAGERS

Prologue

THE BOOK IN BRIEF

How can executives and managers of manufacturing and supply-chain companies predictably achieve high cash flow, low cost, and excellent customer service? This book describes how forward-thinking managers use Factory Physics science to cut through the clutter and confusion of competing options. Typical management efforts currently lack any comprehensive, practical science and are almost always hit or miss. Managers commonly move from one initiative one year, such as "Reduce inventory!" to another the next year, such as "Improve customer service!" because they don't have a practical understanding of the underlying natural behavior of the operations they are trying to manage. Meanwhile, software companies are ever touting the next big initiative in software, such as materials requirements planning (MRP), enterprise resources planning (ERP), advanced planning and optimization (APO), cloud computing, and big data, to chronologically name a few, as if more advanced technology is the solution to whatever ails a company. Using *Factory Physics for Managers*, leaders will advance management practice and performance because Factory Physics science objectively describes what will work for them and what will not. The practical Factory Physics approach helps managers decide whether and when to use the excellent Lean, Six Sigma, and Theory of Constraints operations tools to drive company business strategy implementation while predictably and repeatedly achieving their business goals. Managers innovatively use Factory Physics science to drive higher performance using existing ERP or legacy information technology (IT)—no major IT investments required.

With *Factory Physics for Managers*, Ed Pound and Jeff Bell, executives each with over 20 years of experience in operations, and Dr. Mark Spearman, with over 30 years of experience in research and consulting and coauthor with Wallace Hopp of the world-renowned, award-winning textbook *Factory Physics* (Long Grove, IL: Waveland Press, 2008), describe the manufacturing and supply-chain management summit: a comprehensive, practical, and scientific approach to managing manufacturing and supply-chain operations. This approach directly addresses the inherent variability and risk in business. Typically, executives apply some bundle of popular initiatives, mathematics, and software—the results are unpredictable and often disappointing. This book provides a fundamental science in a very practical framework that will immediately improve executives' and managers' intuition, change how they view their world, and enable them to lead their organizations much more effectively.

WHY IS THIS BOOK NEEDED?

There is widespread confusion about what works and what doesn't work in manufacturing and supply-chain operations. As a result, operations strategies and plans often do not achieve what they promise. Software companies sell applications that just perpetuate what clients already do—regardless of whether or not the software does what the client needs. Lean proponents promote the Toyota Production System and its tenets in the vein of an operations theology. Six Sigma proponents insist on the rigorous statistical analysis required to identify and root out variability. Theory-of-Constraint adherents continue to focus exclusively on bottlenecks. In response to the uneven success of these efforts, Lean and Six Sigma proponents simply concatenate those two initiatives (Lean Six Sigma) in a continuing search for a comprehensive solution to achieve business results. Meanwhile, the academic community, and industrial engineering in particular, has lost its way. Many curricula teach the Lean and Six Sigma approaches but are following industry rather than leading. All this creates enormous confusion. What are executives or managers of manufacturing, service, or supply-chain companies to do in determining how to best lead their companies to achieve marketing and financial goals?

Wally Hopp and Mark Spearman, both with degrees in physics, had a firm grounding in the scientific method when they started as assistant professors in industrial engineering at Northwestern University in the 1980s. They surveyed the state of the field and wondered about a basic applied science and mathematical framework to describe operations. Most of the field was too deep and technical—operations research—or too unstructured and smacking of folklore—continuous-improvement zealotry—to be of good, sustainable use to manufacturing, service, and supply-chain executives. They set out to describe a fundamental, practical science of operations in a manner that would be useful to executives leading operations in support of a business's marketing and financial goals. One executive attending a nascent training session observed, "This is like physics of the factory," and the name Factory Physics stuck.

Messrs. Bell and Pound were students of Spearman and Hopp in Northwestern's MMM program in the early 1990s when the book *Factory Physics* was written. In 2001, Dr. Spearman left academia and devoted his time exclusively to industry and perfecting the science in practice. The authors have applied the principles relentlessly in companies large and small and have advanced the science to elegant leadership practices—both simple and effective. The result is the Factory Physics framework.

This framework shows that vague strategies such as "Eliminate waste" and "Reduce variability" are so general as to be nearly useless—except for companies that have done little or nothing for operations improvement. In the case of companies just starting their journey to systematically improve performance, there's usually so much waste and variability that merely focusing an organization's attention on those issues will generate good results. Beyond initial efforts, limited practical understanding of the Factory Physics science of operations often produces tremendous wasted effort and uneven results. Sound Lean and Six Sigma methodologies are often misapplied. Moreover, most manufacturing and supply-chain operations have high complexity as a result of product mix, process intricacies, and demand variability. This complexity cannot be handled effectively with simple Lean techniques such as value-stream mapping or 5S. Using simple techniques to handle complexity is like paying a financial advisor to tell you to "buy low and sell high." In addition, how does copying another company's best practices provide a *unique* competitive advantage? While the Toyota Production System works very well for Toyota and similar operations, there are better approaches for running a chemical plant or a job shop.

The Factory Physics framework enables managers to calculate risk and act decisively. They make operational decisions that are tuned to and inform their company's business strategy to ensure success in operations leadership. The strength of the Factory Physics approach is that it is based in science. It is not "initiative by imitation" or something managers think they might try because a friend, or colleague, or an industry analyst said that it worked somewhere else. Executives and managers reading this book will be inoculated against the lull of bland slogans through an improved knowledge of operations behavior from the practical science learned. The book will explore that science in a plain and uncomplicated fashion. It will discuss some of the math behind the science at a basic level (those interested can refer to *Factory Physics* for a more mathematical discussion). *Factory Physics for Managers* will take the concepts and apply them to the task of designing and executing operations control to achieve a company's business goals. The closed-loop control approach described for operations strategy and execution is fundamentally different from most, if not all, contemporary approaches. It will fundamentally transform a company's information technology practices from transaction tracking "financial ERP" to an integrated control system connecting executive strategy to day-to-day execution. Additionally, the book addresses the change-management challenges that every executive faces. After reading this book, executives and managers will be much better prepared to lead. They will have much improved intuition and be able to apply practical science to translate business strategies into operations tactics and controls—tactics and controls that can be executed with confidence to achieve a company's marketing and financial goals.

CHAPTER 1

Science—Use It or Lose

There is nothing more practical than a good theory.

—Kurt Lewin

"Oh, that is just a theory!" When we hear this, it usually means that the speaker thinks that the theory in question is not true and not useful. Indeed, the word *theoretical* has come to mean an idea that is not practical. The U.S. National Academy of Sciences' definition of *theory*, however, addresses this issue:

> *The formal scientific definition of theory is quite different from the everyday meaning of the word. It refers to a comprehensive explanation of some aspect of nature that is supported by a vast body of evidence. Many scientific theories are so well established that no new evidence is likely to alter them substantially. For example, no new evidence will demonstrate that the Earth does not orbit around the sun (heliocentric theory). . . . One of the most useful properties of scientific theories is that they can be used to make predictions about natural events or phenomena that have not yet been observed.*[1]

Interestingly, almost everything people do is based on some kind of theory—most aspects of which are intuitive. People intuitively believe that the floor will remain solid when they walk on it—that is a theory. Drivers intuitively believe that the car will slow down when they hit the brakes—another theory. If the brakes are broken, the theory is wrong, and the consequences can be severe. As the U.S. Academy of Sciences says, "The most useful property of a theory is *the ability to make predictions about natural events . . . that have not yet been observed*" [emphasis added].

But not all theories are good. Some are simply false. For instance, the theory that the Sun moves around the Earth is not true; instead, it is the other way round. Other theories may be true but really tell us nothing. These are known as *tautologies*. For instance, "All time in a factory is either value-added time or non-value-added time." This is just as valid as the statement, "All time in a factory is either spent in the cafeteria or not spent in the cafeteria." Because the truth of the statement is contained in the statement itself, it tells us nothing about the real world.

OF THEORIES AND BUZZWORDS

There are many theories about production management. However, managers usually don't argue about theories per se because they do not want to sound too theoretical; instead, managers often argue about *buzzwords*. Merriam-Webster online defines a *buzzword* as "an important-sounding usually technical word or phrase often of little meaning used chiefly to impress laymen."

However, some truly remarkable innovations occurred at the beginning of the twentieth century, before buzzwords became common. *Mass production* was developed by Henry Ford. *Scientific management* was pioneered by Frederick Taylor and Frank and Lillian Gilbreth. And by the 1930s, *quality control* became important with the invention by Walter Shewhart of the control chart. Interestingly, many of these innovations morphed into buzzwords once the use of the computer began to take off in the 1960s. The first was as manufacturing requirements planning (MRP), followed quickly by the more encompassing manufacturing resources planning II (MRP II), business resources planning (BRP), and others. The 1980s introduced just in time (JIT), total quality management (TQM), business process reengineering (BPR), flexible manufacturing system (FMS), and a host of other three-letter acronyms (TLAs) (see Table 1-1). In the 1990s, a new TLA appeared: the all-encompassing enterprise resources planning (ERP) system. The 1990s also introduced two new buzzwords that were not TLAs and, given that they are still on the scene today, have had great endurance—*Lean* and *Six Sigma*. Indeed, given the success of Lean and Six Sigma, they are more like the historic initiatives of the early twentieth century than like the buzzwords of the 1980s and 1990s. What makes them different?

Lean took the best of JIT and combined it with practical methods such as value stream mapping (VSM) and 5S. Numerous "how-to-do-Lean" books made Lean more than a buzzword—it became a

TABLE 1-1. Examples of Three-Letter Acronyms

TLA	Full Phrase	Description
MRP	Materials Requirements Planning	Computer software for production planning and control
MRP II	Manufacturing Resources Planning	Next generation MRP
BRP	Business Requirements Planning	Another extended version of MRP
FMS	Flexible Manufacturing Systems	Highly automated production system that can switch to different products quickly
BPR	Business Process Reengineering	An approach for redesigning work processes
JIT	Just In time	A production management approach for quick delivery
TQM	Total Quality Management	Management approach to improve quality of products and processes

phenomenon. Today, Lean is being applied in everything from factories to offices and even hospitals; the participating organizations perform scores, if not hundreds, of *kaizen* events (improvement projects) each year.

The other methodology with staying power has been Six Sigma. A common saying before Six Sigma was "KISS—Keep it simple, stupid!" But Six Sigma dismissed this axiom, recognizing that manufacturing systems are anything but simple and sometimes require a more sophisticated approach. That Six Sigma unapologetically applies extremely sophisticated statistical methods shows how far management has moved from KISS. Like Lean, Six Sigma has become almost universal, with most companies having trained numerous *black belts* (a more captivating name than "statistics expert") and performing hundreds of Six Sigma projects each year. The fact that Lean Six Sigma is now being used by the U.S. Department of Defense and other government agencies indicates how ubiquitous it has become.

If you are looking for the next great buzzword, this book is not for you. If you are looking for a book that will tell you when and why Lean and Six Sigma work well as well as when and why they will not work, then read on. If you are looking for a book that allows you to understand the basic principles of production and supply chain so that you can design a management system that may or may not look like Toyota or Apple but is uniquely suited for *your* particular business environment, read on.

While we appreciate and strongly support the appropriate use of Lean and Six Sigma techniques, no matter the label, we have found that Lean and Six Sigma approaches do not provide a *comprehensive* theory for managers to use in charting a course for business performance. Additionally, there are some principles of Lean and Six Sigma theory that consider neither the reality of the business environment nor the natural behavior of production/inventory systems. Very often, Lean practitioners consider the Toyota production system with its focus on achieving one-piece flow as the *end* rather than as a *means* to the ultimate end which is long-term profitability. Likewise, Six Sigma will assert that all variability is "evil" and that it should always be as low as possible. History shows us that this is not always a good approach.

Compare the strategies of Henry Ford and Alfred P. Sloan. Ford produced a single model of automobile (Model T from 1908 to 1927) offered to the customer in "any color he wants so long as it is black."[2] Ford was a fanatic about driving variability out of production. In 1921, GM had been a distant second to Ford with 12.3 percent of the market compared to Ford's 55.7 percent. Sloan became president and CEO of GM in 1923 and set a goal to provide "a car for every purse and purpose" thereby greatly increasing the variability in the GM supply chain. But the strategy worked, and by 1929 GM had eclipsed Ford in the market, later becoming one of the largest corporations in the world.[3]

Unfortunately, the methods that enabled Sloan to create one of the world's largest corporations sowed the seeds of its own destruction. GM's centralized management and focus on finance made it appear profitable when it was not. Moreover, the strict requirement for a positive return on investment (ROI) prevented GM managers from seeing the need to implement changes that would be required to exist in a market that offered better cars for less money. In this case, the return on investment was necessary for survival. But after years of increasing profits and market share, hubris set in, and the question of survival was never raised.

Moreover, it is not because GM did not embrace Lean that it failed. Indeed, GM not only embraced Lean, but, in a somewhat ironic twist of fate, is listed as an example of "Lean Manufacturing and Environment" under the "Case Studies and Best Practices" web-site of the U.S. Environmental Protection Agency.[4] Nonetheless, on June 1, 2009, after almost 101 years, Alfred P. Sloan's GM ceased to exist. GM declared bankruptcy, and all shareholders were essen-tially wiped out. The new GM was owned by creditors, the largest being the U.S. government. Today, the "new" GM is back on its feet after the U.S. Treasury sold its last remaining shares in December 2013. Whether it withers or flourishes will depend on how well its management understands the underlying principles of automobile production and marketing.

One problem facing the new GM and most managers in any large corporation is a constant need for action. This need breeds new "ini-tiatives" whether they are appropriate or not and leads to a flurry of activity. The new activity often diverts attention from the fundamen-tal problems rotting a company's financial core. The Factory Physics approach avoids such activities by focusing only on those that are directly related to cash flow, customer service, and long-term profit-ability and by considering the tradeoffs among these.

Continuous improvement programs can be quite powerful, but simply having activities labeled as "continuous improvement" does not make a company successful. Next we consider one of the most successful (and long) continuous improvement programs in history—the Toyota production system. A scientific analysis of the Toyota production system provides a peek behind the curtains of folklore that have been laid over the secrets of Toyota's success.

TOYOTA AND SCIENCE

Toyota is the archetype of Lean. In the 1960s and 1970s, Toyota was a car company that competed by producing inexpensive cars. However, quality was not a strong point. In a 2007 article in *Automotive News*, Max Jamiesson, a Toyota executive in the 1970s and 1980s, provided the following assessment:

> *"Back then, the car was a piece of junk." When he left Ford Motor Co. for Toyota, his Detroit colleagues made jokes about Toyota being little more than recycled beer cans. They weren't far from wrong, Jamiesson admits.*
> *He recalls that Toyota engines back then would "grenade" at 50,000 miles, and the brake pedal would "fold into the floor." At high altitudes, Toyota carburetors needed to be propped open with Popsicle sticks,*

or the engine would starve from insufficient air-fuel delivery. But the exterior fit and finish was [sic] *good.*

"The outside of the car was like a show car," Jamiesson says. "All the lines and tolerances were perfect, so that when the salesman showed the car, it was beautiful. And the interiors were great, too. So we told Japan, 'This is great; it shows we can make a quality car. Now make the rest of the car like that.' The rest of the things need to function."[5]

From this inauspicious beginning, Toyota transformed itself into one of the most successful companies in the world and has offered one of the best-selling cars in America, the Camry, for nearly three decades. Those of us old enough may remember the saying from that earlier time, "Cheap stuff . . . made in Japan." Toyota played a huge role in changing that perception.

How Toyota Did It

So how did Toyota do it? One of the first things was to take a scientific approach and recognize that the manufacturing environment itself was not a static given but could be *changed*. Like Einstein, who rejected the notion of a fixed space and time, Taiichi Ohno and Shigeo Shingo rejected the notion that the mass-production practices of their day were the best practices possible. Instead of seeking to find the optimal lot size for a given setup time, they sought to reduce setup times until the optimal size was *one*! Indeed, "one-piece flow" became a hallmark of the Toyota Production System (TPS). This idea of focusing on the details of the environment was applied to such an extent that Toyota's 5S process for making an operation clean and organized became an important part of TPS implementation. Toyota recognized that controlling work in process (WIP) with supermarkets (i.e., *kanbans*) and measuring output (i.e., *takt* time) worked better than trying to control output with a schedule and measuring WIP. Toyota also recognized the precedence of quality before production. An operator could stop the line if bad parts were being produced. "If you do not have time to do it right the first time, when will you find time to do it over" is a pithy aphorism that hits at the heart of this concept (and the basic concept of Six Sigma as well). Finally, Toyota empowered its employees to redesign workplaces over and over again until they found the most efficient configuration for the given task.

While these steps sound simple, and perhaps even obvious in hindsight, it is important to realize that while Toyota was perfecting its production system, equally "obvious" and *opposite* steps were being pursued in the United States. Ohno began developing Toyota's system in the late 1940s and continued to perfect it into the 1970s. Thus, while Toyota considered *overproduction* to be a key waste, Detroit was happily pursuing mass production as the key to reducing costs. Long runs of millions of automobiles were produced by U.S. automakers in the belief that if the inventory did not sell when produced, it would eventually move when discounted at the end of the model year.

Given the results, it seems clear that although Ohno and Shingo never described the TPS in *scientific* terms, they understood the behavior of production systems at a very basic level. Shingo described practices in extremely poetic and flowery terms, for example, "The Toyota Production System wrings water out of towels that are already dry."[6] This description is catchy but difficult to implement.

Many managers read about the almost miraculous results obtained by Toyota and are eager to put in a similar system and reap the rewards. They are often disappointed when they cannot achieve the same results in a few months. What they do not realize is that Toyota perfected its system over a period of more than 25 years. Of course, with the plethora of Lean literature available, one should expect results more quickly than that. Even so, it is likely that the journey will require a sojourn through the desert before reaching the Promised Land. For instance, if the production environment produces poor-quality products, the line will stop quite frequently as a manager begins to implement the TPS practice of stopping the line whenever there is a defect. This means that a defect that causes a problem for one station in a 10-station assembly line stops the *entire line* for some period of time. This can amount to a great deal of downtime.

Obviously, any lost time to address quality problems must be made up. One way Toyota did this was to schedule 10 hours' production into a 12-hour time slot. In this way, an extra 2 hours were available, if needed, for stopping the line, and yet the line could nearly always achieve its daily requirement needed to meet demand. Stopping the line was not costless. Toyota paid for its quality focus by paying for more capacity than it actually used. In contemporary parlance, this is called "undercapacity scheduling."[7]

While this sounds like a great deal of extra time, a 2-hour makeup period for a 10-station line absorbs relatively few stoppages. If each station had only one problem per hour and this problem could be remedied, on average, in 1 minute, the time lost on a 10-station line would be 2 hours for every 12 hours of production. This is exactly the makeup period that was described in Schonberger's best-seller of the 1980s, *World Class Manufacturing* (New York: Free Press, 1986). Producing for 10 out of every 12 hours yields a capacity utilization of 83 percent. If one line could not meet demand working 83 percent of the time, another line or overtime (with all the attendant expenses) would be required. But Toyota recognized that by allowing line stoppages for quality problems, the tension created would motivate people to eliminate the root causes of the line stoppages and thereby require fewer shutdowns and less makeup time. For a company just beginning its Lean journey, we would expect to see more issues per hour, and most would take more than 1 minute to resolve. Thus 2 out of every 12 hours represented world-class performance, which is why Schonberger reported it in his book.

The other hallmark of the Toyota Production System, one-piece flow, also comes with a cost. While one-piece flow results in minimum WIP and minimum cycle time for a given output rate set by the *takt* time, it requires additional makeup time. (We use the term *cycle time* to indicate the time required to produce a part from raw stock until completion. Other authors may use cycle time to indicate the process time on a machine. We prefer to call this *process time* and recognize that other authors may use such terms as *production time*, *throughput time*, *flow time*, and even *sojourn time* to mean what we are calling *cycle time*.) Indeed, if one watches an automotive assembly line operate for any length of time, one will typically see workers complete their tasks and have time to stand back and wait for the next vehicle. Unlike the two extra hours of makeup time used to accommodate line stoppages as a result of quality defects, these few seconds of makeup time are used to accommodate the variation in the task times.

For example, suppose that the demand for the Camry is 600,000 units per 250-day year. This translates to 2,400 units per day or 1,200 units per 12-hour shift. For a manager scheduling the line to work 10 hours each shift, the *takt* time will be 30 seconds ([10 h × 3,600 s/h]/1,200 = 30 s). This means that the time available at each workstation is 30 seconds. However, if the line's manager adds enough workers to the line so that the *average* task time is 30 seconds, there will be trouble. If the average task time is equal to the *takt* time, a station worker will be able to complete the task within *takt* only 50 percent of the time. This means that as the line continues moving, the worker will have to continue working into the next workstation, thereby disrupting that worker's work.

There are two ways to avoid such problems: (1) stop the line every time a worker faces a task that takes longer than the average or (2) set the *takt* time to be somewhat longer than the average task time. Thus, in the first case, the line will move at the pace of the slowest worker and will stop from time to time. However, if a manager uses the second option and sets the *takt* time to be somewhat longer than the average, some extra time is allowed for each station, thereby providing a very regular output for the entire line.

Now consider the histogram of task times in Figure 1-1 showing the distribution of times for tasks on an assembly line. About 5 percent of tasks take less than 20 seconds, 45 percent take from 20 to 25 seconds, another 45 percent take from 25 to 30 seconds, and the last 5 percent take more than 30 seconds. The average is 25 seconds, and the standard deviation is 3 seconds. Therefore, if the *takt* time of the line were set to 30 seconds, 95 percent of tasks would be completed in the time allotted. The workers should be able to deal with the 5 percent of occurrences that take longer than 30 seconds as long as they do not all happen at the same time.

While 5 seconds does not sound like much, the extra time adds up. Moreover, performing a 25-second task in a 30-second *takt* time is equivalent to having an extra 2 hours available for each 10 hours

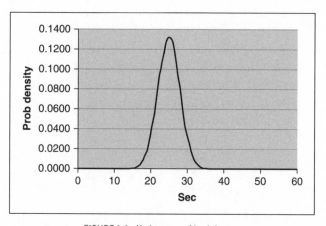

FIGURE 1-1. Histogram of task times

of production because 25/30 = 10/12 = 83.3 percent. And since managers commonly employ the first method for long disruptions and the second for variations in task times, this results in useful production time from less than 70 percent of the scheduled production time (0.833 × 0.833 = 0.694). This means that for a 12-hour shift, a manager gets around 8 hours and 20 minutes of productive time, not including lunches, breaks, and shift changes. In this case, if the manager scheduled workers to cover lunches and so on, the result would be around 1,200 parts produced per shift, the amount needed to cover demand.

Batch and Queue Production

On the other hand if a manager uses a different line control approach by decoupling the line and allowing WIP to flow freely and accumulate between processes, the system would run at the rate of the slowest process, that is, one part every 25 seconds (plus the extra minute once per hour). In this case, however, when one station had a problem, other stations could continue to run as long as there was WIP. Now, what about those disruptions? Recall the 10-station assembly line having, on average, a single 1-minute disruption per hour. Over a 12-hour period, this would add up to 2 hours of disruption time (2 h = 10 stations × 12 disruptions each × 1 h/60 min), and this is what was planned. However, if the stations of the line have been decoupled, each station only "sees" its own disruptions. The production time now would be 11 hours and 48 minutes (losing only 1 minute per hour per station), and the production rate would become around 1,700 parts every 12 hours. This means that the decoupled line produces 41 percent more than the line with one-piece flow.

But, again, there is a cost! The extra production was achieved by allowing a great deal of extra WIP above what would be required for one-piece flow. The extra WIP entails a longer cycle time to get through the line. The one-piece flow line takes 5 minutes to produce a part (10 stations with 30 seconds per station). If the decoupled line has 5 units of WIP for each station, the cycle time grows from 5 to 25 minutes. If the WIP required were 15 units, the cycle time would be 75 minutes. The problem with all this WIP is that it hides problems. The line can happily run *with* the problems, and there is no need (much less urgency) to eliminate them. Moreover, if bad parts start being produced at the first station and they are not discovered until the last station, then the line has just produced 150 units of *scrap* or *rework*. A line with such a high scrap (or rework) rate can easily end up with productivity levels below that for one-piece flow despite all its makeup time.

A Balanced Approach

Fortunately, one-piece-flow and unlimited WIP are not the only options. There is a middle way. If a manager limits the WIP at each station, the decoupled line's productivity is only *slightly* reduced while retaining the ability to quickly detect problems when they occur. What should this WIP limit be? As usual, "It depends!"

It depends on how much *variability* there is in the system. Variability will be an important concept in this book and will be discussed in more detail later. Any variability in production time or part quality will have a negative impact on productivity. This doesn't mean that all variability is bad—more on this later. However, a little extra WIP can greatly buffer variability, thereby increasing productivity without overtly increasing cycle times or substantially hampering defect detection. The key is to understand how throughput is related to WIP and variability—and this is one of the major insights of Factory Physics science.

THE TRACK RECORD: LEAN AND SIX SIGMA

While Lean and Six Sigma have seen tremendous success in reducing waste and improving profits in many companies, success is not always ensured. Indeed, a recent *Wall Street Journal* article indicated that 60 percent of Six Sigma projects did not yield the expected benefits.[8] The record for Lean is worse, with only 2 percent of projects achieving their anticipated results.[9] The low hit rate for Lean projects may be due, in part, to the huge number of *kaizen* events (i.e., improvement projects) that are attempted by many companies. Another reason is that Lean promotes improvement by imitation. "This is what Toyota did, so this is how you must also do it!" Managers do not understand how the TPS works, only that it worked for Toyota. Then they apply it to a business very different from Toyota's, and it does not always fit.

A CONFUSED LANDSCAPE _____

While many people understand the basic relations of accounting and finance, too few similarly understand basic relations found in production and the supply chain. Everyone understands that if revenue increases with no increase in costs, profits will rise. When we ask our seminar participants to describe the basic relation between the time it takes a part to move through a factory and the number of parts within that factory, less than 1 percent have been able to do so correctly. We have observed a similarly low percentage among university researchers, the analysts (e.g., Gartner, Forrester, Solomon, and others) and the vast majority of consultants. Why is this? It is certainly not because these people are stupid. It is because these relations are seldom taught either in universities (that have not adopted *Factory Physics*) or in short courses. *Factory Physics for Managers* seeks to remedy this deficiency.

This lack of basic understanding results in much confusion. We call it *Newton's third law of experts*: For every expert, there is an equal and opposite expert. For every Lean consultant espousing the benefits of level production, there is an information technology (IT) salesman pitching advanced planning and scheduling (APS). Even among Lean experts, there is little agreement on how the science of the TPS works. Ask a room full of Lean masters to describe what makes a pull system a pull system, and you will get a room full of different answers. Even the definitions given by the Lean Enterprise Institute (LEI) and the American Production and Inventory Control Society (APICS) do not agree—nor do they make sense. The classic definition is given by the founder of LEI, James Womack, and spelled out in his book with Dan Jones, *Lean Thinking* (New York: Free Press, 1996).

> Pull *in simplest terms means that no one upstream should produce a good or service until the customer downstream asks for it.*

But this definition is quite different from that offered by the dictionary produced by APICS:

> Pull: *(1) In production, the production of items only as demanded for use or to replace those taken for use. (2) In material control, the withdrawal of inventory as demanded by the using operations. Material is not issued until a signal comes from the user.*[10]

The Womack definition implies that pull systems are essentially make-to-order systems. The APICS (production) definition is vague. The first phrase, "productions of items only as demanded," is similar to Womack's definition (i.e., make to order), whereas "replace those taken for use" suggests a supermarket or a make-to-stock system. Meanwhile, the APICS material definition is rather tautological because "issuing material" inventory and "withdrawing inventory" are essentially the same. That the definitions by the two expert organizations in the field are so different is very troubling in and of itself. More troubling is the fact that if managers were to choose one or the other, they are faced with the question, "What is the big deal?" Make to order and make to stock have been around for more than 60 years.

In our opinion, a bigger deal is that both organizations appear confused regarding the science underlying what they label as a pull system. Otherwise, they would not describe it using the same terms as those used to describe make-to-stock and make-to-order systems, which have been around for many years, because the pull concept *is essentially different* from both make to order and make to stock.

In Chapter 3 we will show that WIP control provides a way to achieve minimum cycle time with maximum throughput, regardless of its label. Neither of the preceding definitions discusses WIP control as a way to control performance. Both definitions state that producing or using only what is demanded is the defining characteristic of a pull system. If a million customers asked for a part at once, either definition requires an attempt to produce all 1 million parts at once. The classic pull implementation known as *kanban* does limit the amount of WIP of each part to the number of production cards (be they physical cards or electronic ones). The benefits are shorter cycle time, less WIP, and a stable flow. While *kanban* is the best-known method, the limiting of WIP can be done in many ways. After we describe the dynamics of production systems, it will become clear that classic *kanban* (the original pull system) is overly restrictive, and we will describe a way that is much simpler and more applicable to complex environments such as those with low volume and a high (and changing) mix. Finally, the use of a pull system often becomes an end in itself in many Lean implementations. This loses sight of the fact that the goal for a business is to sustain high profitability over the long term, not implement pull.

Many more things are confused besides the definition and purpose of pull. For instance, many people believe that increasing capacity at bottlenecks will result in greater output of the factory (not always true). Others believe that reducing cycle time will increase output (not true). Line balancing is the idea of setting up all stations in a line so that they have the same levels of capacity, and many believe that line balancing will minimize costs (also usually untrue). It is not surprising that such beliefs are held—production *seems* relatively simple, and these assertions *seem* intuitively true.

The problem is that most people's manufacturing, service, and supply-chain intuition is based on what happens *on average.* People understand mean effects. But when variability becomes the issue, their intuition is much worse. Why is this? *Because there has never been an adequate science of operations* or, in other words, a *theory* of operations that managers can use to reliably predict the results of actions before the actions are taken. Factory Physics science provides a remedy to this problem by providing a practical set of theories that have been tested and validated through relentless analysis and practice.

We believe that basic knowledge of the way production and inventory systems behave should be a prerequisite for anyone seeking to design, control, or manage such a system. This does not mean that the manager or vice president needs to have a Ph.D. in industrial engineering or logistics, only a keen intuition about how such systems behave. Managers should know the relationships between WIP, cycle time, throughput, variability, and capacity in an intuitive way. They should appreciate the importance of using a computer to model the process because it is better to experiment with a model. With a valid model, many options can be tried quickly to see which works best. Conversely when experimenting with the actual production of service operations or a supply chain, mistakes are frequently career-limiting. The purpose of this book is to teach managers and executives these basic relationships so that they can make better decisions. If you remain unconvinced, consider what happens when a large company attempts innovation by imitation—setting a huge project into motion because that is the way Toyota did it.

Boeing's Moving Assembly Line

Boeing's creation of a directly coupled moving assembly line to produce its 777 jet airliner was a huge mistake. This view may be a bit controversial. Boeing has made presentations around the country extolling its accomplishment of this impressive *technological* feat. Our contention is that although it is technically impressive, it did not make business sense, and the results obtained were available using much less flashy and *much less* expensive methods. Moreover, by blindly copying Toyota, Boeing not only spent a great deal of money but also was shut down for long periods of time during a period of peak demand. While we are big admirers of Boeing as one of the world's leading aerospace companies, this particular decision was ill-advised. Executives at large companies such as Boeing make decisions with big and expensive consequences. The 777 moving assembly line story provides an example of why a solid, fundamental understanding of the science behind operations is vital—especially for executives.

We begin in March 2007, when two of the authors attended a conference where the keynote speaker was from Boeing. His talk, "Transformation of a Factory—The 777 Moving Line," had created quite a buzz. How would such a line work? Planes are not cars. One might roll a car off an assembly line every 30 or 45 seconds, but the *takt* time for an airplane is three days.

Of course, putting a 777 on a moving assembly line was not easy, but then the Japanese consultants Boeing had hired never said that it would be easy. They only said that, "It must be!" because their contention was that a company could not be lean without a moving assembly line. Boeing management was not only going to make Boeing lean, but Boeing was also going to be a Lean leader. Already Boeing was teaching its suppliers to become leaner. Ohno had defined seven forms of waste (or *muda* in Japanese), and Womack and Jones had added one more to make it eight. By 2001, Boeing had defined ten. The search to eliminate waste became a way of life, and much waste had been discovered and eliminated, leading to great productivity increases.

The implementation cost for the 777 moving assembly line turned out to be around $250 million (from 2006 to 2007), plus the lost revenue in shutting down the plant several times for a number of weeks. It was also not easy. The first attempt was in 2006, but there were problems. A moving stand had to be created for access. Standard heights had to be established and implemented. Several plant modifications later, the line began moving in 2007, just in time for the conference. Boeing provided the following explanation on its website for why moving assembly lines are a good idea for planes.

Moving assembly lines, and the accompanying Lean techniques, enable a smooth, continuous production flow, enhancing the quality and efficiency of production processes. The line is stopped when an abnormal condition occurs. Stopping the line is the visual that tells us an abnormal condition exists and needs to be quickly addressed. In addition to reducing flow time and production costs, moving assembly lines also create an environment that makes it easier for employees to do their jobs. All the tools, parts, plans and work instructions are delivered to employees so they have everything they need where and when they need it.

The only problem with this explanation is that the line moves at an average rate of 1.8 inches per minute. In practice, it was not a continuous movement, but the line was periodically pulled forward. This meant that no one would notice for quite a while if the line were stopped. Thus one of the key benefits of a moving assembly line was lost from the beginning.

One of the key results reported at the conference was a reduction of square footage of 72 percent. But then there was a question from the audience—by how much time was the 777 assembly cycle time reduced? "It used to take 50 days to complete one 777—we have reduced that to 48 days." It was clear that divulging a meager two-day cycle-time savings was an awkward moment for the speaker. On a break, we were chatting with the speaker and asked for additional information in an attempt to further understand the tradeoffs of the endeavor. We said, "Our understanding is that the greatest variability in process time for plane assembly is due to the type of seats that are installed. A plane for a budget carrier having basic seats will take much less time to install than one for a plane with first class, business class, and basic seats. What did you use for the *takt* time?" The speaker replied, "Well, we tried to use the average but, as you might expect, that did not work too well. So we ended up using the longest *takt* time."

So an evaluation of the implementation's effectiveness must include

- Cost of $250 million to modify the plant
- Lost revenue while the plant was shut down
- Reduced throughput to enforce the longest *takt* time required for the most complex of the 777 models

This was an example of what one wag calls, "Type III error—solving the wrong problem." Cycle-time reduction was not the issue.

More throughput—making more planes—was the issue. By install-ing a moving assembly line that had to accommodate complicated planes as well as simple ones, Boeing reduced the output of the 777 plant. While it is impossible to correlate directly, during 2007, the company's total backlog grew from $250 billion to $327 billion, the largest increase since the company began reporting the statistic.[11] Coincidental or not, implementation of the moving assembly line occurred at a time when demand was very high for Boeing.

This was 2007. By 2009, Boeing was reporting better results[12]:

- Factory build-time reduction: 24 percent
- Factory unit hours: 34 percent
- Inventory turn rate: 71 percent
- Lost-workday case rate: 37 percent

We are not sure how they went from a 4 percent reduction in cycle time to a 24 percent reduction, but, again, cycle time is not the point, and the 2009 description provided no indication of an increase in throughput. The *takt* time remained at one plane every three days.

More recently, Boeing has made improvements to the line and has significantly reduced the *takt* time to 2.5 days and thereby increased throughput by 20 percent. How did Boeing do this? A 2012 blog on the *Aviation Week* website described the following changes:

1. Made process improvements such as automated "flex track systems" that fit on the airplane and drill holes more accurately and faster than a human worker can do
2. Prebundled and preinstalled the wires in a stand that goes directly into the cockpit instead of installing individual wires on the assembly line
3. Changed the design to allow wiring subassemblies to be made offline and then inserted in a fraction of the time required previously[13]

Perhaps it was necessary to have the plane moving on an assembly line to highlight the need for these improvements, but we think not. Preparing subassemblies offline essentially removes tasks from the critical path by doing them in a parallel operation. Another benefit publicized by Boeing at a 2013 conference, which two of the authors of this book attended, was that installing a moving assembly line enforced the production discipline needed to be more productive. Again, enforcing good management practices does not require a moving assembly line. Interestingly, Boeing had already been extremely successful using decoupled assembly lines and offline subassembly to increase the rate of B17 production back in World War II.[14]

The fact that it took six years to implement the 777 moving assembly line, not to mention the huge cost of implementation, shows how important it is to perform improvements based on a theory that can "make predictions about phenomena that have yet to be observed" and not because "that is the way Toyota does it."

Remarkably, Boeing is not using a moving assembly line to build the new 787 Dreamliner.

LOOKING AHEAD

This book is about increasing your knowledge and, more importantly, your intuition. Consequently, Factory Physics should not be a buzzword although that will not prevent some from trying to make it so. Indeed, that is a danger that we often warn our clients about. We recommend against using the classic company-wide rollout of a Factory Physics "initiative." Not everyone in the company needs to master Factory Physics science. Certainly the concepts should be taught at an appropriate level when implementing design changes to production or inventory control processes. Those involved in changes identified through application of the science should have at least a cursory understanding of why the changes are being made and an opportunity to provide feedback. The great thing about this approach is that it's highly objective. Combined with a genuine appeal to the intelligence of the average worker, the Factory Physics approach works well because people like doing things that make sense. If someone can objectively show that one of the concepts does not make sense, something has been learned and the science advances. Factory Physics science is not the "next best thing." It represents the underlying principles of whatever "best thing" you are currently using and is the knowledge of the next best thing you create for your particular business.

The remainder of this book will describe Factory Physics science as a comprehensive, practical science of operations for managers. Using this science will enable managers to design, implement, and control a production or service system uniquely suited to their particular business—while avoiding the pitfalls of initiatives by imitation, buzzwords, and poorly defined or bad theories. To do this, we begin with the most basic business goal—to make money now and in the future. The goal should be achieved through moral means and to noble ends, but if a company does not make money now and in the future, it jeopardizes any noble ends its owners and employees desire. We will describe the inherent conflicts between sales and operations that arise in most businesses in pursuit of the most basic goal. We seek to resolve these conflicts not by making them go away (because they will not) but by providing a means to establish an integrated *strategy*. By *strategy*, we mean to plan where to operate in the cost, inventory, and customer service constraint space that makes the most money. We will develop this strategy definition as we introduce new concepts. We then will describe how to translate such a strategy into real-world *tactics* that achieve the strategy. Finally, we will describe a groundbreaking approach to execution that establishes *controls* and *measures* to show when the business is in control and when it is out of control. Only when it is out of control do managers need to make adjustments. The result is a much more stable operations system that achieves its strategic objectives in the face of demand variability, production complexity, and product complexity *and* is easier to manage than most contemporary approaches.

In later chapters we address leadership and change-management issues. Throughout this book, we provide examples from a number of different industries and from large and small companies. Finally, we provide a recommended approach for readers to use in implementing the Factory Physics framework in their particular companies and examples of companies that already have implemented the Factory Physics framework. Using the recommended approach and studying these examples will give any manager the ability to (1) design a production and supply-chain management system uniquely suited to his or her particular business and (2) drive predictable, significantly improved performance.

CHAPTER 2

The Nature of Business—A Secret Hidden in Plain Sight

The best way of keeping a secret is to pretend there isn't one.
—Margaret Atwood

Sustained operations leadership success requires understanding the natural behavior of business. This natural behavior is a secret hidden in plain sight. We will talk a fair amount about natural behavior of operations and businesses in general because we see so very often that executives do not clearly understand the natural behavior of the operations they are trying to manage. If they did, they would not use brute force approaches such as:

- Install a directly coupled moving assembly line for airplane production
- Have an organization that uses spreadsheets extensively to plan and schedule production and manage inventory when they have already spent large sums of money on the "latest" information technology (IT) such as enterprise resource planning (ERP) *or* spend large amounts of money on add-ons such as advanced planning and scheduling (APS) to "fix" their planning and scheduling
- Promote "eliminate waste" or "one-piece flow" as an ultimate goal or even as an ideal goal
- Tolerate dysfunctional use of performance standards such as "earned hours" for evaluation and motivation of employees

- Manage by proclaiming such things as, "Our suppliers better get their parts in on time or tell them that I will be showing up at their door with a truck to get the parts myself." (actual quote from a vice president of operations of a multibillion-dollar manufacturing company to employees during a company meeting)

Understanding the natural behavior of operations first requires a clear understanding of the environment every manager has to navigate. Understanding a company's products, customers, people, and competitors provides necessary but not sufficient information for successfully creating and implementing strategies that provide predictable results.

Positive cash flow and long-term profitability are the primary business goals. Certainly these goals can be achieved in many different fashions, including criminal practices, so we do not recommend profit for profit's sake. Justice, temperance, prudence, and courage must be applied when determining how to best achieve the goals in concert with the leader's own values. Profitability is accomplished by increasing sales while reducing cost. A good-quality product is required. However, all too often we see companies focused on being the *leanest*—take your pick of definitions—or on achieving the least amount of variability—if that is even desirable—or on being demand-driven, and who isn't?

Unfortunately, constant conflict is the nature of business. Achieving lower costs generally requires low inventory, high utilization, and high throughput, a combination requiring low variability. Pursuit of high sales drives a requirement for fast response. Fast response requires low utilization; consider the utilization of a fire truck or an ambulance. Ambulance services attempting increased utilization with fewer vehicles while promising a fixed response time of five days or less are not doing much business. The drive to increase sales also usually results in more products and variants of existing products, which means more inventory and more variability. Therefore, as illustrated in Figure 2-1, there are conflicts between high and low inventory, high and low utilization, and more or less variability. Short cycle times contribute to both higher sales (beat the competition on lead time) and lower costs (find defects before running up scrap and rework costs), but the pursuit of short cycle times can be driven to highly unproductive extremes, as we shall see later.

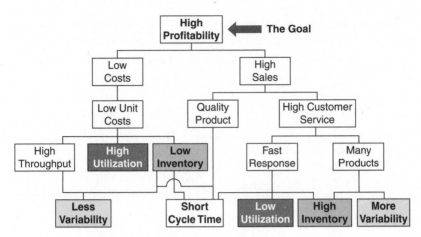

FIGURE 2-1. The tradeoffs in any company's environment

These natural conflicts exist in virtually any business, and they will *not* be eliminated. This is the nature of business. These natural conflicts need to be *managed*. For most companies, this is a secret hidden in plain sight, obscured by political battles or the chaos of weak or dysfunctional business control. When the natural conflicts are not managed, an organization can become bipolar.

1. Executives direct the organization to work on an initiative, for example, inventory reduction.
2. Inventory gets really low, and customer service starts to suffer.
3. Executives now focus on customer service. Inventory rises, and costs go up.
4. Executives now focus on cost, and so on.

We call this *whack-a-mole management*; some executives call it *continuous improvement*. Experienced managers in manufacturing or supply-chain leadership positions have probably experienced the drill.

LEADING PERFORMANCE IMPROVEMENT MORE PRODUCTIVELY

Don't misunderstand; there is plenty of excellent work being done by continuous-improvement personnel such as Six Sigma black belts and Lean masters. The problem is that their efforts shouldn't be directed based on the problem du jour (although quick-response teams for emergency situations are certainly appropriate), or stretch goals, or number of projects per year, or *kaizen* events per year, or cumulative projected savings per project.

Take for example, Jabil, a successful $17 billion contract manufacturer. On the company's website, the following is posted:

- 13,000+ *kaizens* to date (as of July) in 2013
- 32,000+ *kaizens* completed in 2012
- 15,000+ *kaizens* completed in 2011
- 9,500+ Lean bronze practioners
- 200+ Six Sigma black belts

Mike Matthes, Jabil's senior vice president of worldwide operations, said the following: "We are not promoting a Lean Six Sigma program. We are transforming the company by instilling a mind-set and culture of continuous improvement that is evident in everything we do."[1] We think that this is a good goal—it's just not directly connected to the corporate goal of long-term profitability and positive cash flow. Jabil has been a successful contract manufacturing company and has obviously benefited from its continuous improvement approach. However, the number of *kaizens* and people trained are measures not directly connected to long-term profitability and cash flow goals. These measures encourage more *kaizens* and training classes, whether they are needed or not. We do think that training your employees in problem-solving and teamwork techniques is vitally important. The problem is that training for training's sake and conducting projects so that there are more projects ultimately lead to frustration and wasted effort—continuous-improvement exhaustion. This is a major problem with typical Lean Six Sigma implementations.

In a June 14, 2012, *Wall Street Journal* article titled, "Where Process Improvement Projects Go Wrong," Dr. Satya S. Chakravorty reported the results from a study of process-improvement programs at large companies over a five-year period. His conclusion: "They [process-improvement programs] typically start off well, generating excitement and great progress, but all too often fail to have a lasting impact as participants gradually lose motivation and fall back into old habits." After the kickoff and excitement of the typical initial success of the programs under study, projects were conducted more generically without expert guidance. Then ". . . implementation starts to wobble and teams may find themselves struggling to maintain the gains they achieved earlier." The continual-project mind-set instills a mind-set of continuous improvement but doesn't necessarily lead to better results. "The improvement director, whose salary and bonus depended on the success of the company's Six Sigma initiatives, highlighted projects that were showing great progress and ignored those that weren't." This is a classic case of poor measures alignment; there is a disconnect between the goals of the corporation and the goals of the continuous-improvement programs. Rather than looking at the tradeoffs inherent in business and determining the best set of projects to support business goals, the management directive is to do lots of projects and measure results as determined by the number of projects and savings from projects. Why does this disconnect occur?

Measures alignment refers to the process of ensuring that the measures by which people are evaluated are aligned with the overall goals of the organization. Measures are usually set at the upper levels of organizations and therefore require strong, informed leadership to ensure a strong alignment between individual performance measures and overall organizational goals. In our experience, a major contributor to poor measures alignment and uneven continuous-improvement program results is that leaders lack a good method to quantify and understand the tradeoffs so that they can prioritize efforts and align measures appropriately. Tim Main, chairman of the board of Jabil, says, "As far as I know, we are the only company in the world in our industry that requires our management to be Lean Six Sigma certified. I think that it will significantly increase the number of *kaizen* events and focus that will lead to extraordinary quality levels. The real objective there is not just to be Six Sigma Black Belt Certified but to have a clear, demonstrable difference between Jabil's operating performance and capabilities over our competition."[2] This is what leaders do. They decide on a productive course of action for a company and move the company along that course. However, if a company's actions are not directly connected to desired business outcomes, the actions are much less certain to produce the desired results.

Mr. Main's comments illustrate our point. Jabil is promoting company-wide training—a good thing. See the January 29, 2013, *Forbes* article by Victor Lipman, titled, "Why Employee Development Is Important, Neglected and Can Cost You Talent" for more discussion on the value of employee training and development. However, assuming that more *kaizen* events will lead to extraordinary quality levels is a stretch. Finally, how much of a competitive advantage is provided by doing training that is available to all companies and practiced by most of the competition? Both Flextronics and Sanmina, two of Jabil's big competitors, practice Lean Six Sigma.

It is reasonable to argue that instituting a continuous-improvement program is neither a necessary nor a sufficient condition for achieving a company's business goals. (For those employed to support some type of continuous-improvement program, bear with us. We are not going to recommend elimination of continuous-improvement programs.) The main tenet of our argument is that achieving a goal requires actions that directly support that goal. Companies can achieve financial and marketing goals without a continuous-improvement program. A better approach and key concept of this book is to first understand the science that describes the natural behavior of operations and how it connects to financial performance and customer service. From there, a manager can *design performance* to achieve desired results. In Chapter 5 we will discuss the connections between the science and financial statements, but for now, suffice it to say that a scientific approach to performance design is the most direct way to connect actions to desired goals successfully. We do think that standardized training is a powerful factor in developing, retaining, and focusing skilled employees. We also believe that training can indeed be a big contributor to successful business results, but at the same time, company-wide training in continuous-improvement programs is not sufficient to attain predictable results over the long term.

Leaders should deliver messages on continuous improvement like the following hypothetical example:

> *We firmly believe in the power of our employees to drive excellence in our processes. We provide training for all employees on the tools and techniques of continuous improvement and teamwork. Further, we apply a practical, scientific operations management approach. This enables best possible adaption to the inherent conflicts between customer demand, cost, and service. This advanced, continuous improvement management approach provides effective and relatively simple focus of efforts. We prioritize application of continuous improvement tools and techniques to get the biggest bang for the buck. Simultaneously, the science ensures that we provide what our customers want when they want it by*

connecting business strategies directly to day-to-day activities. Finally, we use the practical science to design performance uniquely tailored to our company's strengths. This helps us serve our customers faster and better than the competition.

TRADEOFF ILLUSTRATIONS

Chapters 3 and 4 will discuss what we mean by practical science in more detail. Here we provide some illustrations of how to evaluate tradeoffs.

Consider a simple problem involving bank teller staffing. A bank manager wants to have enough tellers to service customers in a relatively short period of time to ensure customer loyalty. Attempted options are:

1. Minimum teller capacity
2. Maximum teller capacity
3. Flex capacity

Following is a description of a progression to a solution:

1. Keep the number of tellers to a minimum. This keeps each teller busier on average and thereby maintains lower labor cost per customer visit. Rather than hiring four tellers, the manager hires two.
2. After a while, customers start to balk at the lengths of lunchtime lines, and the manager's boss even receives a few calls from customers who are irate about the long lines. In this case, the manager has made a decision to maintain a small amount of capacity to keep costs down. The tradeoff is that the bank's customers have much longer wait times and are not happy about it.
3. The manager then decides that the low-cost option is not working so well. Two more tellers are added, resulting in a drastic drop in customer complaints about long wait times. The tradeoff, of course, is that teller labor cost has now doubled.
4. After getting a few concerned inquiries from upper management about teller labor cost, the manager comes up

with a different approach. One of the four tellers quits to go back to school, and the manager steps in when needed to help keep wait times down when a long line starts to form. Rather than hiring a fourth teller as a replacement, the manager decides to function at *flexible capacity*. While this takes time out of the manager's day, it proves to be the best balance of tradeoffs for capacity (cost) and service.

Now imagine that you are a production manager and your boss demands that operations provide a one-week cycle time and 3,000 units of product per week with no overtime. What is the correct reply? For operations managers, even those with limited experience, the answer is, "Sure. We can do that" because a response of "I don't know" or "I don't think it can be done" will cause the boss to look for someone else who will get the job done. That is perhaps a little facetious, but in operations it's not uncommon to be held to goals that are wildly optimistic.

This is the *stretch-goal approach*. Vince Lombardi's quote illustrates the idea, "Perfection is not attainable. But if we chase perfection, we can catch excellence." While we agree that it is better to set high expectations rather than low expectations, the stretch-goal approach is too often applied in a general and arbitrary fashion. Overuse or poor stretch-goal application leads to burnout and is ultimately counterproductive. Repeated stretch-goal use also calls into question a leader's knowledge and credibility. We have found, as will be explained later, that asking people to attain the best possible performance is a more productive approach. This is especially effective when accompanied by a credible model describing best possible performance.

In addressing the production performance demand just mentioned, what if the graph in Figure 2-2 were available? Now, even if the boss was originally told "Will do" in response to his directive, there is the option to go back and make the case with data. As the top curve shows, the cycle time at a production rate of 3,000 units/week and zero overtime is well over two weeks. However, with only four hours per week of overtime, the original goal of a one-week cycle time can be achieved. Further, suppose that the model used to generate the curves provides insight that indicates areas where continuous improvement efforts should be focused on being more productive. Once the process is up and running, continuous improvement efforts will lead to the required end state of having no overtime.

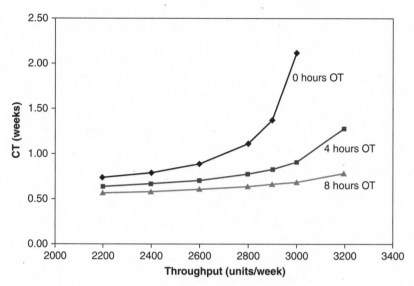

FIGURE 2-2. Production tradeoff curves

Another interesting aspect of Figure 2-2 is that it provides a visual illustration of tradeoff behaviors that are encountered throughout any operations environment.

1. As an operation's utilization rates rise higher and higher, cycle times increase rapidly and nonlinearly.
2. Initially adding a little bit of extra resource (capacity in Figure 2-2) results in significant improvement in performance. Adding the same incremental amount of resource a second time results in a much smaller additional improvement. Going from 0 hours of overtime to 4 hours of overtime decreases cycle time from over 2 weeks to about 0.8 week. Adding another 4 hours of overtime per week only decreases cycle time from about 0.8 to about 0.6 week.

It is vital that managers understand these and other tradeoffs inherent in their environment to gain improved skill in managing and leading organizations. Quantifying these tradeoffs is also important. As important as the ability to quantify tradeoffs is, more important is a manager's ability to internalize these relationships so that better decisions can be made on the fly through better intuition.

LEADERSHIP AND TRADEOFFS

Profitably harnessing natural business behavior and establishing competitive advantage requires executives to objectively and quantitatively understand the natural conflicts in their businesses and master the tradeoffs necessary for addressing those conflicts. Only then can strategies be designed properly and tactics, projects, and controls executed predictably to achieve marketing and financial goals.

Leaders can choose to:

1. Manage chaos by capitulating to conflict, establish random stretch goals, rely on brute force and expediting, and hope for good results, or
2. Implement a copycat initiative that has some good ideas and may or may not fit the organization, or
3. Institute predictive control of a desired business strategy by offering strategic, comprehensive, and quantitative understanding of competing alternatives (This enables well-informed, objective decision making to drive high performance on profitability and cash flow.)

All paths involve challenges. For options 1 and 2, a manager could be a rising star—this is often someone who gets promoted so quickly that the disasters left in that person's wake do not get attributed to him or her. Too often, though, the end result is a job change or pursuit of other career interests. Option 3 will typically encounter cultural-change resistance and will require skill as a consensus builder and leader to navigate the change successfully. The big upside with option 3 is that it provides excellent control over results and predictive understanding to make the decisions that offer the best chance at long-term success.

THE FACTORY PHYSICS APPROACH

The Factory Physics approach is to understand the natural conflicts in business through a practical, comprehensive science of operations. With tradeoffs understood and quantified, leaders can choose strategy, develop appropriate tactics and controls, and execute to achieve targeted business goals with a high degree of success.

A *strategy* is a plan of action designed to achieve a specific end. Executive strategy typically involves long-term, large-investment decisions such as "What are our markets?" "What is our technology?" and "How much installed capacity do we need?" *Tactics* are polices or actions implemented to accomplish a task or objective. Management tactics typically involve medium-term decisions such as "What do we need to make or buy?" "When do we need to make or buy it?" and "Do we need recourse capacity?" Tactics are often deployed with planning rules the organization follows and often puts into its ERP systems. *Controls* in an operations world are methods or systems used to implement tactics for achieving desired performance. Controls check such things as "Is demand within planned limits?" "Is inventory position within limits?" and "Is work in process (WIP) below its maximum limit?" Figure 2-3 provides a very high-level illustration of the *Factory Physics* approach. In the rest of this book, we lay out the science behind the tradeoffs and outline how to deploy the *Factory Physics* approach.

There are usually good reasons for the various conflicts in businesses. A case can be made for high inventory and low inventory, more variability and less variability, high utilization and low

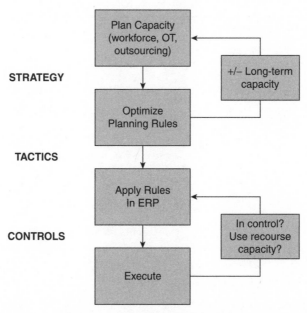

FIGURE 2-3. The Factory Physics approach

utilization, and fast response and slower response. But for managers, *the secret to formulating and implementing successful operations plans is to understand and quantify the natural conflicts in business and make appropriate tradeoffs to achieve marketing and financial goals.* In the end, it is a business design problem. Good business design and leadership require that managers understand the science governing their business. This begs the question of how to understand and quantify these conflicts and tradeoffs—which, it turns out, was the genesis of the *Factory Physics* approach.

The Nature of Business

1. Focus on profit, cash flow, quality, and customer service. Reducing waste is too general to be a strategy. However, don't discard process-improvement concepts and tools. If none exist, get them. They will be needed.
2. Simultaneously manage the tradeoffs between inventory, capacity, response time, and variability. Management efforts become whack-a-mole management if managers focus only on one or two of the elements at a time.
3. The *Factory Physics* approach offers managers a practical, scientific approach to understanding their business environment so that they can choose strategy, develop tactics, and execute with predictive controls.

CHAPTER 3

Practical Science for Leaders

All of physics is either impossible or trivial. It is impossible until you understand it and then it becomes trivial.

—Ernest Rutherford

When building an operations plan, the focus is usually on such things as profitability, cash flow, revenue growth, and customer service. We see many executives proceeding down the operations plan path by setting ambitious goals, such as "Double inventory turns" or "Cut cycle time 50 percent."

It's important to both the company's performance and a manager's personal performance to know if such goals can be achieved profitably before a manager commits to them. As discussed previously, managers naturally encounter conflicts and tradeoffs in leading organizations. This chapter lays down a framework that will work both strategically and tactically to describe those tradeoffs. Our framework enables managers to quantitatively and predictively determine how ambitious their and their organization's goals should be—just what good theory should do.

KNOWLEDGE AND SCIENCE

Management would be much easier if managers were simply required to memorize facts, follow defined procedures, or enter data in software programs to get desired results. Experienced managers know this is not the case; management is most often a fairly chaotic pursuit requiring accurate intuition to profitably interpret information and apply procedures. Managers face a plethora of theories, procedures, and software promoted as providing desired results. There is a significant difference between having the skill to apply scientific methods, follow procedures, or use software and having accurate knowledge of operations behavior.

Widespread confusion abounds regarding what works and what doesn't work in manufacturing and supply-chain operations. As a result, operations strategies and plans often fail to achieve what they promise. Chapter 1 discussed confusion in the knowledge landscape. Here we describe the various knowledge landscape constituencies that managers have to navigate in determining the best predictive theories to apply:

- Software companies are motivated to sell more software applications. The applications often only perpetuate existing client practices—regardless of whether or not the software does what the client needs. Software and software implementations are sold as solutions to handle all the complexity of business. Software often merely enables the user to see all the complexity faster and more completely than ever without helping the users to manage that complexity any better. The result is that the users of manufacturing requirements planning (MRP), enterprise resources planning (ERP), or advanced planning and scheduling (APS) systems are typically overwhelmed with complexity in real time.
- Continuous-improvement programs promote a myriad of philosophies. Lean and Six Sigma have already been discussed at length in previous chapters. Theory-of-Constraint (TOC) programs focus on the importance of managing the bottleneck—a primary concern for good control. However, there are many other concerns for a comprehensive theory of operations.
- Large consulting companies hire multitudes of bright, relatively inexperienced new graduates and send them into companies to analyze and recommend solutions. This becomes particularly problematic when the new grads are not paired with seasoned veterans or the seasoned veterans do not fully engage. Consulting companies, big and small, typically base their business model on billable hours, another misalignment of measures. The consulting company makes

more money by billing more hours. The client is better served by getting a solution as quickly as possible. Meanwhile, the consultants typically create extensive spreadsheets and databases for analysis—with all the accompanying error opportunities in complicated analytics. The process is repeated over and over at each client, and there is a fair amount of "reinvention of the wheel."

- Analyst companies such as Gartner, Aberdeen, Forrester Research, and Solomon generate endless surveys and white papers of so-called best-in-class performance with wildly varying levels of statistical rigor. Analyst companies are for-profit organizations. Client companies that spend the most money sponsoring analysts' surveys seem to get the most press from analysts. Analysts have sales quotas that are met by generating and selling ad-sponsored research reports. We wonder about analyst objectivity when their business is supported by the companies they should be objectively evaluating and their business model is driven by selling more research whether it's needed or not.

- Meanwhile, the academic community, and industrial engineering (IE) in particular, seems to have lost its way. Many curricula teach the Lean and Six Sigma approaches, with some queueing theory thrown in for good academic rigor, but they are following industry rather than leading. There is no well-defined science of industrial engineering or a standard core curriculum for mastering that science and its application in industry.

- Operations research (OR) continues to be the field for rigorous research on industry problems, but one typically needs an advanced degree to do OR analysis because the methods are heavy on complex math. This means that the average business leader typically doesn't read OR journals. Business leaders employing OR experts usually have to take analysis results on faith because the leader typically won't have the time or inclination to understand the math.

- Academic research in general is driven by the need to publish on topics that are new or undiscovered. Given the ratio of practical academic papers to academic papers published, these types of topics rarely correspond with topics useful to business leaders. This does not mean that the articles are useless. On the contrary, academic research and publishing are in large part how science advances. Our point is that the output of academic research is largely directed toward topics that do not apply to practical business management issues. To provide an idea of denominator of that ratio, Jinha[1] estimated that about 1.5 million scholarly articles were published in 2009, with an annual growth rate of around 3 percent per year. The reader is left to determine the numerator from personal experience.

What is an executive or manager of a manufacturing or supply-chain company to do in determining how to best lead his or her company to achieve marketing and financial goals? One thing is for certain: rewriting the landscape of the continuous-improvement, analyst, or academic communities is not an option—at least not a short-term option. As it turns out, a basic science of operations *does* exist, and we will state it in this chapter. Further, we think that an understanding of this science will provide managers with improved decision making in evaluating tradeoffs. This, in turn, improves a manager's chances for achieving sustained success over the long term. Finally, improved decision-making ability improves a manager's ability to lead.

Science, Math, Software, and Intuition

In talking about a science of operations, we should distinguish between science and math. *Science*, as we are using it, is the process of making an observation about the behavior of nature and then relentlessly testing that observation to see if it holds up as a predictive law. If the observation holds up under extensive testing, it is provisionally accepted as a scientific law—the provision being that some future test might disprove the observation as a universal law. Karl Popper, in his book, *Conjectures and Refutations: The Growth of Scientific Knowledge* (New York: Routledge, 1963), describes the pursuit of knowledge as a series of conjectures (guesses at causes or solutions) and refutations (tests to disprove the conjecture). Conjecture and refutation have very practical applications for managers.[2]

One of the popular problem-solving techniques used in contemporary management practices is *brainstorming*. Employees perform stream-of-consciousness generation of ideas for solutions. Brainstorming can be a very useful way to generate ideas and potential solutions, but it then typically degenerates as a solution-implementation exercise because people become emotionally attached to their ideas. The adage "All ideas are good ideas" is a haven for protecting weak ideas. *Not all* ideas are good ideas. How could that be? That's like saying, "All children are above average." Managers can lead employees to productive generation of strong solutions by having employees apply conjecture and refutation to ideas and proposed solutions. The point is to come up with conjectures *as well as* strong refutations. Every successful refutation creates learning and knowledge is advanced. From a psychological standpoint, commending employees for generating strong refutations and improved conjectures sends a much different message from having employees defend their ideas—good or bad. Through conjecture and refutation, good ideas naturally emerge through survival of the fittest. An example follows from a nonautomotive business considering the application of automotive techniques to its business:

> **Conjecture:** The goal is the Toyota Production System (TPS).
> **Refutation:** The goal is not to be like Toyota; the goal is to have the highest cash flow and profitability for our business while providing desired customer service.
>
> **Conjecture:** Okay, the goal is to achieve our business goals using TPS.
> **Refutation:** TPS is just one operations logistics design and is particularly designed to be successful in automotive assembly. Our business shares few characteristics with automotive assembly.
>
> **Conjecture:** Well, TPS has many useful and productive practices that we can use. We should use TPS practices that best help us to achieve our business goals.
> **Initial conclusion:** Agreed that we should use the most useful and productive practices that help us to achieve our business goals. However, Toyota is not the only company that has useful and productive practices. We need a way to determine the most useful and productive practices for our business. TPS offers many good ideas for consideration.

This leads to conjectures about a way to determine the most useful and productive practices for a business to use in meeting its business goals. We shall provide this conjecture as a science of operations shortly.

Another example:

Conjecture: "Variation is evil."[3]

Refutation: For clarification, we're using *evil* in an economic sense as detrimental to profit, cash flow, or service. *Variation* includes customers wanting to have more than one type of product and wanting to order that product whenever they want. Those are not intrinsically evil variations.

Conjecture: "Lean means speed,"[4] so any variation that results in reduced speed of delivery of a product or service to a customer is evil.

Refutation: If the cost to reduce variation, and thereby increase speed of delivery, is greater than the revenue generated by the increased speed, then *reducing variation is evil.*

Initial conclusion: Variation is only evil if it reduces a manager's desired combination of profit, cash flow, and service.

We use math to quantify conjectures and refutations, but science and math are not the same thing. Commonly, there is confusion between what is scientific and what is mathematical. One of the greatest scientists who ever lived, Sir Isaac Newton, stated his first law of motion as: "Every object perseveres in its state of rest, or of uniform motion in a right (sic) line, unless it is compelled to change that state by force impressed thereon."[5] In other words, an object will remain at rest or will continue moving in a straight line unless acted on by an external force. Newton's first law of motion is a fundamental scientific principle, yet it uses absolutely no math.

Enough philosophy! Our point is that we are more concerned that managers understand the behavior of operations in a practical, scientific framework than that they understand complex mathematical formulations. Implementing the latest software program is also not a substitute for understanding the behavior of operations. Certainly, math has led to many insights into the natural behavior of operations. Software has greatly increased the ability to do complex analysis, but the usefulness of either in operations management is greatly diminished without a good understanding of the science of operations. As a matter of fact, we regularly see managers use a combination of complex software, ill-informed science, and inaccurate mathematical models for planning and control of operations. This approach greatly diminishes performance. We move to a science of operations shortly and cover some basic mathematical relationships at the end of this chapter. Much more mathematical detail is provided in Chapter 4, but as in the original *Factory Physics* book, we mainly want managers to develop better intuition about the world they manage.

Merriam-Webster defines *intuition* as "quick and ready insight" and as "the power or faculty of attaining to direct knowledge or cognition without evident rational thought and inference."[6] Good intuition leads to better decisions because good intuition is predictive. As discussed in Chapter 1 on the definition of theory, everyone has some degree of intuition. Managers' intuition about operations performance is based on their experience and training. We want to improve managers' intuition though a better understanding of the science governing operations. Better intuition enables managers to make better decisions on the fly and lead more effectively. Better intuition allows managers to better manage software systems and interpret software recommendations. Better intuition provides managers with the ability to better interpret others' recommendations in pursuit of a company's marketing and financial goals. Better intuition allows managers to interpret and use the practices, recommendations, and ideas of the continuous-improvement, academic, and analyst communities more effectively. Better intuition leads to increased confidence in decision making.

Recall the example of jet airliner production on a moving assembly line in Chapter 1. Almost any manager would ask, "Why should we do this?" If given the answer, "That is the way Toyota does it," a confident manager would continue to press to understand why doing something that Toyota does is good to do in a completely different production environment such as Boeing's. More detailed intuition is required for the less obvious example given in Chapter 1 of one-piece flow with average process times of 25 seconds and a *takt* time of 30 seconds. Off hand, this arrangement may seem okay or even desirable, but the confident manager will question whether 83 percent

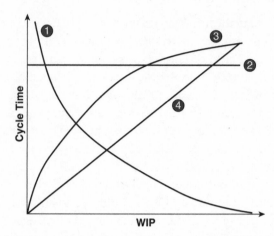

FIGURE 3-1. Common guesses concerning the relation between WIP and cycle time

utilization of available capacity is acceptable. The answer may be yes, but the question should be asked.

When we train managers in Factory Physics principles, we often ask the class to draw a simple curve illustrating the relationship between work in process (WIP) and cycle time (time to go through the line). We give the simplest example of a production flow as four identical process centers in series with identical capacity and zero variability. Even in this simplest of examples, we get a variety of conjectures as to what kind of curve describes the relationship between WIP and cycle time. Many incorrect guesses are put forth (see Figure 3-1 for an illustration):

1. Cycle time decreases nonlinearly as WIP increases.
2. Cycle time does not change as WIP increases. This is the inherent assumption of *all* MRP/ERP systems.
3. Cycle time increases nonlinearly as WIP increases.
4. Cycle time increases linearly from zero as WIP increases.

Only two or three people out of well over 1,000 polled have had the correct response. We will describe the correct relationship shortly.

How can this be? How can experienced managers of manufacturing, service, and supply-chain operations not know such a fundamental relationship? The answer, sadly, is that the relationship is not widely taught. It should be intuitive, but it is not until it is taught. Once it is explained, it makes perfect sense, and then intuition grows about more than just a simplified case (we will cover this in more detail later).

Knowledge and Science

1. Science is not the same as math or information technology (IT).
2. Science describes the natural behavior of the business environment for business leaders.
3. A basic intuitive understanding of the fundamental relationships is much more important for a leader than complex math or the latest IT.

PRACTICAL THEORY

In formulating a science of operations, we need a framework in which to test our theories. Remember, we are after theories as defined by the U.S. National Academy of Sciences. A theory is "a comprehensive explanation of some aspect of nature that is supported by a vast body of evidence." In the Factory Physics approach, the framework we use is the demand-stock-production (DSP) framework (see Figure 3-2). As we describe the Factory Physics approach, we are essentially stating conjectures that have undergone extensive refutation testing over

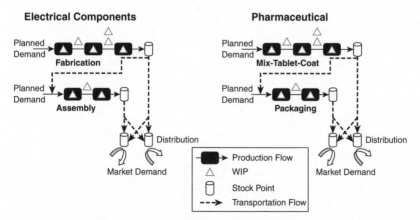

FIGURE 3-2. Demand-stock-production diagram examples

the last 20 years. We begin with some fundamental statements about the structure of businesses.

The Value Stream: Demand, Stocks, and Production

Every value stream is made up of two essential parts: *demand* and *transformation*. The essence of any production or service is to transform material or other resources into goods or services to meet demand.

Without demand, there can be no revenue, no matter how efficient the operations. In this use of demand we are talking about external demand to a company—customer demand. There is also internal "demand," but this is also handled by the demand and transformation construct, as discussed below.

While we are on the subject, it is a counterproductive practice that functions within a company insist that other company functions be treated as "customers." For example, customer service insists that customer service "demand" takes precedence over production's requirements because customer service is the "customer." This often corrupts pursuit of the company's goal of profitability and cash flow. Customer service is often understandably focused on satisfying the external demand at all costs, which is not always a good decision for company profitability and cash flow. Customer service and production are teammates or associates, or whatever cooperative label is suitable, working toward a common goal.

Obviously, with no revenue, there can be no profit. Transformation provides the ability to satisfy the demand. At this point, one might be thinking, "What about supply? After all, don't value streams involve supply?" It turns out that one person's supply is used to satisfy another person's demand, so supply is simply the transformation on the part of the supplier, with the demand coming from the consumer's production needs. Within a company, a subassembly line supplies the internal demand of the final assembly line. The subassembly line is transformation, and the assembly line requirements are demand. Transformation is composed of *production* and *stocks,* as illustrated in Figure 3-2.

Production represents materials, resources, or information moving through a sequence of operations performed by machines, people, natural processes (e.g., water turning a turbine), or some combination of the three. We distinguish between services production and product production. *Service production* is a sequence of actions to meet demand. Demand is not met until the complete sequence of actions is complete. *Product production* is a sequence of actions producing intermediate physical or virtual products resulting in the final product demanded. Factory Physics science is comprehensive and applies to service production or to physical or virtual product production. The material moving through product production could be a physical product such as a casting or a virtual product such as a part design or a planned work order. An example of service production is the sequence of actions in recognizing a power outage, responding to the power outage, and restoring power.

A *flow* is a collection of production routings or a collection of demand streams. Both production and demand are represented by a rate of flow and so are considered to be examples of flow. On the other hand, a *stock* represents material, resources, or information waiting for a production or service process. Stocks are what separate flows. Demand is typically a flow out of a stock to satisfy a request (be it for a product or a service). Production is usually a flow into a stock, although it can flow *through* a stock without stopping, as in the case of a service. Net flow is production minus demand. If the net flow into a stock is positive, the inventory will grow; if negative, it will fall.

Stocks occur whenever two or more flows meet. If two or more parts need to come together in an assembly, for instance, there will be a stock for the parts to match up. Raw materials and finished goods are also examples of stocks. Note that services cannot be stocked because demand for services can only be satisfied by providing the service. For instance, the demand to put out a fire cannot be met (at this writing) by having a fire truck show up exactly as the fire starts. For some services, we could consider their demand to be always backordered. In other words, the demand must occur some time before it can be satisfied—a fire starts, and someone recognizes it and calls the fire department. In this case, the backorder time is from when the fire starts (whether someone sees it or not) to the time the fire is put out. The stock in this case has no physical inventory but still has a status containing information about the service production process (amount and length of backorders). Only product production systems can satisfy demand essentially immediately by pulling material (a completed part) or information (a completed computer-aided design drawing) from a stock. *Stocks* is the general term for inventory buffers. Stock points are logical constructs used to create classifications for planning and control of physical items (e.g., parts by supplier or by lead time or demand volume); more on this will be presented later in this chapter.

If the demand is for a product, then certain raw materials must be transformed into the finished product, expending company resources in the process. These resources do not become part of the final product and may include supplies (consumed but still not part of the final product), machines, labor, utilities, engineering services, and management. If the demand is for a service, then company resources must be applied to provide the requested activity, but no raw materials need be used. Consequently, transformation always involves the use of some type of company resource and may or may not involve raw materials. This very simple model of demand and transformation (composed of stocks and production) can be used to represent any manufacturing or service value stream.

In Figure 3-2, the only things that change between the two diagrams are the labels. This illustrates an advantage of the Factory Physics framework—it provides one scalable construct for virtually any production/service system. A more complex network is shown in Figure 3-3.

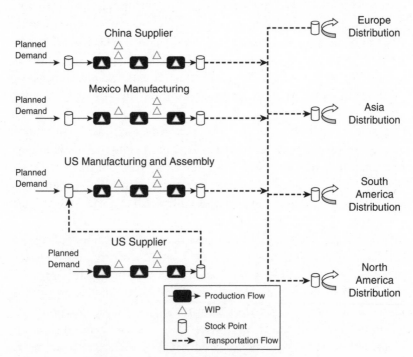

FIGURE 3-3. A network of production flows and stocks

The *demand-stock-production* (DSP) structure is a vital concept because it provides a way to think about and model businesses to create the best plan for leading a company to achieve its marketing and financial goals. Anyone familiar with value-stream mapping (VSM) or process mapping in general will recognize DSP as a variation on those themes. Indeed, companies with good value-stream maps are well on their way to employing Factory Physics science to accelerate their improvement efforts. The reasons the DSP construct is so powerful include the following:

1. Performance boundaries (best case to worst case) for production flows and for stocks can be described using practical science and applied math.
2. An operation's current performance given its cost and variability constraints can be determined relative to those performance boundaries.

In addition, performance boundaries and a range of strategic options can be illustrated graphically using efficient frontiers and performance graphs. Experienced Lean practitioners are well aware of the power of visual management in improving and maintaining high performance. Demand also can be described quantitatively with straightforward statistics, that is, mean and variance. The result is that the construct of demands, stocks, and production provides a framework that yields very powerful predictive analysis and intuition for leaders.

The Value Stream: Demand, Stocks, and Production

1. All value streams or processes or supply chains can be divided into two parts: demand and transformation.
2. Transformation can be further described as a combination of productions and stocks.
3. Demand and production are flows. Production flows into a stock point, and demand flows out of a stock point.
4. The behavior of demand, production flows, and stocks can be described practically and quantitatively to provide more powerful analysis and intuition for leaders.

Buffers

In a perfect value stream, a unique and perfect-quality product that has never been made before is produced, and at that instant, a customer shows up and says, "That is exactly what I want. How did you know?" The customer then pays for the product and leaves. This is the perfect situation: the customer does not have to wait, and yet there is no inventory. If the operation could operate so that capacity was there only when it was needed, both labor and machines would operate at 100 percent efficiency. In this perfect world, customer service is 100 percent, no stock is required (zero finished goods and zero raw material because they show up exactly when they are needed), and there are never any backorders. This is an example of both perfect customers (demand) and perfect transformation. In this perfect world, profit is as high as it can be because costs are at a minimum, and all demand is being met.

Unfortunately, this perfect world does not exist. Customers do not show up right when a part is completed; many times they don't even show up when they say they are going to. Sometimes customers don't tell us anything about when they are going to show up. They just do—and they expect the product to be there!

But customers are not the only source of imperfection. The plant or a supplier might deliver a part on time or might not. Service technicians might be available when needed or might not be. Quality of a part or service could be good or could be unacceptable. Things happen! Managers don't manage in a perfect world. Managers manage in the real world, and an important characteristic of the real world is *variability*. Variability is anything that departs from regular, predictable behavior. Variability provides both problems and opportunities when trying to synchronize demand and transformation.

It is clear, then, that demand and transformation cannot be perfectly synchronized in the presence of variability. When trying to synchronize demand and transformation in the presence of variability, *buffers* are required. From *Factory Physics*:

> *A buffer is an excess resource that corrects for misaligned demand and transformation.*

Moreover, *there are only three kinds of buffers: inventory* (when product is finished before demand), *time* (when demand waits for parts), and extra production *capacity* (which reduces the need for the other two buffers).

Buffers are like shock absorbers on cars. Instead of reducing bumps in the road for a car, buffers reduce or dampen the effect of variability when trying to synchronize demand to transformation. For instance, if a manager decides to hold 200 pieces of finished-goods inventory (one type of buffer) even though average demand is only 10 pieces per month, a highly variable spike in demand, for example, an order for 100 pieces, can be handled with ease. Does it make sense to hold 200 pieces of inventory, even though average demand is 10 per month? That is a design decision that management must make.

How well a manager understands relationships between buffers and understands buffers' effects on business performance will go a long way toward determining the manager's success as a leader. Interestingly, managers will use some combination of buffers to synchronize demand and transformation whether they like it or not. Despite the propaganda and the preaching and the promised magic of zero inventory, produce to demand, just-in-time, mass customization, and the desire to be lean, leaner, leanest, managers *need* buffers. Buffers are not a cool new trend one might read about in the *Harvard Business Review*. Buffers are a fact of life.

The Factory Physics Mindset

An operational excellence leader we met said, "I consider buffers to be necessary evils; we have to live with them, but less are better." This is like saying, "Fat is evil." Our view is that managers should employ the right combination of buffers and an optimal quantity of each buffer to help achieve their companies' financial and marketing goals. Approaching buffers as evil destructively narrows options for success in pursuit of your goals. If your goal is to live a good life, focusing only on reducing your body fat limits your options for reaching your goal—but you may end up skinny.

Types of Buffers

Buffer management has major implications for managers trying to achieve business goals. The fact that *there are only three forms of buffers* for synchronizing transformation and demand is a good news, bad news situation. Buffers are not the same as waste. Consequently, there are not seven buffers or eight or even ten. This is the good news. There are only three buffers, and they are as follows:

1. **Inventory.** Extra material in the transformation process or between it and the demand process.
2. **Time.** Any delay between a demand and satisfaction of it by the transformation process.
3. **Capacity.** Extra transformation potential needed to satisfy irregular or unpredictable demand rates.

Because pure service operations, such as diagnosis and healing of injuries in hospital emergency rooms, do not provide items that can be physically stocked, service operations have only two types of buffers: *time* and *capacity*. Granted, there are physical inventory items such as bandages and medications, but the end product is the healed injury, and that is not an item that can be inventoried. The bad news is that there are only three forms of buffers, and managers who don't like the choices are out of luck. We are describing Factory Physics science for operations, not "factory magic." There are no magic solutions to instantaneously make things or enchanting spells to resolve conflicts and tradeoffs. Harry Potter never worked in manufacturing, service, or supply-chain operations. Unfortunately, it is common to see managers, particularly executive managers, ignore the science of buffer behavior in trying to attain their goals.

Examples of buffer use include carrying "just-in-case" inventory for when machines go down, working overtime or outsourcing to satisfy a jump in demand, and adding a lead-time "cushion" to make sure that a part finishes on time. Buffers sometimes can be swapped. For instance, we can essentially eliminate the lead-time buffer by building to stock and using finished goods as an inventory buffer. The secret is to know the most *economical* combination of buffers for a given situation.

Common continuous-improvement programs address these buffers in different ways—and usually one at a time. TOC's drum-buffer-rope control is one of many methods for controlling buffers. Toyota's seven forms of waste can all be reduced to one of the three buffers—over a 50 percent reduction in classification terms. Many Lean advocates unwittingly decrease performance and profitability by fanatically focusing on reducing cycle time—as we will see later, this mistake is easily diagnosed and avoided. Six Sigma's define, measure, analyze, improve, and control (DMAIC) methodology typically focuses on the causes of variability that increase the requirements for buffers but offers no advice as to what the best combination of buffers might be.

Designing, implementing, and controlling the best combination of buffers and variability constitute a primary task for successful management. One or more buffers will be required to synchronize demand and transformation in the face of variability. If nothing is done about variability, downplaying, restricting, or ignoring the use of one buffer will guarantee increased amounts of one or two of the other buffers. It is Nature's way. Typically, executives don't want to invest in a larger-capacity buffer because capacity (i.e., more machines, more people, overtime, or outsourcing) tends to be expensive. At the same time, there always seems to be a push to reduce inventory, so inventory is reduced, often with no insight into the effects of lower inventory. The result? Time becomes the default buffer. In other words, orders are shipped late, and customers are forced to wait. This is probably not the best use of a company's buffers. As it turns out in the real world, something or someone is always waiting.

Buffers

1. Buffers are required to synchronize demand and transformation in the presence of variability.
2. There are only three buffers: inventory, time, and capacity.
3. Properly sized and positioned buffers are not waste.
4. A primary challenge for leadership is determining the best combination of buffers and variability to employ in meeting a company's financial and marketing goals.

Conceptual Illustrations: Something or Someone Is Always Waiting

One way to consider how the interactions of buffers work is to consider that in the presence of variability, someone or something is always waiting. Our thanks to Dr. Antonio Arreola-Risa of the Mays Business School at Texas A&M University for the idea of describing buffer portfolio design as a question of who or what is waiting. Strategic decisions for managers include determining what amount of resources to put in place, knowing that some of those resources are going to be idle at some time or another. Once the resources are in place, managers make tactical decisions about how to minimize wait time while delivering products or services as closely synchronized to demand as possible:

- When there is variability, then either machines wait on parts or parts wait on machines or both.
  - Parts waiting for machines adds to cycle time—the time buffer.
  - Machines waiting on parts decreases utilization—the capacity buffer.
- When there is variability, then either customers wait for parts or parts wait for customers or both.
  - Customers waiting for parts represents the time buffer.
  - Parts waiting for customers represents the inventory buffer.

Managers almost always see a combination of buffers. Even when parts are usually waiting for machines, there are times when the machines are idle. This is the way random systems behave. Likewise, even when inventory is almost always available, there will be times when it is not, and customers must wait.

A serious mistake that managers commonly make is to try to force capacity utilization so that machines and people are always busy. Most managers get nervous when people are not working or machines are sitting idle. But, if people and machines are not waiting, then parts and/or customers will be. This is especially acute in low-volume, high-mix "job shop" environments but can be addressed rationally and profitably.

As described in Chapter 1, Toyota used capacity buffers liberally. Yet, somehow, operations and supply-chain managers commonly view anything less than 100 percent utilization as a failure of effort. As we will discuss in Chapter 5, a big driver of this is the use of the standard-cost model to determine operations and supply-chain decisions even though that model does not reflect the natural behavior of business. There is hope, though. We have of late encountered managers who tell us, for instance, "I want to know the *right* amount of inventory I should have on hand, not just how to reduce inventory." The recognition here is that it may actually make sense to increase inventory if that provides better service and thereby leads to additional revenue. The same is true for utilization concerns. The question is, "What is the level of utilization that makes a company the most money?"

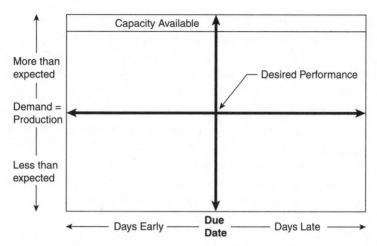

FIGURE 3-4. What waits and when—a basic business model

In the rest of this section we will cover a conceptual discussion of Factory Physics science in the context of why all this waiting occurs. Figure 3-4 shows a basic model of the challenges a business manager faces whether in a production business or a service business. The challenge is to provide the right amount of product or services (*demand*) on the promised due date. The *due date* is the planned due date for completion of a quantity of product or service. In a perfect world, the due date would be the same day that the demand appears. As discussed earlier, we don't live or manage in a perfect world, so the due date in this discussion corresponds to when managers plan for the product or service to be delivered based on management assessment of demand or actual demand. Capacity is the upper limit of a business's ability to provide product or services. Desired performance is pretty simple. This is where the amount demanded is delivered on the due date. For services, it's the date when the service requested is delivered on the due date.

It seems so simple. The fact that desired performance seems so simple is one of the reasons that companies and leaders often make a mess of it. We are periodically reminded that executive managers do not appreciate the inherent complexity of achieving such a simple result. Career-development moves are made by putting, for instance, a fast-rising marketing person in charge of production to give that person experience. Even within operations, a person who has been a faithful, smart line employee is moved into management with absolutely no training in the science of operations. This is akin to putting a good quality inspector in charge of heart surgery because the inspector is smart and will "figure it out." It is our contention that *no* manager should be allowed to manage operations or supply-chain functions without a basic understanding of the science of operations covered in this book. This doesn't prevent career-development moves such as just described. It only means that appropriate training and education in operations science are required before someone is put in charge of an operations or supply-chain environment. The world has been getting along without this requirement for some years now, but major reductions in chaotic and dysfunctional management are possible through application of the concepts in this book.

In considering why desired performance is not so simple, Table 3-1 provides an incomplete list.

The reasons for less than desired performance never really go away. However, we have found that the causes of poor policy and control can be readily corrected, leading to much better performance. Figure 3-5 illustrates the effects of randomness and variability using a cloud to indicate the range of possible performance.

The cloud in the figure represents possible outcomes of a particular order for a product or service—each point in the cloud is represented by the coordinates of time and amount, plus a third: the probability of that particular time and amount.

TABLE 3-1. Causes for Less than Desired Production Performance

Early to Due Date	Late to Due Date	Too Little Production	Too Much Production
• Demand is unknown but requires quick response	• Customer promised delivery before lead time date	• Capacity constrained can't meet all demand	• Want to keep machines or people busy so make more than demand
• Demand is known but "drops out" after production or service starts	• Problems with capacity availability cause delays	• Scrap or rework	• Poor policy decisions – incorrect lot sizes
• Want to keep machines running so make more than demand	• Scrap or rework	• Poor policy decisions – incorrect lot sizes	• Minimum lot size limits
	• Customer change requests during production or service	• One piece flow, poor WIP control	• Poor control – "ganging" setups

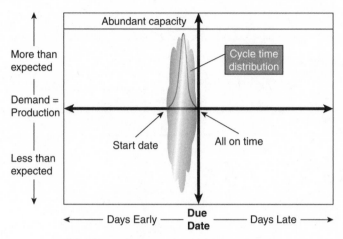

FIGURE 3-5. Production results in the real world

The cycle-time distribution shown illustrates that with abundant capacity, the range of cycle times is relatively small. Knowing this distribution, we can schedule a start date for production or promise a completion date for a service and always meet the required due date. We distinguish between cycle time and lead time. *Cycle time* is the time required to go through the process (a random variable). *Lead time* is a management policy decision about what amount of time to use in determining a promise date for a completed product or service. For customer delivery performance to be 100 percent, lead time must *always* be greater than or equal to cycle time.

Now watch what happens when we restrict capacity for the same process. Figure 3-6 shows the cloud being compressed on the production axis, and consequently, it expands horizontally. The average cycle time required for completion has now gotten longer, and the variability of cycle time has also increased (cycle-time distribution has spread out). As a result, we are much more likely to deliver products or services late using the original lead time.

The cloud concept of variability provides one illustration of why someone or something is always waiting. We will be more quantitative (while remaining highly practical) shortly. The possible outcomes of this variability effect are summarized in the figures that follow.

Figure 3-7 shows the matrix of potential outcomes for a service or make-to-order (MTO) business. The choices are due date, backorders, and unneeded consumption of resources.

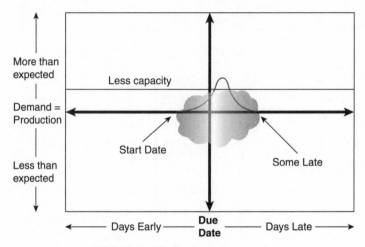

FIGURE 3-6. Effects of reducing capacity

A backorder means that the service job or MTO product is late. Extra consumption of resources is an interesting result. For instance, if a company sends two technicians on a service call and only one is actually needed, the extra tech tagging along is an unneeded consumption of resources. Does this incur extra cost? Not necessarily. If the extra tech goes along on the call because there is not some other service call that needs attending, there is really no extra cost. If the extra tech is part of the service company's base-capacity configuration, that is a capacity buffer the company has strategically decided

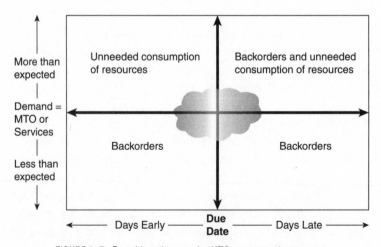

FIGURE 3-7. Possible outcomes for MTO or service businesses

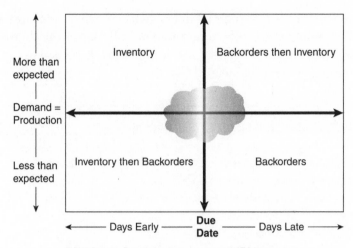

FIGURE 3-8. Possible outcomes for an MTS business

to maintain to address variability in demand. The fact that the second tech is able to go along on the service call even though an extra tech is not needed is just a result of random variation. If a second tech can go along on nearly every call without affecting service to other clients and that second tech is not really needed to complete the service calls, the capacity buffer is probably too large.

Figure 3-8 shows possible outcomes for make-to-stock (MTS) businesses or processes. The choices are due date, inventory, and backorders. Is too much inventory a significant extra cost? Maybe; it depends on how long the extra inventory sits around without being sold. Are backorders on inventory extra cost? Maybe; certainly if they result in missed sales. If the backorder is only for a day or so and replenishment inventory arrives in time to deliver product within the customer's expectations, there's negligible cost. As a matter of fact, the regular occurrence of backorders is a common result of operations planning. This is reflected in the fill rates that companies set as policies. *Fill rate* is the probability that there will be no backorders. If a company sets a fill rate of 99 percent and one of every 100 orders is not filled out of on-hand inventory, it is backordered. That's okay, though, because one of 100 being backordered is a 99 percent fill rate. The "variability cloud" is usually denser in the middle, indicating that the probability of meeting a due date is higher closer to the due date.

Managers who deal with variability by proactively designing their portfolio of buffers will be better able to lead organizations to successfully attain their business goals. So what's the best way for determining the optimal portfolio of buffers and variability for desired performance? We start with a high-level discussion of performance and how it is influenced.

Something or Someone Is Always Waiting

1. A conceptual illustration of the behaviors of buffers and variability is that something or someone is always waiting.
2. Time buffer— the customer waits.
3. Inventory buffer—parts wait.
4. Capacity buffer—machines or workers wait.
5. Variability creates a "cloud" of possible outcomes in the interplay of demand and delivery.
6. The size, shape, and position of the cloud depends on the level of variability and the types and amounts of buffers chosen.

A Manager's World: Environment, Tactics, Controls, and Measures

Most managers want performance that is characterized by high profit, high cash flow, and excellent service. Variability and randomness make this a difficult task. To develop a more quantitative framework for evaluating the tradeoffs in pursuing best possible performance, we describe performance in terms of four components. Performance is a function of:

- **Environment.** The amount and variability of transformation resources and the level and variability of demand.
- **Tactics.** Policies or actions implemented to accomplish a task or objective.
- **Controls.** Controls in an operations world are methods or systems used to implement tactics for achieving desired performance, for example, an MRP system or upper and lower limits on inventory position. The most effective controls provide some sort of feedback mechanism to indicate the status of the performance being controlled.

- **Measures.** For an operations plan, measures are quantities used to report performance characteristics of a process, for example, on-time delivery, capacity utilization, or number of parts within policy compliance.

Strategies are the plans a manager makes to control a company's environment and accomplish its business goals. Because tactics include implementation of controls and measures, we will reserve discussion of controls and measures until later on when we are ready for a more detailed discussion. For now, a discussion of environment and tactics provides a good high-level illustration of some basic management options available for controlling performance.

The importance of the description of a manager's world as being composed of environment and tactics is that companies can typically improve performance quickly simply by changing the tactics that are currently in use. An example includes the policies embedded within most ERP systems that signal *when* to order and *how much* to order. Another production example of a tactic is maintaining extremely low WIP levels in an attempt to achieve or emulate one-piece flow. Too little WIP results in reduced throughput because the process or supply-chain constraint starves for work frequently. For service businesses, a policy example would be promising delivery times to the hour. If it doesn't make a significant difference to customers, promising delivery times to the day or half-day should result in fewer late deliveries and less resource use (cost) per delivery.

Changing tactics is typically a low-cost action, although managers should not underestimate the change-management effort involved. It is common to find that companies are not using the inventory policies already in their planning system, even though those policies may be pretty good. It is also common to find management that has trained its organization to ignore the policies in its planning system. For example:

1. An executive dictates a 30 percent reduction in inventory without understanding the customer-service implications.
2. Policies (e.g., safety-stock levels) are loaded into the system that roughly reduce inventory by the required amount.
3. Inventory is reduced, and customer service suffers.

4. Planners and buyers would rather be beat up once at the end of the month or at the end of the year for having too much inventory than be beat up every day for missing deliveries.
5. More inventory is ordered than system policy requires.
6. Policies become points of reference and lose any usefulness as rules for achieving a strategy.

It is no small task to successfully change employee behavior to use the ERP system as an actual planning and control system when employees have been trained to use it mainly for data storage and order tracking.

In Chapter 2 we said, "Understanding the natural behavior of operations first requires a clear understanding of the environment every manager has to navigate. Understanding a company's products, customers, people, and competitors provides necessary but not sufficient information for successfully creating and implementing strategies that provide predictable results." Here we add some specificity to the additional information referenced as being required for sufficient understanding of the environment and predictive management control.

To characterize the environment, we usually consider a mean and a variance of the key environmental parameters,

1. Demand
2. Replenishment time

Cost is definitely a consideration, but it is not a basic element of performance mechanics. For instance if a manager wants a 99 percent fill rate on a particular finished goods item, the amount of inventory required depends solely on the item's demand and the replenishment time for that item. It may be that the item is very expensive and the required inventory is more than the manager wants to stock. However, the amount of inventory required to meet the fill rate is independent of the cost of the item. Certainly, the cost of an item will influence the demand for the item. The cost of resources required to replenish an item will influence its replenishment time. Cost is an important consideration but, as we shall see later, managers can often use cost improperly in trying to achieve the most profitable control of their environment. This is analogous to a scientist assessing the behavior of gold electrons differently from the behavior of carbon electrons because gold is more valuable. It happens all the time in operations management.

Affecting the environment is usually a much more difficult proposition than just changing tactics. Changing the environment means doing such things as:

- Adding capacity (machines or people)
- Increasing run rates
- Reducing variability in demand or replenishment time
- Increasing average demand
- Reducing average replenishment time
- Reducing setup times
- Improving uptime

In considering performance control and improvement of a production or service or supply-chain environment, the following sequence of steps should be taken:

1. Determine how well the process of interest is performing compared with how well it could be performing. This means compared with the best possible performance in the current environment. We call this *absolute benchmarking.* Benchmarking against competitors or best-practice companies can provide interesting ideas and insights, but a manager never really knows how well those companies are performing compared with how well they could be performing. With absolute benchmarking, a manager can determine whether the manager's best possible is good enough to meet the business goals. If so, the pursuit is how to get to the best possible performance. If not, steps have to be taken to improve the environment.
2. Change tactics in the current environment to achieve the best possible performance.
3. If best possible in the current environment is not good enough or if further improvement is desired, the environment must be changed.

We have now described a scientific theory of operations. Specifically:

1. All business is a structure of demand and transformation.
2. Transformation is composed of stocks and production flows.

3. Buffers are required to synchronize demand and transformation in the presence of variability.

For a theory to be useful, it must provide a "comprehensive explanation of some aspect of nature that is supported by a vast body of evidence." The discussion thus far has focused on a comprehensive description of the behavior of operations. We turn now to the mathematical concepts that represent a vast body of evidence supporting Factory Physics science.

Practical Theory

1. The knowledge landscape is highly fragmented for managers who try to use it to lead organizations to achieve business goals.
2. There is a practical science that describes the performance of operations and supply chains. Understanding that science provides better intuition for managers. Better intuition makes managers better leaders.
3. Understanding the practical science enables leaders to navigate the knowledge landscape and design a combination of tools and controls that works best for their specific business conditions.
4. The science starts with a description of all businesses as a combination of demand and transformation.
5. Transformation is a combination of production flows and stocks. Thus all businesses can be described by demand-stock-production diagrams. The behavior of production flows, stock, and demand can be described and evaluated quantitatively.
6. Highest profitability and cash flow are achieved by meeting the most demand with the lowest cost while achieving desired service to customers.
7. It is impossible to perfectly synchronize demand and transformation in the presence of variability. When trying to synchronize demand and transformation in the presence of variability, buffers appear.
8. There are only three types of buffers: inventory, capacity, and time.
9. Increasing variability increases the quantity of buffers required to synchronize demand and transformation.
10. A manager's job is to determine the best combination of buffers and variability for achieving business goals and then to lead the organization to implement the design and achieve the goals.
11. Another way to think about buffer design is as a question of who or what waits?

12. Performance is a function of tactics and environment. It's generally much easier to change tactics than environment. Absolute benchmarking is the comparison of current performance with best possible performance in the current environment.

PUTTING PRACTICAL SCIENCE TO PRACTICE

As we said earlier, "attaining better intuition requires that managers align their understanding of their environment with an accurate scientific understanding of the natural behavior of that environment." We realize that the construct of demand, stocks, production flows, and buffers may be new and still somewhat unclear to readers. In this section we will move more deeply into the science of the natural behavior of operations and supply chains. We introduce some fundamental mathematical equations that describe this behavior and provide visual, quantitative descriptions of this behavior using performance graphs. The math covered here and the performance graphs:

1. Provide the basis for managers to ensure that their intuition coincides with the natural behavior of their environment
2. Lay the groundwork to establish quantitative evaluations of the tradeoffs

For some managers, this might be enough. If not, Chapter 4 provides a much more detailed discussion of the math to provide more technical information should that be desired for either validation of the concepts or more detailed application in practice. However, the balance of this book will discuss the science of operations at the level provided here in Chapter 3. In other words, we are not going to overload you with technical or mathematical jargon. However, we do have to provide some definitions for consistency.

Definitions

We do not claim that these are the only possible definitions of the terms defined. We are only trying to use them to make sure that we are consistent in the use of terms for defining and using the science described herein:

- A *production job* refers to a set of physical materials that traverses a routing along with the associated logical information (e.g., drawings, work orders, inspection procedures). Although every job is triggered by a customer order or anticipation of a customer order (e.g., forecasted demand), in production, there is frequently not a one-to-one correspondence between jobs and orders. That is so because (1) jobs are measured in terms of specific parts (uniquely identified by a part number), not the collection of parts that may make up the assembly required to satisfy an order, and (2) the number of parts in a job may depend on manufacturing efficiency considerations (e.g., batch-size considerations) and thus may not match the quantities ordered by customers.
- A *services job* is the service that is delivered (e.g., putting out a fire or diagnosing and treating a broken arm) and includes the associated logical information (e.g., insurance forms, blood pressure results, X-rays for diagnosing and treating a patient's broken arm).
- *Production routings* describe the sequences of workstations or process centers passed through by a part for production. Routings begin and end at stock points. For example, in Figure 3-9, Cell 19's routing is Cell 19 $\rightarrow$ Aqueous $\rightarrow$ Laser $\rightarrow$ Ship. There is no stock point shown at Ship, although materials get stocked prior to shipping if for no other reason than getting the product packed for shipping.
- A *service routing* is the list of steps that must be completed to provide a service. Figure 3-10 shows routings for a service flow for admission of a walk-in patient to an emergency department at a hospital. The routing is simply to and from the respective steps (e.g., tracking board, triage, etc.) to a physical waiting area. In this case, the specific waiting area is treated as a stock point. There's a "Care Center" set up to handle patients who don't require expensive emergency room beds (e.g., a patient having a hard-to-remove splinter removed).
- *Cycle time* is the average time from release of a job at the beginning of a routing until it reaches a stock point at the end of the routing (i.e., the time the parts spend as WIP or the amount of time a patient spends in triage).

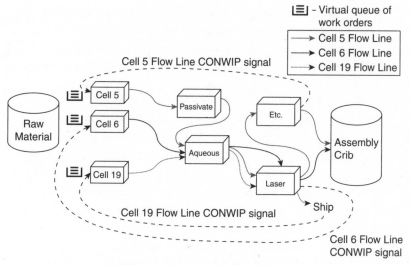

FIGURE 3-9. Production routings (flow lines)

- The *lead time* of a given routing is the time allotted for production of a part on that routing or line or completion of a service. As such, it is a management constant. In contrast, cycle times are generally random. The methods by which managers set and maintain lead times in MRP

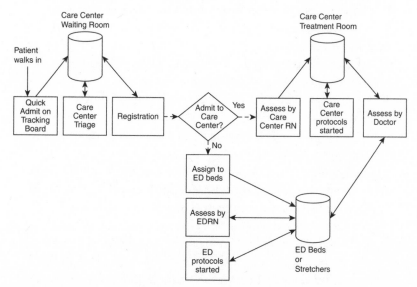

FIGURE 3-10. Service routings for walk-in patient admission to an emergency department

systems are vital to maintaining good control over a process. Our experience has been that lead times get set in practice when an IT system is installed or updated and sporadically thereafter. This causes fundamental performance problems, which we shall discuss later.

- *Replenishment time* is used in describing inventory systems and is the time from when the inventory position (on hand + on order – backorders) reaches the reorder point and triggers a reorder until that reorder quantity is in stock and available for use.
- *Throughput* is the average output rate of a product production flow or a service production flow (e.g., parts per hour, liters per hour).
- *Capacity* is the upper limit on throughput.
- The *utilization* of a workstation is the fraction of time it is not idle for lack of parts. This includes the fraction of time the workstation is working on parts or has parts waiting and is unable to work on them because of a machine failure, setup, or other detractor. It is quite telling that many of the leaders we train as part of *Factory Physics* short courses have a very imprecise understanding of how to compute capacity and its utilization. This is a serious problem in establishing predictive control of any flow and, by implication, a serious problem for successfully leading a business.
- *Process time* is the time required to complete a job at a process center.
- *Nominal process time* is the time to complete a job at a process center with no downtime.
- *Effective process time* is the time required to complete a job including downtime at a process center.
- *Interarrival time* is the average time between arrivals of a job to a workstation.
- The *coefficient of variation* is a way of normalizing levels of variability and is equal to the standard deviation of a random variable divided by the mean. Thus, if the coefficient of variation of the diameter of a hole on a printed circuit board is 1.5 and the coefficient of variation for the length of a jet airplane is 1.5, we know that the relative variability of those two dimensions is the same, even though they are on vastly different scales.

- *Fill rate* is the probability that a part is not backordered. In other words, it's the probability that a part is on hand in inventory when demand for the part occurs. Note that customer service can be 100 percent even if the fill rate is less than 100 percent—for example, if a product is out of stock when an order is received but the order lead time is five days. If the product arrives in stock and is shipped to the customer within the five-day lead time, customer service is 100 percent for that order.

Factory Physics Science: As Simple as Possible but No Simpler

In working with Factory Physics science in practice over two decades (dating from the formulation of the book *Factory Physics*), we have found that executives and managers are predisposed to favor simple solutions over complex ones. A simple solution or plan is much easier to communicate and execute across a large organization. Executives in particular are often accused of promoting mindless platitudes in an effort to rally an organization to improved performance. The earlier discussion of conceptual illustrations provided an introductory explanation of Factory Physics science (i.e., something or someone is always waiting), but that level of discussion doesn't provide much guidance for running a business. Also, neither mindless platitudes nor conceptual illustrations provide information that can be used to directly connect executive strategy to day-to-day execution. The following discussion provides a more detailed explanation of Factory Physics science and demonstrates the models we have used in practice for the last two decades, give or take, to successfully understand, manage, and improve businesses. We will work with this level of detail throughout the rest of this book (except for even more detail in Chapter 4) to demonstrate the concepts of Factory Physics science for successfully managing and leading businesses.

In making the simplest explanation for Factory Physics science when we teach it, we cover three equations and four performance graphs in addition to the buffers and DSP concepts. We realize that this is not quite as simple as saying, "Reduce waste." On the other hand, we didn't say it would be as simple as falling off a floating boat and hitting water. Product mix, process complexity, and demand and replenishment variation cannot be described and predictively modeled by something as massively simple as a value-stream map. As Albert Einstein once said, "A theory should be as simple as possible but no simpler." The three equations and four performance graphs provide managers with a practical scientific basis for an approach to handling complexity and variation predictively and successfully. Just as important, when you finish the remainder of this chapter, your intuition should be improved or affirmed regarding the conflicts that compose the natural behavior of business.

Advancing the Practical Science of Management

As you will discover, the equations that we are about to cover are not new. At the same time, the research carried out by Factory Physics, Inc., is pushing the boundaries on the science of manufacturing and supply-chain dynamics. See "Toward a Standard Model of Supply Chain Dynamics," by Mark Spearman, presented at the Institute for Operations Research and the Management Sciences (INFORMS) annual meeting in October 2013. As it turns out, application of the "principle of least action" from fundamental physics to the supply chain naturally results in a Brownian motion model that explains the basic Factory Physics tradeoffs among the variability buffers of inventory, capacity, and time. This level of physics with stochastic partial differential equations and its Hamiltonian-Brownian motion model are way beyond the scope of this book. At the same time, managers can take comfort in the fact that there is basic and comprehensive science underlying their efforts to reduce waste and increase profitability, cash flow, and service.

The basic construct of a demand-stock-production (DSP) structure for designing capacity, inventory, and time buffers is a tried-and-tested science of management. At the same time, it is a relatively unique understanding of operations management science. Spearman and Hopp were the first to propose this approach in *Factory Physics*. At the same time, they proposed another new scientific idea, which was the idea of best-case, practical-worst-case, and worst-case performance boundaries. See Chapter 7 of *Factory Physics* for the details, but this concept of performance boundaries has far-reaching implications for managers attempting to lead their organizations successfully. Given (1) the DSP structure to design a buffer portfolio for most profitable variability management, (2) performance boundaries for predictive determination of optimal performance of inventory, capacity, and time (service), (3) the ability of managers to strategically select a position within or on performance boundaries, (4) translation of the selected position into optimal policies for desired performance, (5) tactics and controls to ensure that the organization, down to an individual level, is performing within the ranges specified by the manager's strategic choices, and (6) standardization of control in the organization's IT system (regardless of IT vendor), managers now have an applied science of operations at their disposal to lead organizations more efficiently and effectively than ever before.

We have only talked about the first item in any detail so far. As we turn to discussion of the three equations and four performance graphs, we are moving into a discussion of items two through four. As mentioned, the equations are not new. However, each equation leads to a graph (except for the last graph, lot size versus cycle time) that provides a visual illustration of performance. The equations and graphs help to develop managers' intuition on buffer interactions and the boundaries of performance. The equations and performance graphs illustrate the natural behavior of the fundamental scientific structure of DSP, buffers, and variability so that an executive can develop an operations design for the best possible profitability, cash flow, and service. As icing on the cake, this approach only serves to strengthen existing performance-improvement efforts that managers have in place, such as Lean, Six Sigma, TOC, or whatever company program may be in use. We are not advocating starting over on performance improvement, although in some cases dysfunctional efforts should be abandoned. We want to advance the practical science of management to help managers work better with existing resources.

For the three equations and four performance graphs, we will present each equation, discuss its components and background, and then look at the graph related to the equation as a visual exercise in understanding performance management. Each equation provides a double-edged sword. On the one hand, by itself, each equation is too simple to model complex manufacturing and supply-chain processes. On the other hand, each equation provides very powerful insights that can be used to improve a manager's intuition and leadership ability. Later in this book we will describe a practical approach for putting these concepts into practice in the face of all the complexity and confusion encountered in day-to-day management—an approach based on our experience in working with our own and other companies over the past two decades.

The *VUT* Equation

The *VUT equation* (also know as the *Kingman equation*) describes a relationship between waiting time (cycle time in queue), variability *V*, utilization *U*, and processing time *T* for a single process center. The *VUT* equation is a model of an open queueing network. In other words, jobs released to a flow can grow without bound, depending on demand and flow performance. WIP control systems (pull systems) mitigate unbounded growth of WIP and cycle time, but the underlying behavior never goes away.

Cycle time at a single process center is equal to the time in the station t_e (effective process time) plus the time waiting CTq, that is,

$$CT = t_e + CTq$$

This description of cycle time is straightforward and quantitative, as we shall see. We are discussing natural behavior of processes at a high level. The *VUT* equation, which models CTq, provides just the right amount of detail for now. Chapter 4 provides more detail on the fundamental components of cycle time. Note that this is very different from describing cycle time as CT = value-added time + non-value-added time, a highly subjective and uninformative definition. We call this approach to cycle-time analysis the *value-added fantasy* and discuss it in more detail in Chapter 5.

As value-stream maps typically show, a major amount of time in almost any flow is time spent waiting (CTq). In its most general form, the *VUT* equation is written as

$$CTq = VUT$$

This form of the equation shows that CTq has three elements: (1) a variability component V, (2) a utilization component U, and (3) a time component T.

Without going any further, we observe a fundamental characteristic of cycle time: the components are multiplicative, not additive. A practical implication of this is that businesses with high variability should carefully consider the effects of trying to drive high utilization levels. Conversely, businesses that want high utilization of resources should be well aware of the effect of increasing variability when doing things like increasing the number or variety of products offered.

For further explanation, we consider the industrial engineering version of the *VUT* equation:

$$CTq = \left(\frac{c_a^2 + c_e^2}{2} \right)\left(\frac{u}{1 - u} \right)t_e$$

Here we see that the components of the *VUT* equation can be further described as

$$V = \left(\frac{c_a^2 + c_e^2}{2} \right)$$

where c_a^2 = squared coefficient of variation of interarrival times, an indicator of demand or flow variability, c_e^2 = squared coefficient of variation of effective process times, an indicator of process variability; u = utilization, as defined previously (also calculated as time used divided by time available), and t_e = effective process time, as defined earlier.

Now, referring back to the practical implication of increasing utilization in businesses that also have inherently high variability, we see that the cycle-time implications are major. If a manager of any low-volume, high-mix business wants to increase utilization from 70 to 95 percent, ostensibly to get a better return on assets, the increase provides a 36 percent increase in utilization. This means that the machines are busier, but note what happens to cycle time by looking at the U factor in the *VUT* equation:

At 70 percent, $U = 0.7/(1 - 0.7) = 2.3$.
At 95 percent, $U = 0.95/(1 - 0.95) = 19!$

So the manager has traded a 36 percent increase in utilization for a 714 percent increase in cycle time. Is this a good trade? Only the manager knows for sure. We mentioned low-volume, high-mix businesses in particular because they typically already have a high *V* factor (high variability), which leads to even higher cycle times. Having a large-capacity buffer—that is, low utilization—might result in machines sitting idle, but it provides a much needed buffer against variability if short lead times are important. This is in sharp contrast to the classic view of utilization, but we will address that shortly.

Another insight from this behavior is that cheap capacity is highly valuable for improving responsiveness. In other words, if there is a 20-year-old machine that will still hold quality standards, don't throw it out just because it's slow. As a matter of fact, a manager may want to go to the used machine market and buy more. Manufacturing people in particular like to have the latest and greatest technology, which almost always translates to expensive machinery. The proposed benefit of this additional expense is usually increased efficiency. Use of outdated, cheap capacity can provide increased responsiveness (i.e., shorter cycle times) by enabling desired output at relatively low utilization levels. Moreover, the increased responsiveness could be much more valuable to retaining customers and increasing demand than just buying expensive, more efficient capacity.

Cycle Time versus Utilization Graph

Figure 3-11 is a visual representation of the *VUT* equation. It vividly and simply illustrates the natural behavior of a business as utilization increases toward 100 percent. Cycle time blows up.

When we think about performance boundaries, the shining star in Figure 3-12 shows "perfect world" best-case performance. This would be the zero-variability scenario discussed in the first paragraph of the buffers section. Best-case performance is 100 percent utilization, where cycle time for the process center is a zero-variability nominal processing time *t*. In a more complex process with multiple process centers, the best-case cycle time would be the sum of the best-case process times at each process center—value-added time in Lean parlance.

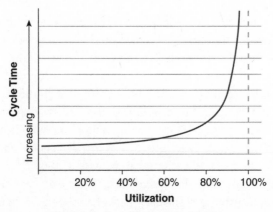

FIGURE 3-11. Cycle time versus utilization

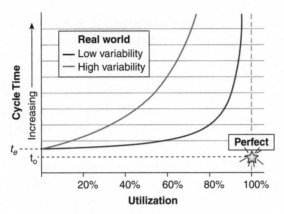

FIGURE 3-12. The corrupting influence of variability

With variability, actual performance will never match best-case performance, so there's no sense in planning for or trying to achieve best-case performance. *A manager's first step in planning is to figure out which curve describes the current environment and select the utilization level that meets business cycle-time goals—a policy decision.* Of course, if the process is on the high-variability curve shown in Figure 3-12, there might be problems with finding a financially suitable utilization level; setting the right utilization policy won't work. In this case, the environment must be changed. Either variability has to be reduced, or the capacity buffer has to be increased to bring utilization down while still achieving the throughput needed to meet demand. This is where it is imperative for managers leading organizations to understand the effects of these interactions among variability, utilization, and time.

In pursuit of perfect performance, we have seen leaders drive organizations into management chaos. In one such example, the executive vice president (a Lean expert) in charge of manufacturing for a multibillion-dollar aerospace business had the multimillion-dollar planning system loaded with requirements that were 30 percent greater than any output the business had ever demonstrated. For managers who understand the real-world behavior of cycle time versus utilization, this is a disturbing thought. As expected, the requirements in the planning system could not be met, so the planning-system signals were largely ignored. War room meetings were a regularly planned occurrence year round. The vice president even hired a programmer to develop a Microsoft Access hot-sheet database for the weekly publication of priority parts because the MRP planning system "didn't work." At a quarterly all-hands meeting, the vice president praised the manufacturing organization for its work in driving Lean efforts. WIP and cycle time had been reduced through hard work and many *kaizens*. Unfortunately, inventory was too high in the assembly stores area (after manufacturing and before assembly); on-time delivery was not as good as it needed to be, and the vice president said, "We need to figure that out." This was a classic case of ignoring the natural behavior of operations.

There were plenty of parts being made—and made with fairly short cycle time—but they were not the right parts. So production cycle time was shortened, but the overall cycle time, including the time sitting in inventory, was much longer. As the graphs in the preceding figures show, maintaining 130 percent utilization is impossible. Because the planning system had an infeasible plan, the hot-sheet system was used to determine production requirements. Production managers looked at the MRP production plan and at the hot sheet and then attempted hot-sheet requirements within the general overload of requirements. The planning system load of 130 percent utilization should have resulted in complete loss of control and extremely high cycle times, but that did not happen. The results were achieved through a huge amount of brute-force activity. Besides the continual war room meetings, there were individuals whose job it was to do nothing but expedite parts. In addition, production managers made liberal use of overtime and outsource capacity (at extra cost) at a cottage industry of small machine shops in the community of the main manufacturing facility. The business results were less than desired and much less profitable than could have been achieved, but there was plenty of Lean activity to highlight.

The effect of all this extra activity was twofold:

1. The overtime and outsourcing efforts provided more capacity, which meant that overall utilization was lower.
2. Use of the hot-sheet system helped to filter out unnecessary demand, which also lowered utilization.

A valuable part of this approach in the vice president's eyes was that there was always a high level of activity. People were busy all the time. This gets to one of the physcological impediments to managing utilization properly—managers hate it when people or machines

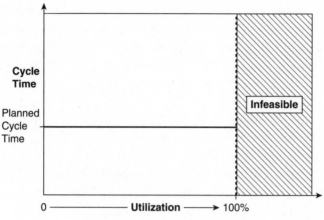

FIGURE 3-13. Classic view of cycle time

are idle. It's hard to reconcile idle capacity with good business practice. As described in Chapter 1, managers look to practices such as moving assembly lines as the ultimate in manufacturing systems. The impression is that capacity utilization is nearly 100 percent in these systems, when, in fact, this is not the case. Managers must understand the tradeoffs between capacity, inventory, and response time to design and maintain a capacity base that provides the best financial return for their businesses. Unfortunately, the model that typically informs management decisions is the classic view of utilization. Figure 3-13 illustrates that thinking.

The idea is that a company plans on a particular cycle time, and as long as 100 percent utilization is not exceeded, that cycle time will be good for planning purposes. This is reinforced by two other common conventions:

1. **The standard cost model.** This model says that total cost is a function of fixed cost plus a variable cost. Unit costs are determined by allocating the fixed cost across the number of units produced. More units produced leads to less unit cost whether all the units are sold or not. The conclusion often drawn from this model is to drive production to 100 percent utilization to achieve the lowest possible unit cost.

2. **Contemporary MRP, ERP, and advanced planning and scheduling (APS) systems data-entry requirements.** If a manager is going to set lead times for a part for planning

purposes, that information is typically entered as a fixed value into a planning system in the item master screen or a similar screen. It is not a common practice to go in and adjust part lead times on a regular basis. Using fixed lead times is essentially based on a system assumption that capacity is unlimited. Attempts to address this flaw in MRP or ERP systems resulted in the development of capacity-planning modules and APS systems. However, APS systems use optimization heuristics, that is, approximations, to figure out an "optimal" schedule and then provide the ability to constantly reassess and change that schedule. This provides a Sisyphean task for planners and managers. It is impossible to determine an optimal schedule for anything but the simplest of processes (see the section "Why Scheduling Is Hard" in Chapter 15 of *Factory Physics* for a detailed discussion). APS systems typically try to compensate for this by allowing managers to adjust the schedule daily or more frequently to compensate. If today's powerful computers do not have the power to determine optimal detailed schedules, does it make sense that a planner or manager will be able to compensate by manipulating all the jobs, job statuses, purchase orders, and process center statuses manually? We think that it obviously does not make sense. Yet companies still buy APS systems and wonder why they don't solve their inventory and customer-service problems.

The *VUT* equation is just one model illustrating the practical science describing real-world behavior of production flows, stocks, and buffers. As mentioned earlier, the *VUT* equation is an open-queueing-network model. In other words, WIP and cycle time can grow without bounds. For flows, Lean advocates well know that there is a big benefit to controlling WIP: it prevents cycle-time explosions. This type of control is what is known as a *closed queueing network.* We will look at WIP control in the next section on Little's law. We will also see how the cycle time for flows (either open or closed queueing networks) contributes to the requirements for inventory in stock points when we cover the equation for variance of replenishment-time demand. Thus the *VUT* equation provides a wealth of insight into the dynamics of flows and stocks and the tradeoffs between buffers that managers must master to lead and suceed over the long term.

A final observation from the *VUT* equation: if a manager attempts to push too far down on one of the buffers (e.g., run at 100 percent utilization with no capacity buffer), one or both of the other buffers will blow up. If the capacity buffer is reduced to nothing, shipments will either be late or there will be lots of inventory or both. We don't make the rules; we're just explaining them. Managers should not follow the classic view that cycle time remains fixed until 100 percent utilization is accomplished. This will drive constant failure of a manager's efforts to provide high customer service while tying up minimum cash inventory.

"Realism is the heart of execution, but many organizations are full of people who are trying to avoid or shade reality. . . . Sometimes the leaders are simply in denial. When we ask leaders to describe their organizations' strengths and weaknesses, they generally state the strengths fairly well, but they're not so good at identifying weaknesses."[7] Our experience is that many managers are not aware of the natural behavior of buffers and variability. As a result, they try to manage based on financial or software models that are not realistic predictors of performance. A manager's intuition must be informed by the *VUT* model of performance to reflect reality. If this is done, managers will be more effective leaders because they will be much more likely to execute successfully.

So what happened to the vice president of manufacturing? As it turned out, the brute-force approach worked well for a while in getting financial results, so he enjoyed a run of success. Ironically, he was undone by trying to establish skill-level classifications for production workers as part of perfection of the Lean implementation efforts. This led to a union organization movement that resulted in the vice president's pursuit of other career opportunities. Would the brute-force approach have caught up with him eventually? We'll never know. What we do know is that the next vice president of manufacturing scaled back on the Lean implementation and provided the quote in Chapter 2: "Our suppliers better get their parts in on time or tell them I will be showing up at their door with a truck to get the parts myself." He lasted an even shorter period of time. We firmly believe that organizations should have some standardized process of continuous improvement. However, we also firmly believe that those efforts are typically much less productive than they should be. Without a good understanding of practical science, managers use initiative and action combined with folklore and exhortation to try to get results. As described in Chapters 1 and 2, the results have been mixed at best.

The *VUT* equation and the cycle time versus utilization graph provide instructive illustration of the behavior of buffers and variability. A huge takeaway from the *VUT* equation is that managers should thoroughly understand how to calculate and manage utilization. Capacity is a first-order effect. If managers cannot calculate and manage capacity utilization appropriately, all other efforts at improving performance will suffer accordingly. Focusing on variability reduction when trying to achieve an infeasible (utilization >100 percent) production schedule is a quixotic venture. As we saw with the vice presidents of manufacturing, sometimes the suffering is not even recognized as such. Neither vice president recognized the practice of loading an infeasible schedule into the planning and control system as a major driver of wasted effort. We have found the understanding of utilization to be surprisingly weak in many organizations and will cover it in more detail in Chapter 4.

Production and Stocks

We said that we were going to provide predictive science that would tie directly to execution. For that, we have to include useful analysis of production and stocks because they are the primary components of all processes. The performance graphs in Figure 3-14 are

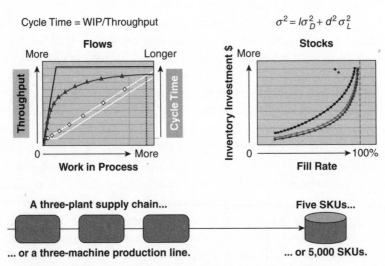

FIGURE 3-14. Performance graphs for production and stocks

a highly useful aid for analyzing production and stocks. For production, Little's law (*Cycle Time = WIP/Throughput*) provides the primary mathematical model. For stocks, the primary equation we discuss is the variance of replenishment-time demand. We cover this topic in much more detail later, but, for an introduction, the variance of replenishment time demand equation shows that the variance of replenishment time demand is a function of the following:

- Average replenishment time (ℓ)
- Variance of demand (σ_d^2)
- Average demand (d)
- Variance of replenishment time (σ_ℓ^2)

This doesn't mean that these are the only equations required. Plenty more are included in Chapter 4, but these two equations lead to an invaluable illustration of the primary behavior of production and stocks.

This modeling of production and stocks enables executives to predictively assess different strategic options and to identify areas for improvement. Determining where a production flow or a stock is performing relative to its respective performance boundaries is the process of absolute benchmarking. For production, it's easy to say that "one-piece flow" or "pull one" is the goal. It's more productive to say, "I will maintain a minimum WIP level of X units to meet demand at a cycle time of Y." For stocks, it's easy to say, "Cut inventory by 50 percent." It's quite another to say, "I can save $3 million in inventory and maintain a 90 percent fill rate with an average backorder time of five days by using more optimal safety stocks and reorder quantities." For both production and stocks, the easy approach is management by directive and hope—the old stretch-goal technique. The latter approach is a science-based analysis leading to predictable results. The Factory Physics approach provides new mathematical models reflecting the science of production flows. It also provides new applications of existing mathematical models for helping managers visualize and use the science of stocks. The result is a very powerful, comprehensive, practical science that enables managers to design production and stocks to achieve desired business performance. We start with the primary model of the science of production flows: Little's law.

Little's Law

In 1961, John D. C. Little published a paper titled "A Proof for the Queuing Formula: $L = \lambda W$,"[8] which described the fundamental relationship between WIP, cycle time, and throughput for production flows. The relationship is typically written as:

$$WIP = Cycle\ Time \times Throughput$$

and as anyone who has done a value-stream mapping exercise knows, it provides a great estimator for value-stream cycle times. If the equation is written in the form $y = f(x)$, the relationship is written as:

$$Cycle\ Time = WIP/Throughput$$

In other words, cycle time is a function of WIP and throughput. From a practical standpoint this means that WIP is a leading indicator of cycle time. As Mark Spearman likes to say, "WIP is visible cycle time." Little's law provides an extremely effective way to determine process cycle times for a manager. The reason is that it makes use of two easily determined quantities:

1. **Throughput.** This equals the demand for a product over the long term. This is always a defined quantity at a company. It's not the quantity needed at every instant in time but the average defined for planning purposes, so it's easy to get. It's a rate, so it is reported as units/time.
2. **WIP (work in process).** This is pretty simple. Go to the production flow, and count the WIP if it's a physical production process. For a service business or virtual production process (e.g., design drawings), the manager is not counting a physical entity. Even so, jobs in process or drawings in process can be counted.

There are some practical issues for using Little's law to calculate cycle time. For MTO jobs, there may be many different jobs with many different rates in the system at any one time. Using one rate and one number for WIP can muddle use of the cycle-time calculation. This can be addressed by converting jobs to units of time at the process constraint—this normalizes the WIP level. When the constraint changes substantially with product mix, typically, software modeling is required.

Another practical issue is that a Little's law calculation for continuous-flow processes (e.g., oil refineries or bottling operations) is often not very informative. Because these types of operations restrict the amount of WIP because of their highly coupled physical structure, the cycle time doesn't vary much. Because WIP is limited by the number of towers or tanks in a refinery or the size of a bottling line, there are often not many options for using WIP to control cycle time. However, the Little's law relationship *can* be used when designing a line to ensure that there are enough WIP locations on the line to buffer against variability of the constraint and ensure adequate throughput.

Little's law is a very powerful model of the science governing flows in any case. As Wally Hopp often says, "It may be little, but it's the law." However, as often occurs with value-stream mapping, managers generalize the Little's law model to inappropriate conclusions that are at odds with the natural behavior of business processes. For instance, Little's law could be interpreted to mean that with constant throughput, less WIP means less cycle time. So some managers jump very quickly to figure what the least amount of WIP on a line could be. Without any knowledge of the relationships between variability and buffers, a common conclusion from looking at Little's law is that one-piece flow should be implemented to provide minimum cycle time.

In *Factory Physics*, Spearman and Hopp showed that attempting one-piece flow is a perilous pursuit. One of the innovations from *Factory Physics* was the understanding of performance boundaries for production and stocks. "Perfect world" best-case performance is not possible. However, we are not recommending setting soft goals. Performance goals should be tough, and they should push people to improve. This requires a predictive understanding of what is possible. As described in Chapter 7 of Spearman and Hopp's *Factory Physics* and also detailed in Chapter 4 of this book, there are boundaries even for perfect performance in production flows. When the unavoidable presence of variability is added to both demand and transformation, *best possible performance degenerates away from best case performance limits*. The questions for goal setting then become "What is the best possible performance?" and "Is the best possible good enough?" For further illustration of the boundaries of performance for production flows and the unique insights that Factory Physics science provides, we turn to another innovation from Factory Physics science—the production-flow graph.

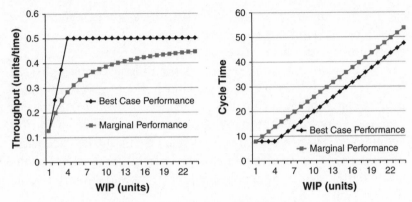

FIGURE 3-15. The components of Little's law

Production-Flow Graph

The production-flow graph provides a visual representation of Little's law. The flow graph is actually a combination of two graphs, as illustrated in Figure 3-15.

1. Throughput versus WIP
2. Cycle time versus WIP

For a reminder of what a production flow might look like, refer back to Figures 3-9 and 3-10. The graphs in Figure 3-15 are from the renowned Penny Fab simulation, as detailed in Chapter 7 of *Factory Physics*. The Penny Fab production flow is illustrated in Figure 3-16.

The reader might question the simplicity of such an example in providing evidence for a comprehensive model of real-world performance. As we shall show later, we have used the concepts derived from this example in massively complex real-world production and supply-chain processes. However, when teaching this example to many, many managers, we regularly see the confusion of intuition, as illustrated in Figure 3-1. So we turn the question around and ask, "If a manager's intuition is poor in predicting the behavior of such

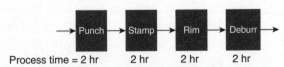

FIGURE 3-16. Penny Fab process centers

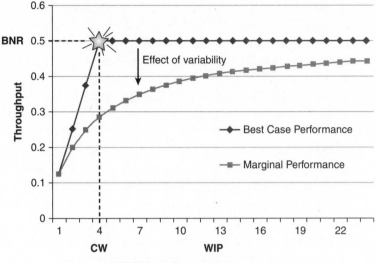

FIGURE 3-17. Throughput behavior

a simple system, how well will that manager fare in dealing with the complexity of the real world?"

In the Penny Fab, the amount of WIP in the line at any one time is controlled, but WIP is allowed to move freely within the flow. This is known as *constant WIP (CONWIP) control*. The characteristics of CONWIP were first described as part of the early development of the Factory Physics approach in 1990 by Spearman, Woodruff, and Hopp.[9] The best case for throughput, as shown by the star in Figure 3-17 is the WIP level at which the flow achieves maximum throughput, the bottleneck rate (BNR), with the minimum amount of WIP, the critical WIP (CW), when there is no variability—the perfect world.

The effect of variability in the real world is to cause less throughput for a given amount of WIP than if there were zero variability. In Figure 3-17 this is shown by the marginal performance curve. Marginal performance shows the effect of introducing variability (exponential processing times) to the Penny Fab. A couple of other things to note about throughput performance in the presence of variability include:

1. Below critical WIP, throughput drops off dramatically as WIP is removed from the system.

2. Above critical WIP, throughput flattens out, so there are only small increases in throughput to be gained by adding more and more WIP to the flow. The bottleneck rate is never achieved as a long-term average throughput. Adding massive amounts of WIP into the flow gets average throughput closer to the bottleneck rate, but the tradeoff, as illustrated next, is a big increase in cycle time.

If we look at the cycle-time graph in Figure 3-18 for the Penny Fab flow, we see that there is a minimum cycle time for a flow, the *raw process time* (RPT), that the flow will generate no matter how little WIP is in the flow. The raw process time is not the same as value-added time. Raw process time includes variability effects such as setups and downtime. For the Penny Fab flow, there are four process centers in sequence with a processing time of two hours at each station.

If there is only one piece of WIP in the system, it will take eight hours at a minimum, on average, even though there is variability. The reason for this is that the fundamental performance parameters for a production flow are its raw process time and its bottleneck rate. Therefore, if a flow's raw process time is eight hours, by definition, one piece of WIP in the system will have an average cycle time of

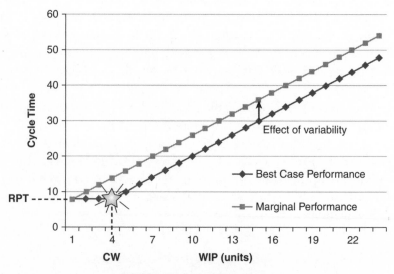

FIGURE 3-18. Cycle-time behavior

eight hours. As WIP levels increase to more than one piece in the system, there arise flow interferences between the two pieces (e.g., one piece is taking longer than average at a station, and the second piece has some wait time for the first piece to get finished). Consequently, as shown in Figure 3-18, best-case and marginal-case cycle times are the same with one piece of WIP in the system, and after that, the curves diverge.

Raw process time and bottleneck rate are the two fundamental performance parameters of a production flow, and a Little's law calculation yields

Critical WIP = raw process time × bottleneck rate

Another application of Little's law puts to rest an old but occasionally seen goal of achieving zero inventory (or zero WIP). If WIP is zero, throughput is zero. This approach is certainly a good way to conserve working capital but not very effective for meeting demand.

Now we combine the cycle-time and throughput graphs to get the production-flow graph, as shown in Figure 3-19, and see the full implications of Little's law for production flows in the real world.

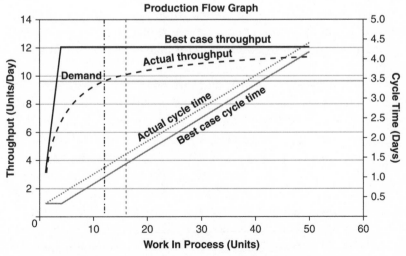

FIGURE 3-19. A visual representation of production-flow behavior

(Courtesy of Factory Physics Inc.)

Some additional detail is added in Figure 3-19 because the graphic is taken from a CSUITE software model used for modeling real-world processes:

- The two preceding graphs are combined, with the left axis corresponding to the values for throughput (the top two black lines). The right axis is for cycle time (the bottom two gray lines).
- The black dashed throughput line tracks *actual* throughput performance with the flow's current variability. This is no longer marginal performance. The same is true for the dotted cycle-time lines. They are for actual performance and can be created for production flows of great complexity, for example, Figure 3-9.
- The solid horizontal line at 9.6 units per day on the throughput axis is the demand.
- The left black vertical line corresponds to the minimum amount of WIP that would be needed to meet demand in a closed-loop flow (a CONWIP pull system that controls WIP).
- The lighter rightmost vertical line is the amount of WIP that would result from having an open-loop flow that releases work at the rate of demand with no control on the amount of WIP in the flow.

Now that we have this combined graph as an excellent visual representation of the natural behavior of production flows, we can lock down important points of intuition for managing performance:

1. Given a level of capacity and variability for a production flow, cycle time *and* throughput vary directly with the amount of WIP in a system. In Six Sigma terminology, WIP is the independent variable. Cycle time and throughput are dependent variables. *WIP is a control parameter for determining the amount of throughput and cycle time a flow will produce.* As explained in *Factory Physics*, the "magic" of pull systems is that they control WIP. Actually, it doesn't matter much whether WIP control is called *pull, push, kick, jump,* or *shout.* The point is that the level of WIP is a design parameter for determing the performance of a production flow. We understand the somewhat intuitive appeal of the term *pull* as

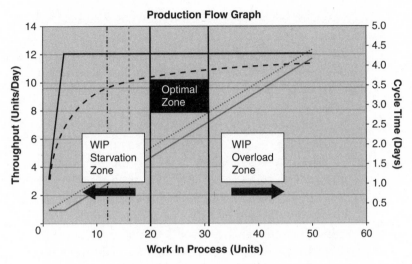

FIGURE 3-20. The optimal WIP zone

used to describe WIP control systems, but in practice, all the definitions we have seen of pull systems are not very precise. Call it by whatever term is preferred, but you need to be sure to understand the behavior of WIP control when designing or controlling production. WIP is an inventory buffer that can be used to great effect when it is used properly.

2. Utilization of the constraint can be seen from the ratio of the demand rate to the bottleneck rate (BNR). In Figure 3-19 utilization of the constraint is 9.6/12, or 80 percent.

3. There is an optimal WIP zone for a production flow that provides maximum output with minumum cycle time. This is shown in Figure 3-20. This is the region where the actual throughput performance curve begins to flatten out. There is not a quantitative definition of the optimal WIP zone yet. The point is to keep the WIP level away from the portion of the curve where throughput drops off the cliff.

    The production flow shown is not operating in the optimal WIP zone because throughput achieves demand with only about 12 units of WIP in the flow, on average, whereas the optimal WIP zone starts at about 20 units. Is this a problem? Maybe, maybe not. The goal is to have best profitability and cash flow. The investment of capacity in Figure 3-20 may be the right amount because demand is increasing or because the demand shown is for a seasonal low period.

4. Specific effects on performance occur as a result of changing the environment, and these are predictable. For instance, what happens when variability is decreased, demand increases, or capacity is decreased?

   a. Decreasing variability moves the actual throughput performance (black dashed line) curve up and to the left. Think of it as reducing variability moves the actual performance curve closer and closer to the "perfect world" best-case performance curve. The actual cycle-time curve also moves closer to best-case performance as variability is reduced. Note that if the production flow in Figure 3-19 were capable of best-case performance, only about four units of WIP would be required to achieve the throughput needed to meet demand. Interestingly, even zero variability would not change the utilization level of the constraint; it would just require less working capital (WIP) to achieve the needed demand and do so at much shorter cycle times.

   b. Achieving throughput to meet increased demand in the current system would require more WIP in the system. For example, in Figure 3-19 if demand were increased to 11 units/day, about 30 units of WIP would be required to meet demand. Similarly, cycle time would go from approximately one day to approximately three days. We don't often see managers who have a good understanding of this dynamic. With contemporary continuous-improvement efforts, we typically see a focus on reducing WIP to a minimum to decrease cycle time and then frustration because customer service suffers, even though the cycle times are short. Efforts then often turn to doing such things as increasing forecast accuracy or putting finished-good inventory in place. This is dysfunctional buffer management.

   c. The effect of decreasing capacity is shown in Figure 3-21. The circles show the points on the actual throughput curve where throughput meets demand. In this case, capacity was decreased from 12 to 10 units/day. Demand is 9.6 units/day. The reduced capacity means that the optimal WIP zone is in the 12- to 17-unit range, but this is now not enough WIP because production doesn't meet demand

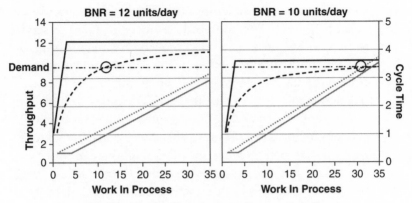

FIGURE 3-21. The effect of reducing the capacity buffer

until about 30 pieces of WIP are on the line. With more WIP, the cycle time has gone from about 1.3 days to about 3.5 days. Is this a good trade? Only the manager can make that call.

5. We have mentioned the perils of pursuing one-piece flow a number of times. The production-flow graph should make this obvious. As production's WIP levels are pushed down in the WIP starvation zone (see Figure 3-20), cycle time continues to drop off linearly, which is a good thing. However, throughput also drops off precipitously. Because throughput equates to revenue, this is generally a bad thing. This strategy effectively starves the bottleneck very often. Bottleneck utilization is low, so parts move through quickly. Another way to look at this is that a manager who pursues such a strategy is effectively placing demand variability directly on the production flow. Because demand variability is typically much higher than production variability, this can have very detrimental effects on customer service. A control-theory analogy is that the manager has implemented a control system in which the feedback mechanism (demand) is much quicker than the response time of the system (production). Engineers who design control systems would consider this very bad practice. A manager might think that the company is better off because the flow can respond quickly with short cycle times. In actuality, the quick response does not make up for the lack of volume. It's like trying to use a very long

garden hose to put out a forest fire. The hose can reach any area of the fire (a flow can produce any type of part or service required). The hose can also be moved very quickly from one area of the fire to another (flow response time is quick because of short cycle times). However, the garden hose is just not going to put out a 1,000-acre fire in time. Think of total customer demand as 1,000 houses, each on a separate acre of the burning 1,000 acres. How well will a firefighter be received when showing up with a single garden hose? "But I can move from one fire to another very quickly," the fireman asserts. This is the situation that Boeing got itself into when it pursued a reduction in cycle time through production of the 777 on a coupled moving assembly line.

Variance of Replenishment-Time Demand Equation

This mathematical model describing behavior of replenishment-time demand (RTD) provides highly useful information to guide managers' intuition on how to manage stocks. We used Little's law to illustrate the behavior of production. We will use variance of replenishment-time demand to provide an introduction to the behavior of stocks and stock points. As we said earlier, *stocks* is the general term for inventory buffers. *Stock points* are logical constructs used to create classifications for planning and control of physical items. Classifications could be parts by supplier or by lead time or demand volume. Common usage in the literature is to use the term *lead-time demand* for what we are calling *replenishment-time demand*. However, there is a method to our madness, as should be apparent from our definitions of cycle time, replenishment time, and lead time below.

Figure 3-22 shows a demand-production-stock diagram of a base stock model. Demand and replenishment time drive the performance of a stock point.

To review:

Cycle time is the average time from release of a job at the beginning of a routing in a production flow until it reaches a stock point at the end of the routing. Cycle time is a random variable.

Replenishment time is the time from when the "system" (in its largest construct) recognizes the need for additional

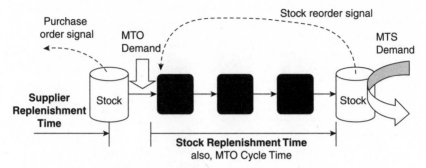

FIGURE 3-22. Base stock model for replenishment time

inventory and when that inventory is available for use.
When we say *system* in this case, we are not referring to
the IT system. The *inventory system* refers to a regularly
interacting or interdependent group of items and actions
forming a unified whole to manage inventory. This
includes status of purchase orders, buyer review time in
processing ERP recommendations, supplier production
time for raw materials, production cycle time for
finished goods, transportation time, and receiving time.
Replenishment time is also a random variable.

Lead time is a management policy that is loaded in the MRP
or ERP system for planning purposes. Lead times are
deterministic.

Based on these definitions, we will be talking about the variance of replenishment-time demand because we are concerned with
behavior of stock points in view of the real world and all its inherent variability. Before we get to the variance of replenishment-time
demand equation, we will provide some examples of stocks points
for grounding your mental images. Figure 3-23 shows a simple DSP
diagram with stock points and production flows. Notice that raw
materials for assembly are also finished goods from suppliers and
from production. Also note that replenishment-time process is apparent for each stock. Production replenishment time is used for the
stock point of production-finished goods; supplier replenishment
time is used for the stock points of raw materials prior to production
and assembly; and assembly replenishment time is used for assembly-
finished goods.

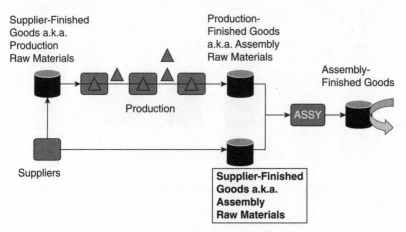

Supplier-Finished
Goods a.k.a.
Production
Raw Materials

Production-
Finished Goods
a.k.a. Assembly
Raw Materials

Assembly-
Finished Goods

Production

ASSY

Suppliers

**Supplier-Finished
Goods a.k.a.
Assembly
Raw Materials**

FIGURE 3-23. A simple supply-chain map

Now, if we look at the supplier-finished goods/assembly raw materials stock point highlighted in Figure 3-23, we show that we can categorize the parts in that stock point in a number of different ways for analysis and control. Table 3-2 shows one approach to classifying the 716 parts in the supplier-finished goods/assembly stock point; the parts are grouped by supplier.

Another approach is shown in Table 3-3. The parts are grouped by demand and lead-time categories. Why this would be a consideration will be apparent shortly. The point is that there are many different ways to group parts in a stock point. We do *not* recommend

TABLE 3-2. Part Classifications by Supplier in Supplier-Finished Goods/Assembly Raw Materials Stock Point

Stock Point ID	Description	Items in Stockpoint	Demand	Actual Fill Rate (%)	Actual Value Inventory
Supplier 1	Supplier 1's parts	151	94,028.89	95.00%	$9,576,990.29
Supplier 2	Supplier 2's parts	462	192,177.78	85.00%	$7,670,690.60
Supplier 3	Supplier 3's parts	78	2,153.33	85.00%	$6,722,185.32
Supplier 4	Supplier 4's parts	13	2,046.67	85.00%	$837,733.72
Supplier 5	Supplier 5's parts	12	8,922.22	85.00%	$969,006.84
		716			

Source: Courtesy of Factory Physics, Inc.

TABLE 3-3. Parts Classified by Fundamental Inventory Drivers: Demand and Replenishment Time

Stock Point ID	Description	Items in Stockpoint	Demand	Actual Fill Rate (%)	Actual Value Inventory
HDLL	High Demand Long Lead Time	159	196,648.89	95.00%	$11,475,357.47
HDSL	High Demand Short Lead Time	112	90,704.44	85.00%	$3,885,519.43
LDLL	Low Demand Long Lead Time	197	5,875.56	85.00%	$2,731,177.43
LDSL	Low Demand Short Lead Time	248	6,100.00	85.00%	$7,684,152.52
		716			

Source: Courtesy of Factory Physics Inc.

using ABC classification—an obsolete and suboptimal approach. More on that later.

This configuration of logical groups for inventory is part of the design process for setting up an optimal control system for inventory, but we're getting ahead of ourselves. Hopefully, these brief illustrations have provided an idea of how the concepts of stocks and stock points apply in your company. If so, that, in turn, should help you to think about how variance of replenishment-time demand can inform intuition for managers working on improving performance.

What is replenishment-time demand? It is simply *the demand that occurs during the relenishment time of a product.* A simple example is as follows: Consider a product that takes three months to procure. If demand is 10 per month, a Little's law calculation yields:

$$Replenishment\text{-}time\ demand = 3\ months \times$$
$$10\ parts/month = 30\ parts$$

If there were no variability, every three months a manager would ensure that an order of 30 parts was placed. The order of 30 parts would arrive every three months just as the last part on hand was used, and the service level for the part would be 100 percent.

In the real world, both replenishment time and demand vary. Replenishment-time demand (RTD) is a random variable with a mean and a variance. The variance of replenishment-time demand V(RTD) is an important parameter in determining optimal inventory management. This is so because one needs to carry enough inventory to cover the variability in demand and in replenishment. For example, if a supplier is late, additional inventory is needed to cover the additional time waiting for the part to arrive. If demand spikes, additional inventory is needed to cover the additional demand.

$$\text{Variance of replenishment-time demand} = \ell\sigma_d^2 + d^2\sigma_\ell^2$$

where ℓ = average replenishment time, σ_ℓ^2 = variance of replenishment time, d = average demand, and σ_d^2 = variance of demand. If the variance of replenishment-time demand increases, bad things happen:

1. Inventory requirements increase.
2. Service levels decrease.

Managers typically have intuition about average demand, although, as we shall see in the discussion on forecast error in Chapter 4, there are problems with the common intuition managers have about demand variability and forecast accuracy. Very rarely, though, do we see managers who have good, or even any, intuition about the effects of replenishment-time variability on inventory requirements and service levels.

Therefore, just as with the *VUT* equation, we have simply stated the equation, and it provides some profound insights about the natural behavior of stocks:

1. To control inventory optimally, a manager must account for *all* components of variance of replenishment-time demand. Most managers focus on average demand, but this is only one driver, although it is a major one. Average replenishment times are also fairly well understood, although they are typically the "stone tablets" of ERP systems and do not get adjusted very often. As mentioned in Chapter 1, most managers' intuition on variability effects is not good. This is a problem that we will attempt to remedy because, as shown in the equation for the variance of replenishment-time demand, variance of replenishment time and variance of demand are drivers of inventory levels and customer-service performance for stocks.

2. *Cost is not a direct driver of inventory-system performance*, although cost can affect both demand and replenishment time. There is no cost component to variance of replenishment-time demand. Given mean and variance of demand and replenishment time, managers have all the information they need to optimally control inventory. This explains one of the reasons why the common usage of ABC classifications in pursuit of optimal inventory management is just wrong. There will be a more detailed case study in Chapter 9, but the common ABC approach is to set inventory policy based on part categories determined by a cost × demand value. For instance, A+ parts are the parts that cover 50 percent of the cost × demand value of all parts managed. To manage cash, these parts are targeted for special treatment, for example, maintain only a couple of weeks of safety stock. The next category is A parts, and they cover the next 30 percent of the cost × demand value and get three weeks of safety stock, and so on. This type of ABC classification is easy to understand, and many managers accept it intuitively as an optimal approach. Unfortunately, it is not optimal, and as a result, many managers are investing incorrectly in inventory and generating costly chaos as the organization tries to meet customer-service requirements with counterproductive inventory-management practices. As an example, a $1,000 part that has an average demand of 1 per period will get the same policy treatment as a $1 part that has an average demand of 1,000 per period. Both parts have the same (cost) × (demand) value of $1,000, but there is no way they should be treated with the same stocking policy. Holding many periods of supply of a cheap, high-demand part is generally a good practice while expensive, low-demand parts might be better off as an MTO part and not stocked at all. Cost reduction generally drives increased profit, but individual part cost does not drive optimal inventory policies.

Chapters 7 and 9 speak to inventory-classification paradigms that are more effective than ABC in today's data-rich world.

As a side note, many of the major ERP software vendors offer some type of ABC approach for inventory management. This points to a few possibilities concerning software vendors:

a. Software companies are only interested in selling software, and they will sell whatever a customer will buy.

b. Software companies don't really understand the fundamentals of inventory management, so they too think that an ABC strategy for inventory optimization is a good thing.

c. Software companies understand the shortcomings of ABC inventory management and may or may not have explained this to their customers. However, customers with bad intuition are hardheaded and are going to buy whatever they want, no matter whether the software vendor recommends against it.

We leave managers to their own assessment of their software vendor. Forewarned is forearmed.

As illustrated in Table 3-3, a more practical approach would be to set policies based on the categories of demand and replenishment times. This is more practical because the classifications correspond to the natural behavior of stocks. Efforts at improvement and management of inventory will then correspond to affecting the natural behavior of the inventory system—it's easier to paddle downstream than upstream.

Tradeoff Plot: Inventory versus Fill Rate Graph

The visual representation of stock-point behavior is what we call a *tradeoff plot*. The tradeoff is between inventory investment and fill rate. This is, of course, another buffer-configuration decision. Should a manager invest more in inventory or let customers wait? How much should be invested in inventory? The tradeoff plot is driven by the dynamics of variance of replenishment-time demand. It provides a look at the behavior of stocks and a means of answering these questions.

The tradeoff plot is also a very special type of Factory Physics performance graph—a set of efficient frontiers. *Efficient frontiers* is a concept developed in finance for evaluating the risk of a portfolio of investments. The development of *Factory Physics* science has resulted in the adaptation of efficient frontiers to greatly improve the ability

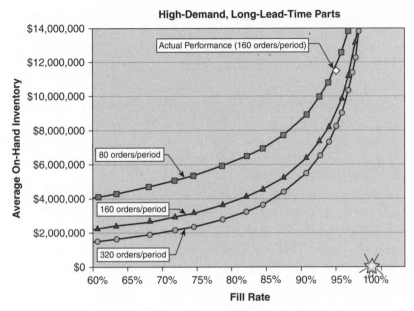

FIGURE 3-24. Inventory versus fill rate tradeoff plot

of managers to rapidly and optimally set inventory policy for the parts in a stock point. More on the concept of efficient frontiers will be provided shortly, but first we introduce the fill rate versus inventory tradeoff plot and see what it tells us about the natural behavior of stocks.

Figure 3-24 provides a tradeoff plot for the 159 parts in the high-demand, long-lead-time stock point in Table 3-3.

First, here is a general description of the tradeoff plot:

- **The y-axis is average on-hand inventory investment.** This is the average amount that will be on hand for financial and sales planning purposes during the planning period for which the plot was generated.
- **The x-axis is the average demand-weighted fill rate.** This is for the entire set of 159 parts.
- **The three curves are efficient frontiers representing different capacity profiles for replenishing parts.** The order profile for each curve is shown in the figure. Eighty orders per period means that each of the 159 parts is ordered, on average, once every two periods. The period could be a week, a month, a year, or whatever fits best in the manager's planning process.

- **Actual performance is current performance reported by the company.** The white diamond shows the current performance as a 95 percent fill rate with about $11.5 million in inventory and ordering, on average, for each part once a period. Is this good? It's not terrible, but it could be better. We'll get to that shortly, but first we provide some description on the efficient-frontiers concept.

Efficient Frontiers

Consider a simple example of one inventory item. Ideal performance would be having inventory 100 percent of the time when needed but with zero inventory on hand. This seems impossible, but it is exactly what MRP would do if (1) demand were known exactly, (2) replenishment times were always exactly equal to system lead times, and (3) we were to employ a *lot-for-lot* order-sizing rule (which simply orders exactly what is needed and no more). Such a system would order the parts so that they arrived just in time to be used. Because they would be consumed the instant they arrived, there would be no inventory, and yet the fill rate would be 100 percent. Figure 3-25 shows the result. This also corresponds to the best-case star on the tradeoff plot in Figure 3-24 at $0 inventory and 100 percent fill rate.

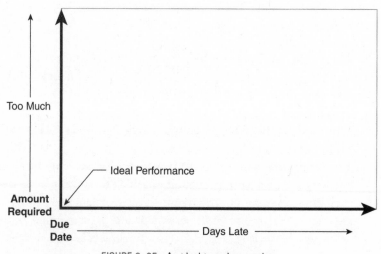

FIGURE 3-25. An ideal inventory system

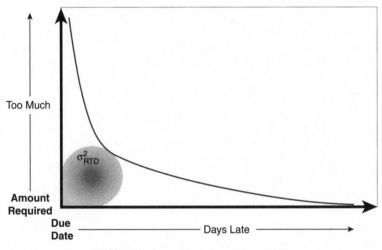

FIGURE 3-26. Inventory system with variability

Now consider what would happen if we were to have randomness in demand and/or replenishment times. Sometimes the replenishment order would arrive early, creating inventory. Other times, it might arrive late, causing backorders. With randomness, it is not a question of having either inventory or backorders; the inventory system will have both.

Figure 3-26 illustrates the effect of the randomness. The variability creates a frontier of possible outcomes that pushes away from the ideal point of exact amount required and exactly on time. Variability produces inventory (more than needed) and backorder time (days late). This variability is characterized by the parameter σ^2_{RTD} indicating the *variance of the replenishment-time demand*, as already discussed in the "Variance of Replenishment Time Demand Equation" section.

If this variance increases, inventory will go up and service will go down. This is illustrated in Figure 3-27.

At any point, both the average on hand (y-axis) and the average backorder (x-axis) are greater than they were in the preceding figure. Besides increasing the variance of RTD, we made an additional change as well. Instead of using a lot-for-lot rule, we are now ordering a fixed order quantity to address the need to control the number of replenishment orders and to minimize inventory. Because the order size is typically greater than the immediate demand, we have more inventory, particularly in the area with poor service (more days late).

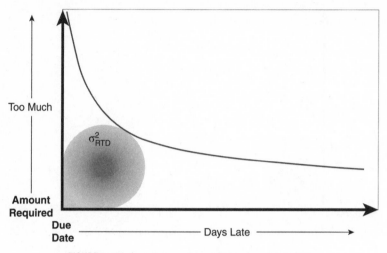

FIGURE 3-27. Inventory system with increased variability

With the use of a fixed order quantity, the curve now shows the relation between average on-hand inventory and average backorder days for a given order size. Of course, *where* we operate on this curve is a *policy* parameter, which, in this case, is the amount of safety stock. This is also a management decision. It's a strategic decision as to what mix of extra inventory (an inventory buffer) and days late (a time buffer) works best for a manager's situation. As safety stock increases, we move to the left on the curve, carrying more inventory, on average, but having less average backorder time.

One curve is all we need for one item. But when we have numerous items, we cannot create a simple two-dimensional plot. Instead, we would need to plot the results of different sets of item policies. For instance, if we had 100 different items, each with a different order quantity and a different safety stock, we would need to specify 200 parameters to describe the inventory policy. Figure 3-28 shows a plot with a number of different policies. Each diamond represents the performance of a given policy. Some policies are closer to a pure MTO system (which carries no inventory), whereas others are closer to a pure MTS system (with no backorders). However, some policies are more *efficient* than others. An efficient policy is one, so plotted, such that no other policy can be plotted that is lower and to the left of the given policy. It is efficient because no other policy is better in terms of both having less inventory and having shorter average backorder times. The set of all efficient policies forms what is called the *efficient frontier*. This

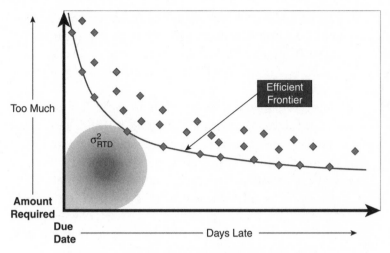

FIGURE 3-28. Plot of inventory policies for numerous items

term is more commonly used in finance to describe various portfolios on a plot of return (y-axis) versus risk (x-axis). In commercial application, companies are more concerned with fill rate than backorder time. Thus, as illustrated in Figure 3-24, the set of portfolios that has the maximum return (minimum on-hand inventory) for a given level of risk (fill rate) contains the efficient policies. The tradeoff plot curves of Figure 3-24 are flipped horizontally from the inventory versus backorder curves discussed in this conceptual explanation.

However the curves are drawn, the Factory Physics approach for system improvement is as follows:

1. Determine where performance is compared with the efficient frontier.
   a. If far away, change policies to get on the frontier.
   b. If performance is on the efficient frontier, the system is performing at best possible given the environment.
   c. Most of the changes a manager has to make to move inventory performance to the efficient frontier are implemented within the production and inventory control systems.
2. Determine how the environment can be changed to improve the efficient-frontier curve.
   a. If the efficient-frontier curve is for a finished-goods stock point such as production-finished goods in Figure 3-23,

changing the environment would mean making changes in production to reduce both the average and variance of replenishment time. For instance, speed up bottleneck machines, reduce setup times, or improve machine availability.

b. Improve demand processes by doing such things as using better forecasting methods, shaping demand, and closely managing and minimizing self-induced variability such as period-ending sales promotions.

c. If the efficient-frontier curve is for a raw materials stock point such as the assembly raw materials/supplier-finished goods stock point in Figure 3-23, changing the environment would mean reducing the average and/or variance of supplier lead times.

3. Repeat.

a. Reoptimize the ERP planning rules given the improved environment.

b. Once the new policies are loaded and executed in the ERP system, performance will migrate to the new efficient-frontier curve.

Insights from the Tradeoff Plot

Now that you are familiar with $V(RTD)$ as describing the fundamental drivers of inventory performance and we have covered the concept of efficient frontiers, let's see what information we can gather from the visual representation of inventory behavior that the tradeoff plot provides us. Figure 3-29 is a repeat of the tradeoff plot here for your convenience.

Observations

1. Inventory requirements increase asymptotically as fill rate approaches 100 percent. This is similar to the behavior that the VUT equation describes for cycle time. As one approaches 100 percent fill rate, it means that there is enough inventory to cover worst-case scenarios in variability, such as a situation where demand spikes just as a supplier is extremely late. Managers must determine the "worst" worst-case scenario they wish to cover with an investment in inventory. Further, this is not as hopeless as it seems for all those managers

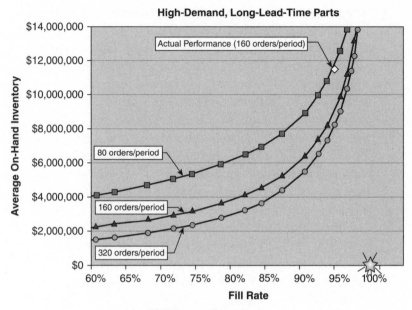

FIGURE 3-29. Tradeoff plot

whose salespeople insist on a 100 percent fill rate for their customers. The difference between a 99.9 percent fill rate and a 99.5 percent can mean a huge difference in required on-hand inventory. As an engineer rounding up, both round to 100 percent. If this is too much sleight of hand, consider that the fill rate is for meeting demand instantly only from inventory. If there is a day to pick, pack, and ship, then there is a time buffer available that also can be used to provide huge reductions in inventory while providing high fill rates.

2. Doubling order frequency from 80 to 160 orders per period provides significant reductions in inventory at a given fill rate. Doubling order frequency again also provides benefit, but not as much. This is the same behavior we saw when we first started describing natural tradeoffs in the production-design example of Chapter 2. As you will see from the math in Chapter 4, increasing order frequency reduces the quantity ordered and thus will reduce inventory on hand. However, as was the case in the production-design example, this has diminishing returns. Eventually, as the order quantity is reduced, the replenishment time of the item becomes a larger determinant of inventory need.

3. The current performance shows a significant opportunity for improvement. The white diamond in Figure 3-29 shows that actual performance is right on the efficient-frontier curve for 80 orders per period. However, the current replenishment frequency is 160 orders per period. So a manager looking at this sees that with the current replenishment profile, the same fill rate could be achieved with nearly $2 million less inventory. Alternatively, the manager could choose to move to the 160 orders per period curve horizontally to the right and pick up a couple of extra points of fill rate with the same amount of inventory ($11.5 million). Where the manager wants to operate is a strategic decision. *Optimal* means optimal for a manager and the manager's company in pursuit of their business goals. Whatever position on whichever curve is selected, the result is designation of the policy parameters of when to order and how much to order for all parts in the stock point. In this example, this would be 2×159 parts, or 318 parameters. Computers can do this very quickly. It beats using spreadsheets and some fairly random ABC-type policy. Full disclosure: the tradeoff plots displayed are from the CSUITE software of Factory Physics Inc. Making this type of calculation on a large number of parts is difficult to do without dedicated software.

Visual Management of Stock-Point Performance

For the final look at stock-point behavior, the comparison in Figure 3-30 is provided to show what happens to the efficient-frontier curves when changes are made to the environment. The upper-left plot (baseline) shows only the 160 orders per period curve from Figure 3-29. With all other plots, this baseline curve is shown as a dashed line. The following changes are made:

1. **Double demand.** Notice that this pushes the curve way up. Much more inventory is needed to provide the current fill rate. The demand term in $V(\text{RTD})$ is squared, so it's no wonder that doubling demand has such a major effect on inventory requirements.
2. **Cut lead time in half.** This is a 50 percent reduction in the average replenishment time on all parts in the stock point.

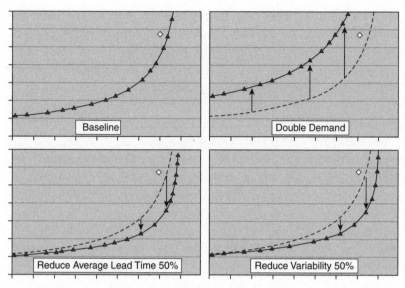

FIGURE 3-30. Results of environmental changes

The result is that the curve shifts down and to the right. At high fill rates, this provides a large opportunity for inventory reduction from current performance.

3. **Reduce variability 50 percent.** In this case, this action means cutting the variance of demand and of replenishment time by 50 percent. The result is nearly the same as reducing average replenishment time by 50 percent. Also, the movement of the curve depends on the characteristics of the parts in the stock point. In this case, the effect of the reduction in variability is similar to the effect of reducing lead time—that is not always the case. Because the variability reduction and lead-time reduction are similar, it presents an interesting option to a manager. Which option should you take if you have to choose one or the other? The evaluation would depend on the resources and effort needed to implement each option. The other thing to consider is the feasibility of either option. Reducing forecast error by 50 percent (a proxy for reducing variance of demand) may well be a bridge too far.

In Six Sigma terminology, this type of comparison is called an *OFAT*—only one factor at a time was changed. There obviously are many combinations of environmental changes that can be made to affect the efficient frontier. Those combinations of changes and anticipated results are exactly the kind of analysis a company's continuous-improvement experts should be working on. While an OFAT is not the most efficient experimental strategy for design of experiments, the comparisons at least provide a directional indication of what type of effect to expect from each change. For instance, if demand is increasing and there is an opportunity to decrease lead time, a manager's intuition should now tell him or her that those are two counteracting effects in moving the curve. Exact determination of the anticipated result will require a detailed analysis, including the amount of the demand increase and the amount of the lead-time decrease. While this type of intuition won't provide an exact answer, it should prevent a manager from committing to a result prematurely. For example, the vice president says, "We're able to cut lead times in half, so I'm going to cut our inventory goals by 50 percent." The response to this should not be, "Aye aye, Captain, full speed ahead." With an informed intuition, the manager replies, "We should do a quick analysis before we go public with that. The lead-time reduction is great and will definitely work to reduce inventory requirements, but demand is also going up, which is going to push inventory requirements up."

Stocks and Flows, the Lot-Size Graph

The final graph for illustrating the science of stocks and production is the *lot-size graph* (Figure 3-31). It is a plot of cycle time versus lot size. There is not a simple equation for the concepts explained here because calculating lot sizes is a dynamic and complex undertaking. Consideration of lot-size optimums involves behavior of both stocks and production. Optimal lot-size calculations have to take into account the following:

1. **Utilization levels.** When utilization is high due to high demand, lot sizes should be large—no time to waste on setups. When utilization is low, lot sizes should be small to minimize on-hand inventory.
2. **Inventory levels.** Larger, less frequent lot sizes will result in more on-hand inventory. Smaller, more frequent lots sizes act to reduce inventory but mean more setups or purchase orders.

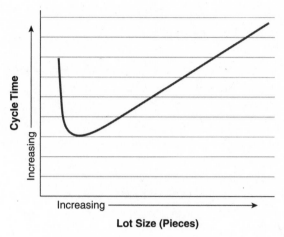

FIGURE 3-31. Lot size versus cycle time

3. **Costs.** Large lots sizes can minimize out-of-pocket costs due to changeover, for example, material wasted on a plastic injection machine when changing from black to white plastic because of the required machine cleaning.
4. **Service level.** Larger lot sizes can mean longer backorder times because each lot has to wait on the large (read *slow*) lots in front of it.

The lot-size calculation is a complex one. It will be discussed in a little more detail in Chapter 4, but the lot-size graph illustrates a few key concepts about the natural behavior of operations as related to lot sizes:

1. There is an optimal minimum for lot sizes. This minimum corresponds to the lowest cycle-time point on the curve in Figure 3-31. It's better to be a little on the large side of lots sizes (to the right of the minimum) because cycle time blows up precipitously to the left of the minimum.
2. Cycle times to the right of the lot size minimum increase because parts wait in larger and larger lots for all the parts that go in front of them at process centers.
3. Cycle times to the left of the minimum blow up because the production flow is setting up all the time.

Putting Practical Science to Practice

1. Factory Physics science is just that—science. We want to make it as simple and as practical as possible but no simpler. While this section did not provide a massively simple explanation, it focused on describing Factory Physics science conceptually and visually without much mathematical complexity. Hopefully this will aid you in internalizing your understanding of natural behavior of operations and thereby confirm or improve your intuition. Improved intution provides better leadership ability.

2. Practical understanding of Factory Physics science requires understanding the behavior described by three equations and four performance graphs and four equations.

3. The three equations are:
   a. The VUT equation.
   b. Little's law.
   c. The Variance of Replenishment Time Demand equation.

4. The four graphs are:
   a. Cycle Time versus Utilization—a graphical representation of the VUT equation.
   b. Production Flow—a graphical representation of Little's law.
   c. Average Inventory Investment versus Fill Rate (Tradeoff Plot)—a graphical representation of the Variance of Replenishment Time Demand equation.
   d. Cycle Time versus Lot Size (Lot Size Graph)—the equations for this relationship are not simply stated because it is a dynamic function of production configuration, variability, and demand.
   e. The Cycle Time versus Utilization graph illustrates why the standard cost model is not an accurate description of production behavior. As utilization approaches 100 percent, cycle time increases nonlinearly to infinity over the long term.

5. The Production Flow graph is an innovative and unique application of Factory Physics science using Little's law. It graphically illustrates why one-piece flow is neither a good nor an ideal goal—true one-piece flow requires zero variability. Best-case performance with real-world variability is maximum throughput with minimum cycle time, the WIP level where the throughput curve begins to flatten horizontally.

6. The tradeoff plot is an innovative application of financial efficient frontier theory to inventory and production control. It graphically illustrates the effect of variability on inventory. At fill rates close to 100 percent, inventory requirements increase nonlinearly to infinity. As a practical matter, leaders

must make a strategic decision about what fill rate is desired in the face of required inventory investment. Also, there is a limit to benefits from increasing reorder frequency. As cycle stock—order quantity—decreases, safety stock must increase to cover variability effects and maintain the desired fill rate.

7. The Lot Size graph results from a combined optimization of stocks *and* flows. It illustrates one aspect (cycle time versus lot size) of the summit of production and inventory objectives: desired customer service levels with the shortest possible cycle times, highest possible utilization of people and equipment, and the lowest possible inventory investment.

In the "Factory Science as Simple as Possible but No Simpler" section of this chapter, we mentioned three equations and four graphs that provide managers with a practical scientific basis for handling complexity and variation predictively and successfully. We have now covered those high-level equations and graphs as a large body of evidence supporting the Factory Physics theory of production and service operations as a construct of demand, stock, production, buffers, and variability. For those of you interested in additional detail, Chapter 4 provides much more mathematical detail. After that, we move to the management concepts and practices that yield the best possible results from the theory we have presented.

Practical Math for Managers

This chapter is designed for two types of readers. For those of you who want to get down and do some computations, who like equations and want to see detailed technical explanations, and who do not trust "black box" explanations, this chapter is for you. If you are one of those people for whom mathematics is not your inclination, please read on—*but skip the math*. Everything in this chapter is explained conceptually and mathematically. The mathematics is for those who want to do the calculations. The concepts are for everyone.

On the other hand, if you are looking for a detailed explanation of the mathematics of Factory Physics, then we recommend consulting that book as a source. This chapter will not replace the detail found there. Instead, this chapter provides a basic mathematical under-standing of the concepts of Factory Physics to enhance intuition. A manager should be careful when applying the math to business per-formance. Unless the business is very simple (e.g., one product or sequence of process centers), the complexity of demand and prod-uct variation requires either a high-level modeling program such as CSUITE to do rapid stochastic approximations or a Monte Carlo dis-crete-event simulation program such as Arena or Simul8. CSUITE is the operations analytics software developed by Factory Physics, Inc., to standardize and advance the Factory Physics framework. It was developed with grants from the National Science Foundation. An efficient approach is to do the rapid modeling with a program such as CSUITE to quickly narrow options for planning or improvement, and then, if a high level of detail is needed, use some type of Monte Carlo simulation. Often the high level of detail provided by Monte Carlo simulation is not needed.

DEFINING TERMS

Many of the terms we will use here come from the science of statistics. To avoid any confusion, we define terms in Table 4-1.

TABLE 4-1. Key Statistical Terms

Term	Definition
Random variable	A mathematical entity that "maps" the outcome of a random event into the set of real numbers. For example, a coin toss could be mapped as heads is 1 and tails is 0.
Mean	The expected value of a random variable. $$\mu = E[X] = \int_{-\infty}^{\infty} s\, f(s)\, ds$$ The letter λ is sometimes used to indicate a mean rate such as demand.
Sample mean	The arithmetic average of a random variable. $$\bar{X} = \frac{\sum_{i=1}^{n} X_i}{n}$$
Variance	$$\sigma^2 = VAR(X) = \int_{-\infty}^{\infty} f(s)(s - \mu)^2\, ds$$
Standard deviation	$$\sigma = \sqrt{VAR(X)}$$
Sample variance	$$S^2 = \frac{\sum_{i=1}^{n} X_i^2 - n\bar{X}^2}{n-1}$$
Coefficient of variation	$$CV = \frac{\sigma}{\mu}$$
Squared coefficient of variation	$$SCV = \frac{\sigma^2}{\mu^2}$$
Mean daily demand	λ
Variance of daily demand	σ_d^2

(continued)

TABLE 4-1. Key Statistical Terms (Continued)

Term	Definition
Mean replenishment time	ℓ
Variance of replenishment times	σ_ℓ^2
Reorder point	r
Reorder quantity	Q
Safety stock	s
Days of supply	DoS
Mean on-hand inventory in a stock point	$\bar{I}$
Mean on order (or WIP)	$\bar{W}$
Mean backorder level	$\bar{B}$
Probability of not being stocked out (fill rate)	$\bar{S}$
Mean effective process time	t_e
Squared coefficient of variation of process time	SCV_e

MODELING STOCKS

Stocks are easier to model than flows, so we will start there. The reason they are easier is that the transformation (i.e., procurement time) required to obtain the inventory is characterized by parameters describing the mean and standard deviation of replenishment times. For flows, these times must be computed from more basic parameters, including, but not limited to, capacity, demand, variability, process times, setup times, and the number of machines. For stocks, they are *given* as parameters.

A Perfect World

In a perfect world, there would be no variability in either demand or transformation. For stocks, this means that a manager would know exactly how many units are needed and exactly how long it would take to get them. If a company purchased (or produced) only exactly what was needed and planned to make it available just in time to be consumed, *zero inventory* would be required. Ironically, even though *just-in-time* is a classic description of the supermarket concept of Lean, what we have just described is also what happens in a material requirements planning (MRP) system operating with no variability and employing a lot-for-lot (purchase/produce only what is needed) lot-sizing rule. Such a system would end up carrying zero on-hand inventory while maintaining 100 percent on-time delivery (or fill rate). Because variability (in both demand and supply) is a fact of life, though, a manager must determine its effects. We begin our description with characterizing replenishment times, then consider demand, and finally describe the combined behavior of the two in an inventory system.

Replenishment Times

The basic stock model presented in Chapter 3 requires knowledge of both the length of replenishment times and how much variation is inherent in them. These indicators are the mean and standard deviation. Off hand, it would appear simple to get the mean and standard deviation of replenishment times, but things can get complicated in the real world. The *replenishment time* is the time from when the "system" (in its largest construct) recognizes the need for additional inventory and when that inventory is available for use. Use of the word *system* here implies everything involved in inventory management, including, but not limited to, any computer system, the people using the system, any offline software, and any other aids that may be applied. For instance, the Oracle enterprise resources planning (ERP) system maintains three components of replenishment time: *preprocessing*, *processing*, and *postprocessing* times. *Processing* is the time actually required to either produce the part (if made in-house) or the time to procure the part (from a supplier). The preprocessing includes time to recognize the need (e.g., if planning once per week, this would add half a week to the total time), to create an order (e.g., purchase or manufacturing order), and to release the order. Postprocessing includes time to receive the order, to inspect the products received, to enter the receipt into the system, and to place it in the proper location to make it available. Other ERP systems are similar to Oracle's, but the names of these fields may differ slightly.

Typically, the values for these components of replenishment time are stored in separate fields in the ERP item master table.

Off hand, it would appear that the mean replenishment time is simply the sum of these component times. However, this may be complicated by certain vendor management policies. For instance, the processing time may not be the average time for the vendor to deliver the part. The vendor lead time might be combined with rules regarding how early and how late a part may be delivered. For instance, if a supplier is allowed to deliver four days early but zero days late to the system lead time, a manager would expect to see the actual average processing time as something less than what is in the system. Also, a supplier who is sometimes late (despite the rule) would end up with an average process time that is somewhat longer than what is in the system. All this can greatly complicate the issue. Fortunately, it is not really necessary to have totally accurate data on replenishment times to do a good job in modeling inventory.

For instance, suppose that we have the following information:

Preprocessing time: 3 days
Processing time: 30 days
Postprocessing time: 1 day

Also, the supplier is allowed to ship five days early and one day late, and this supplier is almost always in range. The replenishment-time parameters would be:

Average replenishment time = preproc + proc + postproc

$$- \text{EARLY}/2 + \text{LATE}/2 = 3 + 30 + 1 - 2.5 + 0.5 = 32.0 \text{ days}$$

Assuming that the replenishment time is uniformly distributed between EARLY and LATE, the standard deviation will be:

Standard deviation of replenishment time

$$= \sqrt{\frac{\text{EARLY}^2 + \text{LATE}^2}{12}} = \sqrt{\frac{S^2 + 1}{12}} = 1.5 \text{ days}$$

If the supplier were out of range a significant amount of the time, we would need to know how far out and for what probability for each range. However, this would greatly complicate the matter.

A practical method is to assume some coefficient of variation with a maximum standard deviation. For instance, we could use a CV = 0.1 and a maximum of two days. In the preceding example, this would yield a standard deviation of two days because 10 percent of 32 days is greater than the maximum value. Another practical consideration is in determining what is acceptable. This is a tactical decision made at the buyer level. For instance, should the buyer with an unreliable supplier plan to always have huge standard deviations of replenishment time and the accompanying increase in inventory? Alternatively, the buyer could set policies in the system based on a standard deviation that produces a more acceptable inventory level in the system. In this case, the buyer would choose to expedite to address demand or accept lower service or both. Because this would not be a long-term solution, the buyer would also be either working with the supplier to improve delivery performance or looking for a new supplier. The same type of decision is required if a normally reliable supplier experiences a one-time disruption in service.

Demand

Like replenishment time, both the average demand and its variation need to be characterized. Unlike replenishment time, the *variance* of demand is considered and not its standard deviation. Also, the characteristics of demand are used to model both *stocks and flows*. For stocks, a manager needs the mean and variance of the demand in a *given period*. The period should be long enough that a significant amount of demand occurs on average (say, around 10 units). The demand shown in Table 4-2 is one that exhibits a Poisson distribution. The Poisson distribution is what would be seen if demand were from the aggregate demands of a large population (e.g., number of Big Macs sold per day at a particular McDonald's). Internet sales often exhibit Poisson demand.

TABLE 4-2. Random but Low-Variance Demand Pattern

Week	1	2	3	4	5	6	7	8	9	10	11	12
Demand	59	48	41	60	48	50	46	54	51	49	39	62

In this case, the mean is 50.6, and the variance is 51.4. If we have a five-day work week, then the mean of the *daily* demand will be:

$$d = \frac{50.6}{5} = 10.1$$

The variance in daily demand is likewise computed as:

$$\sigma_d^2 = \frac{51.4}{5} = 10.3$$

The variance-to-mean ratio (i.e., the variance divided by the mean) is almost exactly 1. This is evidence that the underlying distribution is indeed a Poisson distribution because the Poisson distribution has only one parameter representing both its mean and its variance. Consequently, the variance-to-mean ratio for the Poisson distribution is exactly 1.

To the alert reader, this may seem strange. How can a distribution have a single parameter for both its mean and its variance given that the mean has linear dimensions, whereas the variance has dimensions that are squared? The only way this can be true is if the Poisson distribution models are only random variables that have no dimensions—a pure number. In other words, a Poisson distribution cannot model a random variable for distances, mass, volume, velocity, or even demand *rates*. All these quantities have dimensions (e.g., meters, kilograms, liters, etc.). Even a demand rate has dimensions of parts per day (or some other period). While *parts* has no dimensions, a day certainly does. Consequently, when speaking of demand, the number of units occurring in a *period* is stated without specifying the period. In this way, the demand is a pure number. However, we will often be a bit informal about this and talk about how many units are sold per day or per week.

At any rate, Poisson demand is about as good as it gets in the supply chain. More often we see demand patterns that look like that seen in Table 4-3. There are periods of zero demand followed by periods with a fairly large demand. The mean in this case is 27.7,

TABLE 4-3. Demand Example with Lumpy Demand

Week	1	2	3	4	5	6	7	8	9	10	11	12
Demand	55	51	0	0	0	38	55	0	0	58	0	75

and the variance is 899.9, with a variance-to-mean ratio of 33. This is an example of lumpy demand and is typical of many supply chains. One of the reasons for the lumpiness is known as the *bullwhip effect*.

This type of demand might be seen by an automotive battery producer. The total customer demand for batteries, as seen at the numerous retail outlets, is probably Poisson, where customers purchase one item at a time. But the replenishment for the retail outlets is not one battery at a time but a batch of batteries from a distributor. As demand is accumulated in batches, it increases variability, and so the distributor sees demand that has a higher variance-to-mean ratio than 1. But that distributor purchases an even larger batch from the company that makes the batteries. The effect of this replenishment pattern is that the company will see no demand for several weeks and then a large order followed by no demand, resulting in extremely high variability. This ordering pattern is described as the *bullwhip effect* because a small amount in variability at the source (customer demand is Poisson) results in severe variability at the supply end of the supply chain. Similarly, a small motion of the hand at the end of a bullwhip results in a violent crack at the end of the whip.

Forecast Error and Lead Time

If the lead time to customers is greater than the time required to produce or procure a product, then almost no inventory is needed. The only inventory that would be carried would be any remnants from lot sizes that were greater than demand. In other words, if order quantities are larger than the immediate demand, there will be leftovers in inventory. There would be absolutely no reason to carry any safety stock because all product could be procured or produced before the customer requires it.

However, if lead times promised to customers are shorter than the procurement or production time, inventory will always have to be stocked because end-item demand will have to be forecasted and because such forecasts *are always wrong*. If demand is steady, this forecast can be simply an estimate of the average demand. Otherwise, a forecast will have to be provided for future periods going out as far as the lead time of the supplier.

To determine how much inventory is required, information about forecast accuracy must be specified. The worse the forecasts, the more inventory is needed to maintain a given service level.

For steady demand, only the average and variance of demand are required. But when forecasting period by period, a measure of the forecast error at the lead time of the supplier is needed. If the supplier's lead time is six weeks, then the accuracy of the forecast six weeks out is needed. The accuracy measure should be the mean square error (MSE) at the lead time. Note that this is not the mean absolute error, or the mean absolute percent error, or the mean absolute deviation (all commonly used measures), but the mean square error. Mean square error is computed as:

$$\mathrm{MSE} = \frac{\sum_{i=1}^{n}(D_i - F_i)^2}{n}$$

where D_i = actual demand, and F_i = forecast for period i. Every period i forecast from 1 to n is at the lead time of the part. For example, for a part with a six-week lead time, a forecast is made today for demand in six weeks. This forecast and the actual demand in six weeks are used for $i = 1$. Next week, a forecast is made for demand six weeks out. Next week's forecast and the actual demand six weeks out from next week are used for $i = 2$. When the data are displayed in a spreadsheet, the result is the commonly used *waterfall chart*. Again, if estimating the variance in daily demand, the MSE is divided by the number of days in the period. For a five-day work week, the variance in daily demand taken from the MSE of a weekly forecast will be:

$$\sigma_d^2 = \frac{\mathrm{MSE}}{5}$$

Consider the data shown in Figure 4-1 representing a four-week forecast that is, on average, correct (i.e., it is unbiased). Each diamond represents the actual demand for the week, whereas the straight line is the four-week forecast. In this case, the variance in the forecast itself is 53.1, whereas the MSE is 400.8. The variance of all the data points (actual demand) is 513.4, which is close[1] to the sum of the forecast variance plus the MSE, which is 453.9. Figure 4-2 shows what happens when a forecast is biased high by 20 units. Of course, the variances in the data and the forecast stay the same, but the MSE goes from around 400 to almost 780, higher than the variance in the actual data.

If the MSE is greater than the demand variance, the forecast is an exercise in futility. The MSE should never be greater than the

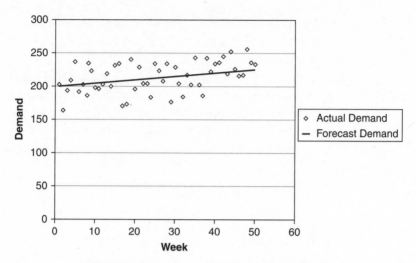

FIGURE 4-1. Forecast and actual data without a bias

variance of the demand data. This would imply that a manager is better off using last period's (week's, etc.) demand as a forecast rather than trying to create a forecast independently. If this is the case, then simply use the variance of the past period's demand instead of the MSE as a measure of the variability in the demand—and try to get a better forecast!

This has major implications for managers trying to lead a business. We very rarely see this understanding of the natural behavior

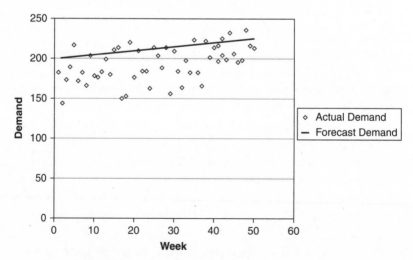

FIGURE 4-2. Forecast and actual data with a 20-unit bias

of demand forecasting. What we almost invariably see is managers trying to get ever more sophisticated forecasting tools and processes as if someday some software will enable a manager to see the future. This will not happen. A manager can greatly increase an organization's effectiveness by:

1. Calculating and using forecast error correctly.
2. Knowing when the forecast error is useless (when MSE > historical demand variance) and switching to the use of historical demand variance for setting inventory policy.

It can be extremely complex to compute a proper MSE of a forecast. To do this properly, the squared errors of the forecast out to a period of the part's mean replenishment time must be summed. If there are many different parts with different replenishment times, this can be very time-consuming. An alternative is to use the variance-to-mean ratio (VMR) of historical demand and then apply it to future demand (or forecast). This should provide an upper bound on the variability because the variance of the data should always be greater than the MSE of the forecast.

The VMR is computed by dividing the variance of demand by the mean demand in a period, that is,

$$\text{VMR} = \frac{\sigma_d^2}{\lambda}$$

For example, suppose that the mean is 215 and the variance is 1,203 for the weekly demands of the past 26 weeks. Now suppose that the forecast for the next 4 weeks is 250 per week. We would estimate the variance in demand during the forecast period from:

$$\sigma_F^2 = 250 \times \text{VMR} = 250 \times \frac{1,203}{215} = 1,398.8$$

Inventory Performance Measures

Now we will provide some of the less complex calculations regarding inventory performance (the more complex are available in the *Factory Physics* text). We will also highlight some of the common errors found in many texts. To make the calculations manageable, we will consider a reorder-point/reorder-quantity (ROP/ROQ) policy. This policy can be used to model other policies as well, such as a *time-phased reorder-point policy*, more commonly known as an *MRP policy*.

Reorder-Point Policies

The policy depends on two policy parameters, the reorder quantity ROQ and the reorder point ROP, and works as follows: Order ROQ parts whenever the *inventory position* hits or falls below the ROP. *Inventory position* is defined as:

$$\text{Inventory position} = \text{on hand} + \text{on order} - \text{backorders}$$
$$= \bar{I} + \bar{W} - \bar{B}$$

Typically, the ROP is given by:

$$\text{ROP} = \text{average replenishment-time demand} + \text{safety stock}$$

or

$$r = \lambda \ell + s$$

where $\lambda \ell$ is the average replenishment-time demand.

When executing this policy properly, the inventory position will always remain between ROP + 1 and ROP + ROQ. This provides an easy way to ensure that the policy is being executed properly. This control-limit approach for managing inventory policy is highly useful for managers, and we will describe its use in detail in Chapter 7.

Replenishment Frequency

It's important to know how often inventory must be replenished. If the parts are purchased items, replenishment frequency describes how many purchase orders must be processed in a period. If the parts are made in-house, replenishment frequency describes how many change-overs must be performed in a given period (say, a week). Fortunately, the calculation is pretty easy. For one item, the frequency is given by:

$$f = \frac{D}{Q}$$

where D = demand for the entire period, and Q = reorder quantity. To obtain the total number of replenishments for a number of parts, simply sum the preceding for each part.

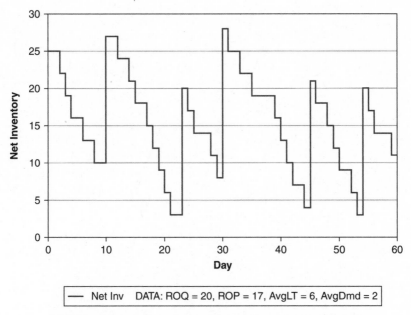

FIGURE 4-3. Plot of net inventory with random demand and safety stock

$$\text{Average no. of replenishments per period} = \sum_i \frac{D_i}{Q_i}$$

Average On-Hand Inventory

Figure 4-3 presents a reorder-point system with random demand and an ROQ of 20 and an ROP of 17. The average replenishment time is six days, and the average daily demand is two. Therefore, the safety stock will be:

$$s = r - \lambda \ell = 17 - 2 \times 6 = 5$$

Note that the net inventory got down into the safety stock for three of the five complete replenishment cycles shown. Because of the randomness and because the safety-stock level is our target, we would expect a system to get into the safety stock for about half of the replenishment cycles. Thus three of five cycles would not be unusual. This is another important point for managers. We have seen organizations where managers strongly emphasize a desire not to use safety stock. Safety stock is a buffer against variability. Variability is unavoidable, so use of safety stock is unavoidable. *If an organization never gets into its safety stock, it has too much inventory.*

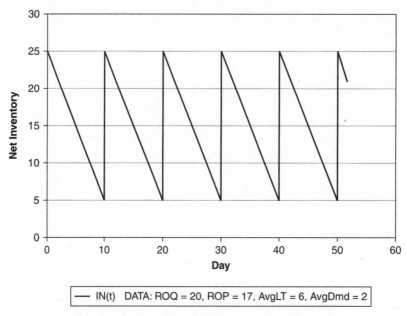

FIGURE 4-4. Net inventory with no randomness in demand

Figure 4-4 shows the same system with no randomness and with smooth demand. In other words, the demand is not two removed per day but a continuous removal of stock resulting in two per day. The plot is less realistic but much cleaner and easier to see. From this plot, it is easy to see that the average on-hand inventory is given by

$$\bar{I} = \frac{Q}{2} + s = \frac{20}{2} + 5 = 15$$

These plots are of *net inventory*, which is on-hand inventory minus backorders. If backorders exceed on-hand inventory, the net inventory would become negative. Thus, to compute average *on-hand* inventory we would need to add the backorders back into the net inventory. However, computing average backorders is difficult because the equations involve probability (see Chapter 2 of *Factory Physics* for a discussion of simple cases). Even so, if the fill rate is high (meaning that there are few backorders), a good approximation of average inventory is simply the ROQ divided by 2 plus the safety stock.

Average on-hand inventory is an important measure, but it needs to be considered with the rate of inventory usage. For instance, having 1,000 units on hand sounds like a great deal of inventory, but if 1,000 parts are consumed per week, having 1,000 on hand is having only a week's worth of inventory. This is why a different measure, called *inventory turns*, is commonly used and is defined as:

$$\text{Inventory turns} = \frac{\text{COGS value of annual sales}}{\text{COGS value of on hand}}$$

where COGS is the cost of goods sold. Of course, the same value of inventory turns occurs if the ratio is calculated using units. Then turns of 12 amount to about one month's demand of inventory on hand. The inventory turns for Figure 4-4 will be around 50, depending on how many weeks are in the fiscal year. Note that inventory turns is *not* a dimensionless ratio, as are many financial ratios. Instead, turns has a dimension of 1/years. Thus the average number of days to sell the existing inventory will be:

$$\text{Average days to sell inventory} = \frac{365}{\text{inventory turns}}$$

Estimating Fill Rate

The *fill rate* is the fraction of the time the system is *not* in a backorder state. It is the *variability* due to the randomness of both demand σ_d^2 and replenishment time σ_ℓ^2 that makes calculations for backorders and fill rate difficult. As we discussed in Chapter 3, a key performance driver is the *replenishment-time demand*,[1] which is a random variable representing the amount of random demand that occurs within a random replenishment time. The mean and variance are given by

$$\mu_{\text{RTD}} = \lambda \ell$$
$$\sigma_{\text{RTD}}^2 = l\sigma_d^2 + \lambda^2 \sigma_\ell^2$$

If X is a random variable representing the replenishment-time demand, then the probability that a system at a certain inventory position x will stock out is given by

$$\Pr\{\text{stock-out with } IP = x\} = \Pr\{X > x\} = 1 - F(x)$$

where $F(x)$ is the distribution function of the replenishment-time demand. Because the inventory position for a reorder-point system is always between $r + 1$ and $r + Q$, yielding Q different values, we can estimate the average fill rate by averaging over this range, that is,

$$\bar{S} = \frac{1}{Q} \sum_{x=r+1}^{r+Q} \Pr\{X \le x\} = \frac{1}{Q} \sum_{x=r+1}^{r+Q} F(x)$$

As an example, consider the system of Figure 4-3, and set the safety stock to zero. We will also need to know something about the variance of the demand and the replenishment time, so let us suppose that the demand is Poisson (meaning that the variance of the demand is equal to the mean of 2) and that the standard deviation of the replenishment time is 1 day. With zero safety stock, the ROP becomes

$$r = \lambda \ell + s = 2 \times 6 + 0 = 12$$

Then

$$\mu_{\text{RTD}} = \lambda \times \ell = 2 \times 6 = 12$$
$$\sigma_{\text{RTD}}^2 = l\sigma_d^2 + d^2\sigma_\ell^2 = 6 \times 2 + 2^2 \times 1 = 16$$
$$\sigma_{\text{RTD}} = 4$$

A standard deviation of 4 is significantly smaller than the mean of 12, and the normal distribution can be used. Continuing with an ROQ of 20 and using a standard normal table (or a spreadsheet function), we can create a table of probabilities for each possible value of the inventory position, as shown in Table 4-4.

TABLE 4-4. Table of Probabilities

x	13	14	15	16	17	18	19	20	21	22
$F(x)$	0.599	0.691	0.773	0.841	0.894	0.933	0.960	0.977	0.988	0.994
x	23	24	25	26	27	28	29	30	31	32
$F(x)$	0.997	0.999	0.999	1.000	1.000	1.000	1.000	1.000	1.000	1.000

Average = 0.9323

The expected fill rate is then calculated be averaging these probabilities, and the result is 93.23 percent. Note that this calculation is the percentage of days that the system is *not backordered.* It is not the percentage of orders that are filled out of stock or even the percentage of demand that is filled from stock (although if the reorder quantity is 1, then all these measures will be equal).

Compare this with what is suggested by many authors of operations management texts (and in numerous "advanced" inventory-planning modules of major ERP systems), namely,

$$\bar{S}_{\text{wrong}} = \Pr\{X \leq r\}$$

$$= \Pr\left\{\frac{X - \lambda\ell}{\sigma_{\text{RTD}}} \leq \frac{r - \lambda\ell}{\sigma_{\text{RTD}}}\right\}$$

$$= \Phi\left(\frac{r - \lambda\ell}{\sigma_{\text{RTD}}}\right)$$

where Φ is the cumulative standard normal distribution (available as Excel function NORMSDIST). If $\bar{S}_{\text{wrong}}$ were used in the preceding example, a service level of one-half would be the result. This creates quite a discrepancy—93 versus 50 percent. What is the problem?

Actually, there are two problems. First, the normal distribution is only valid if the standard deviation of replenishment-time demand is significantly smaller than its mean (not greater than one-third). In this case, this condition is satisfied. In many cases (perhaps most cases), though, it is not. When it is not satisfied, the normal distribution will have significant probability in the region of *negative demand*, something that is not possible. Second, there is a problem of definition. The 93 percent fill rate is what a *customer* would see. That is, 93 percent of the time, the system would not be backordered. On the other hand, 50 percent of the *cycles* should have no stock-outs at all. Figure 4-5 on page 130 shows five complete cycles, and three of them had at least one stock-out—60 percent is not too far from 50 percent, particularly when the possibilities (with five cycles) are 0, 20, 40, 60, 80, and 100 percent. Because managers care more about the customer fill rate than about the cycle fill rate, the customer fill rate should be computed and reported. Another reason that many texts (and ERP systems) use the "wrong" method is because it is simpler—only one probability and no averaging. The implication of using the wrong method is that safety stock would be:

$$\bar{S}_{\text{wrong}} = z_a \sigma_{\text{RTD}}$$

To hit a 93 percent service level, a lookup is done (or use of a spreadsheet function) for the corresponding z-value, which is around 1.5. Thus the ROP would be:

$$r = \lambda \ell + z_\alpha \sigma_{\text{RTD}} = 2 \times 6 + 1.5 \times 4 = 18$$

The corresponding *customer* fill rate for a ROP of 18 would be more than 99.5 percent, and the average inventory would be around 50 percent higher than when using $\bar{S}_{\text{wrong}}$. Consequently, it is very important to use the correct method for calculating average inventory and average service. This has major implications for managers trying to lead inventory-reduction efforts. If the inventory-control system is set to 90 percent using the incorrect calculation, there will be much more inventory than needed to achieve a 90 percent fill rate. This could create a situation where the sales force is actually seeing

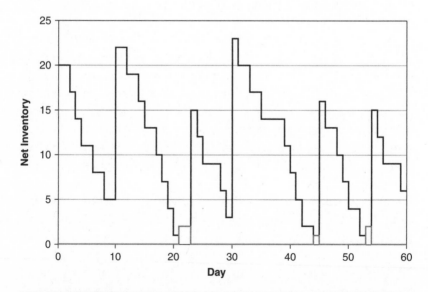

DATA : ROQ = 20, ROP = 12, AvgLT = 6, AvgDmd = 2 —— On Hand —— Backorder

FIGURE 4-5. On-hand inventory and backorders with random demand and zero safety stock

close to a 100 percent fill rate. If the manager switches to a correct calculation for inventory policy, as described earlier, and implements it in the inventory-planning system, the previously accepted fill rate of 90 percent in the system and 100 percent to customers will now be 90 percent in the system and 90 percent to customers. Although inventory will decrease significantly, the company will now stock out 10 percent of the time, much more often than before. Whereas some people in the organization may be happy with the decrease in inventory, sales and customer-service people almost assuredly will be frustrated. We didn't say that it would be easy getting control of poor inventory practices. However, if a manger can provide a predictive warning ahead of time as to the consequences of planned actions, it's in the best interest of everyone in the organization to help mitigate the negative effects. Clearly, the cycle service is a lower bound to customer service because it is less than any of the values averaged. A tighter bound can be obtained from:

$$\bar{S}_{LB} = \frac{F(r+1) + F(r+Q)}{2} = 0.80$$

If the standard deviation of replenishment time demand is less than roughly one-third the mean, the normal distribution works well. However, in many cases, the standard deviation of the replenishment-time demand is on the order of the mean, and so the normal distribution is a very bad approximation (it has significant area in the negative region, and negative demands do not make sense). Unfortunately, many books use the Poisson or the normal distribution to compute inventory performance measures. As with the normal distribution, the variance of the Poisson distribution is almost always too small, particularly when the mean is large. In such cases, one should use a distribution for a non-negative random variable that can be determined with the mean and variance. Possible distributions include the beta, gamma, lognormal, and Weibull distributions, but fitting these distributions is well beyond the scope of both this book and of *Factory Physics*.

Estimating Backorders and Backorder Time

The average backorder amount is the value of the average of the negative portions of the net inventory graph. This is illustrated by taking Figure 4-3 and setting the safety stock to zero. Instead of plotting the net inventory, the on-hand inventory and the backorders are plotted, as seen in Figure 4-5. Wherever the net inventory is positive, there is positive on-hand inventory. Wherever the net inventory is negative, there are *positive* backorders.

The time average of the backorders will be the area under the backorder curve divided by the total time. To compute the expected backorder using probability, see Chapter 2 of *Factory Physics*. However, to compute for this particular case, note that there are three backorder events: two days at a backorder level of two, one day with a level of one, and one day with a level of two, yielding a total of seven backorder days. The average is computed by dividing 7 by 60, which is 0.1167.

From Little's law (defined below), the average backorder *time* is calculated as

$$\bar{T} = \frac{\bar{B}}{d}$$

In this case, it would be 0.058 day. Not very long!

But this is the average backorder time *including all the time when the system is not backordered.* A more interesting measure is the average time backordered *when backordered.* This is given by

$$\bar{T}_B = \left[\frac{\bar{B}}{d(1 - \bar{S})} \right] = \frac{0.1167}{2(1 - 0.93)} = 0.833 \text{ days}$$

which is rounded off to 1 day because that is the period being used.

This knowledge of the behavior of an inventory system provides yet another powerful strategic tool for managers. This is essentially an exercise in managing buffers to reduce cost while maintaining high customer service. For instance, if the starting inventory is $1 million at a 95 percent fill rate, one option for a manager is to use a combination of a smaller inventory buffer and a larger time buffer (longer average backorder days). Thus, if the fill rate were cut to 85 percent, which decreased inventory to $800,000 but increased average backorder time to two days, there is still an opportunity to maintain customer service. If customers are okay with four-day lead times, the lower fill rate could be set, and the following would happen:

1. Eighty-five percent of the time, customers get product shipped to them when they order.
2. Fifteen percent of the time, the product is not on the shelf but arrives and is shipped to the customer within the

four-day lead time. Customer service is 100 percent, even though the fill rate is 85 percent.

3. On-hand inventory is reduced by 20 percent.

Computing Inventory Policies

When we compute inventory policies, we want to consider three objectives:

1. Minimize the amount of money invested in inventory.
2. Maximize the service level, as measured by fill rate, backorder time, and backorder time given backordered.
3. Minimize replenishment frequency.

Because there are three conflicting objectives, we cannot optimize them all unless we add them together using a set of cost coefficients. Because such coefficients are not intuitive and so are relatively meaningless (e.g., what is the cost to be late per unit per day?), we employ a method we discussed in Chapter 3, that of an efficient frontier. We will produce an efficient frontier for a set of order frequencies, with each frontier showing the minimum average inventory investment for a given fill rate.

Figure 4-6 shows the efficient-frontier curves for a pipe manufacturer that has never done any inventory optimization—only heuristic rules. There are three curves, each representing a different replenishment frequency. These are 360 per year, 181 per year, and 90 per year. The one with the highest inventory has the lowest frequency, 90 orders per year. Notice how going from 90 to 181 orders reduces inventory significantly at fill rates below about 98 percent, but going from 181 to 360 orders reduces it much less. This occurs because two things happen when the replenishment frequency goes up. First, cycle stock is reduced (ROQ/2), so we would expect inventory to decrease. But, at the same time, the frequency at which the system reaches its minimum inventory level (also equal to the replenishment frequency) increases. Because of this, the fill rate drops. Therefore, to keep the fill rate the same, safety stock must increase. In the case of going from 90 orders per year to 181 orders per month, the cycle stock decreases more than the safety stock increases. However, when going from 181 to 360 orders, the decrease in cycle stock is almost made up by the increase in safety stock. In general, we

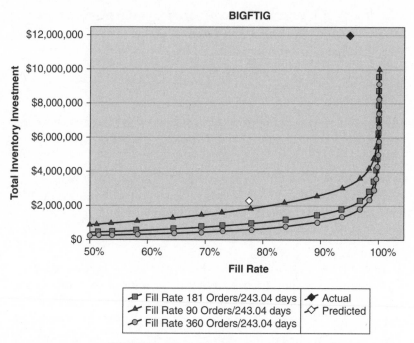

FIGURE 4-6. Efficient frontiers for inventory

find that there is a point where decreasing cycle stock by increasing replenishment frequency ceases to reduce inventory. This is one reason why the goal of having an order size of one can be detrimental. It increases the capacity requirements but does not reduce inventory. The capacity increase depends on whether the situation involves purchasing or production. For purchasing, increased frequency means an increase in the number of purchase orders. For production, increased frequency means more changeovers.

The graph also displays two particular points: a white diamond indicating the expected performance using the given parameters and a dark diamond indicating the current performance of the system (an input to the system). In a well-run system, these will be close. One is the average of the policies (predicted), and the other is a particular instance of the policies (actual). In this case, however, they are far apart. Why?

It appears that the policies in place (predicted) are not sufficient to keep fill rates high enough. Planners know that running out of stock is worse than having too much inventory, so they ignore the policies and use their intuition. They also may be put in the position of expediting. Sometimes, an expedite for a quantity of

1 requires a minimum order of 100. Thus inventory goes up, but the service hit was already experienced. The effects are visible here—more inventory and higher fill rates but much worse than optimal performance. The two diamonds correspond to the 181 orders per year frequency. Consequently, we see that without changing the replenishment frequency, we could drop inventory from $12 million to around $3 million with a substantial *increase* in the fill rate. This would be accomplished by selecting the desired point on the graph that would take the user to a report showing the inventory policy parameters needed to accomplish the desired performance. These parameters are then loaded into the ERP system, which then would execute as before, only with better performance. The bottom line here is that an enormous improvement can be made by only changing numbers in an ERP system.

Inventory in an Assembly System

Assemble-to-order systems can be beneficial in terms of reducing inventory and providing high customer service. A number of decisions must be made regarding the logistical design of a make-to-order (MTO) assembly system:

1. To be able to assemble on *demand* requires an enormous amount of inventory because one would have to have each and every component available *whenever* the end item is desired. What are the tradeoffs between *assemble on demand, assemble to order,* and *purchase and assemble*?
2. What is the proper measure of service—fill rate, backorder level, backorder time, or backorder time given backordered? How do these compare with what is commonly used?

The appeal of assemble to order can be explained in terms of making better use of the available *buffers*, as described in Chapter 3. Thus assemble-to-order control makes recourse to the time buffer in order to reduce the inventory buffer. In other words, by using both inventory and time, the size of a single buffer—either inventory only or time only—can be greatly reduced. By requiring a short amount of time to respond to an order and then assembling the end item, the inventory requirements are much less than in an inventory-only system. Likewise, by maintaining a component inventory, the time buffer (i.e., the longest component replenishment time plus time to assemble) would be much less than required in a time-only system.

An example from *Factory Physics* illustrates this point: consider an end item that requires six components, and there are three options for each component yielding a total of $3^6 = 729$ possible configurations. Suppose that each component costs $150, so each configuration will cost $6 \times \$150 = \$1,900$, and suppose that there is equal demand for each configuration amounting to 100 per year. Components are obtained from a distant supplier with a 90-day replenishment time. If only a time buffer is used to synchronize demand and transformation, the customer would be required to wait at least 90 days for materials to be obtained and then some time to perform the assembly. However, if all 729 of the end items were stocked, an average on-hand inventory of around $11,700 for each configuration would have to be maintained to achieve a 99 percent fill rate for all end items. This adds up to a total inventory investment of $8,529,000.

Another alternative would be to use assemble-to-order control. In this case, the customer would wait only a short time for the assembly, and only 18 different components would need to be stocked instead of 729 different end items. To minimize total inventory, the fill rate of each component is set to be the same, which will be $0.99^{1/6} = 0.9983$. The investment required to do this is $624,000, or 93 percent less than what was required when keeping all 729 end items in stock. Thus an assemble-to-order operation makes better use of the available buffers by employing some of each buffer and not relying on a single buffer.

This concept can be extended further by adding some additional lead time because the typical customer for such an item is not walking into a store and demanding it immediately. For business-to-business situations and even for business-to-consumer situations, when an order is placed by telephone or Internet, there is usually time allocated to perform the assembly before shipping. If there is time to perform assembly, there may be still more time to allow the gathering of components. In other words, if supplier lead times are not long, lower fill rates can be tolerated than in the preceding example. Indeed, if the replenishment times, including the variability around the supplier lead time, are shorter than those offered to the customer, *zero* safety stock will be needed, and the only inventory carried would be that which is left over from an optimal reorder quantity! Employing a time buffer allows the inventory buffer to be much lower than it would be if there were no time buffer (i.e., if the customer were to demand the item immediately).

MODELING FLOWS

Flows are where the action is. It is in a flow that raw material is transformed into something closer to what the customer needs and is willing to pay for. A component might be combined with other components to create a subassembly or even a final assembly. Or a piece of bar stock might be milled into something that a customer will buy.

A *flow* is *a collection of routings*. Each routing takes some material from a stock point and transforms it through a set of at least one processing step into another stock point. In Chapter 3, a number of performance graphs, Little's law, and the *VUT* equation were introduced. Now we are going to see where some of those relationships originate.

Little's Law

There are three important measures of a production line: the rate at which it produces (throughput, or TH), how much work in process there is on the line (WIP), and how long it takes to go through the line (cycle time, or CT). These three are related in a fundamental way.

Consider Figure 4-7, representing the WIP in a single-machine system as a function of time. The jobs have different process times, A and B require four hours, C needs three hours, whereas D takes five hours to complete. Job A arrives at the second hour, B soon arrives at hour 3, C arrives at hour 5, and finally, D arrives at hour 15. The simulation ends at hour 20. What is the average WIP, average CT, and average TH over this period?

The average TH is easy: 4 jobs in 20 hours; TH = 4/20 = 1/5 jobs per hour. The cycle time is also easy. Job A takes 4 hours, B requires 7, C takes 8, and D spends 5 in the system. The average is 24/4 = 6 hours.

FIGURE 4-7. Illustration of Little's law

Average WIP is easy as well: simply add up how much WIP is in each period and divide by the number of periods. It is important to notice that the sum of the WIP in each period is equal to the sum of the cycle times. For cycle times, we were counting from left to right, and for WIP, we count from the bottom up, but the total is the same, 24. So the average WIP will be 24/20 = 6/5. Denote the averages as WIP, CT, and TH. Then $6 \times 1/5 = 6/5$ or, in general,

$$WIP = TH \times CT$$

which is known as *Little's law*. Note that the jobs did not have to have the same process times, nor did they have to arrive in any particular pattern for this to hold. Therefore, it is a very general result. However, there was one sleight of hand performed in the derivation. The exercise started and ended in an idle period (i.e., when there was no WIP in the system). This made the calculations easier but not general. If there were WIP at the end of the period, the averages would be somewhat off. Nonetheless, this term becomes negligible as the period gets longer and longer. Moreover, for the system to be stable, there *must* be some periods of idleness.

Note that the definition of inventory turns is an application of Little's law but with a twist. Using WIP to represent inventory (although WIP is not a stock strictly speaking) and TH to represent sales yields,

$$\frac{TH}{WIP} = \frac{1}{CT}$$

So turns has a dimension of 1/time.

Capacity Analysis

It is always important to know how much capacity a given flow has. This is determined by the bottleneck of the line. The *bottleneck* is defined as the process center that has the highest long-term utilization. As defined earlier, *utilization* is the fraction of time when the process center is not idle for lack of parts. Now consider the two lines shown in Figure 4-8. Which process is the bottleneck in the top line? Clearly, the second workstation will have the highest utilization regardless of the demand because it has the longest process time, and all the workstations "see" the same demand.

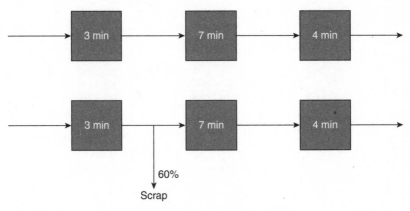

FIGURE 4-8. Two simple production lines

Now consider the second line. After the first workstation, 60 percent of the throughput is thrown away as scrap. Thus the second and third workstations see only 40 percent of the original throughput. In this case, the first workstation will have the highest utilization and so will be the bottleneck. Let's see how that works.

Suppose that 8 parts per hour arrive to the top line. What are the utilizations of the various workstations? In one hour, the first workstation requires 24 minutes, the second requires 56 minutes, and the third 32 minutes. Thus the utilizations are $24/60 = 0.4$, $56/60 = 0.93$, and $32/60 = 0.53$, and the bottleneck must be the second workstation with a utilization of 93 percent.

In the bottom line, the first workstation sees 8 parts per hour, but the second and third workstations see only 3.2 parts per hour (meaning that they could see 3 parts in 80 percent of the hours and 4 parts in 20 percent of the hours; an average of integers can certainly be a noninteger number). Again, the utilization of the first workstation is 0.4. The second is $3.2 \times 7/60 = 0.37$, and the third is $3.2 \times 4/60 = 0.21$, so the first workstation becomes the bottleneck.

Now what is the *capacity* of the two lines? In other words, what is the maximum they could make without worrying about cycle time and WIP? The maximum capacity will be the output of the line when the bottleneck has 100 percent utilization. In the first line, 8 units per hour result in 0.93 utilization. To achieve 100 percent utilization, $8/0.93 = 8.57$ units per hour would have to be started (check it to see if the utilization is now 100 percent). The second line finished only 3.2 units per hour, with 8 units arriving per hour, and

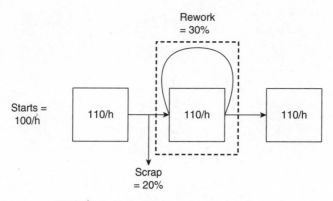

FIGURE 4-9. Production line with rework and scrap

had a maximum utilization of 0.4. Therefore, the capacity of that line would be 3.2/0.4 = 8 units per hour. However, to achieve this throughput, the second line would have to start 8/0.4 = 20 units per hour. Consequently, both lines have almost the same capacity, even though the second line scrapped 60 percent of the incoming product.

What would happen if the scrap occurred *after* the second workstation instead of before it? The second workstation would remain the bottleneck, and 8.57 units per hour would be the maximum *input* rate. But only 40 percent of this input would eventually be finished for a capacity of 3.43 units per hour.

Now consider what happens when there is rework. Figure 4-9 shows a three-workstation line with each machine having a nominal capacity of 110 units per hour. However, 20 percent of the product coming out of the first workstation is scrapped (on average), whereas 30 percent of the units finishing workstation two must be reworked (to keep the example simple, rework occurs, at most, once, so there is no rework of the rework). The last workstation has no such problems. What is the capacity of the line?

An easy way to compute capacity is to assume a throughput and find the utilization and then divide the output by the utilization. So let the input rate be 100 units per hour. Note that the output will be 80 units per hour, on average, and does not depend on the rework. This may seem surprising, but the rework has no effect on the *long-term* throughput. To see this, note the dashed box drawn around the second machine. A law of physics states that "material is always conserved," so that whatever flows into the box must flow out. If we start

100 units per hour but 20 fall out, then 80 must be going in and 80 must be coming out.

So what is the *load*, or the amount of work, seen by each machine? Clearly, the first machine sees 100 units per hour. The second machine sees 80 units coming in, but 30 percent of these get worked twice. So, it sees $80(1 + 0.3) = 104$ units per hour. Finally, the last machine sees 80 units per hour. Then the utilizations will be:

$$\mu_1 = \frac{100}{110} = 0.9091$$

$$\mu_2 = \frac{104}{110} = 0.9455$$

$$\mu_3 = \frac{80}{110} = 0.7273$$

If starting 100 units per hour results in a bottleneck utilization of 94.55 percent, then the capacity of the line will be:

$$\text{Capacity} = \frac{100}{0.9455} = 105.77 \text{ units/h}$$

To check, use this number as the input rate. Of course, only 80 percent, or 84.6 units per hour, arrives at the second machine. These are processed 1.3 times on average, so the load is $84.6 \times 1.3 = 110$ units per hour—exactly the capacity of the second machine.

Now consider a line making more than one product (Table 4-5). Product A takes three, seven, and four minutes, as in Figure 4-8. Product B takes five minutes at each workstation, whereas product C

TABLE 4-5. Process Times for Various Products

| | Product | | |
Machine	A	B	C
1	3	5	6
2	7	5	2
3	4	5	7
Total	14	15	15

takes six, two, and seven minutes, respectively. What is the capacity if A, B, and C have equal demand? The simplest equal demand for doing the calculations is one part per hour for each part. To make one of each part would take 14 minutes at machine 1, 14 minutes at machine 2, and 16 minutes at machine 3. Machine 3 is the constraint with this product mix. The utilization of machine 3 is $[(4 \times 1 \times 0.33) + (5 \times 1 \times 0.33) + (7 \times 1 \times 0.33)]/60 \times 100 = 8.89$ percent, so the capacity of the line would be $1/.0889 = 11.25$ parts per hour. If only part B were made, the capacity would be 12 parts per hour (one part every five minutes). And if only part C were made, the capacity would be the same as making only part A, that is, 60/7 or 8.57. Even though part B requires a total of 15 minutes per part, more of it can be made than either part A or part C because the longest process is 5 minutes and not 7 minutes.

For a final example, if 11 parts per hour are started with a product mix of 25 percent A, 50 percent B, and 25 percent C, machine 3 would be the bottleneck with a utilization of 96.25 percent. Machines 1 and 2 would each have a utilization of 87 percent. For illustration, the calculation for utilization of machine 1 would be: $[(3 \times 11 \times 0.25) + (5 \times 11 \times 0.5) + (6 \times 11 \times 0.25)]/60 = 0.87$ or 87 percent.

The capacity of the line would be $11/0.9625$ or 11.4 parts per hour.

Other "detractors" include setup times and downtimes. Table 4-6 adds setup times, lot sizes, and machine availabilities to the preceding example.

The availability of the machine indicates the percentage of time it is available for production, so the greater the availability, the less is downtime. Availability A can be either given or computed from the

TABLE 4-6. Table of Run Times, Setup Times, Lot Sizes, and Availabilities

Machine	Avail	Process Times			Setup Times		
		A	B	C	A	B	C
1	0.90	3	5	6	55	60	75
2	1.00	7	5	2	55	20	45
3	0.95	4	5	7	50	75	30
Lot Size		70	200	50			

mean time between failures (MTBF) of the machine and its *mean time to repair* (MTTR), that is,

$$A = \frac{\text{MTBF}}{\text{MTBF} + \text{MTTR}}$$

If a machine has 90 percent availability, then its *effective run rate* will be 90 percent of its nominal run rate. Likewise, its *effective run time* is the nominal run time divided by 0.9. In the example, this would mean that the effective run time for one unit of product A made on machine 1 would be 3/0.9 = 3.33 minutes. If 100 parts were made, the total production time (without setups) would be 333 minutes.

Setup times are usually done when the machine is not running and so are not affected by availability. The total time spent doing setups depends on the number of lots run with one setup per lot. If 500 units of *A* are made per month and the lot size is 70, on average, 500/70 = 7.14 setups per month will be done per month. Most months will have only seven setups, whereas 14 percent of the months will have eight. If the setup time for *A* on machine 1 is 55 minutes, on average, around 393 minutes per month will be spent doing setups. Thus, if *Q* is the lot size, *T* is the process time, and *S* is the setup time on a machine with an availability of *A*, the time to produce *D* units will be

$$\text{Process and setup time} = \frac{DT}{A} + \frac{D}{Q}S$$

where the first term is the time to make the units (including the machine downtime), and the second term is the total setup time. To get the total time for a given machine, simply add up the times for each product, that is,

$$\text{Total time} = \sum_i \frac{D_i T_i}{A} + \frac{D_i}{Q_i}S_i$$

Then, to obtain the utilization of a machine, the total time needed is divided by the time available. Table 4-7 shows the details of the calculation for the preceding example with a total demand of 2,000 units split as before with 25 percent A, 50 percent B, and 25 percent C. The time available is 14,994 minutes per month, in which 21 days are worked, and each day has 14 hours of work

TABLE 4-7. Utilization Calculation for a Multiproduct Three-Machine Line

Total Demand		2,000	25.0%	50.0%	25.0%		
Time Available		14,994	A	B	C		
Product Demand			500	1,000	500		
No. Batches			7.143	5.000	10.000		
Process Time	1	1,666.67	5,555.56	3,333.33			
(incl. downtime)	2	3,500.00	5,000.00	1,000.00			
	3	2,105.26	5,263.16	3,684.21			
Setup Time	1	392.86	300.00	750.00			
	2	392.86	100.00	450.00			
	3	357.14	375.00	300.00			
Total Time	1	2,059.52	5,855.56	4,083.33	11,998.41	80.02%	
	2	3,892.86	5,100.00	1,450.00	10,442.86	69.65%	
	3	2,462.41	5,638.16	3,984.21	12,084.77	80.60%	

time and an 85 percent efficiency factor. The highest utilization is 80.6 percent, which implies a capacity of $2,000/0.806 = 2,481$ units per month. Of course, with variability, throughput will be constrained to something somewhat less than this number.

Overall Equipment Effectiveness

Before departing from the capacity issue, let us comment on *overall equipment effectiveness* (OEE), first popularized in the 1980s. The purpose of OEE is to identify the sources of lost production so that they can be addressed and remedied. While there are many definitions, we will use one that appears to be the most common, that is,

$$OEE = A \times P \times Y$$

where A = availability, as before, P = production efficiency, given by the actual run rate divided by the theoretical run rate, and Y = yield, computed from good parts produced divided by total parts produced.

TABLE 4-8. Which Machine Is the Problem?

	Machine 1	Machine 2
Actual run rate (i.e., demand)	800 units/h	800 units/h
Theoretical run rate	1,094 units/h	1,249 units/h
Availability	100 percent	79 percent
Yield	100 percent	94 percent
Setup, lot size	8 h, 25,000	0 h, 1,000

One big problem with OEE is the P factor. If demand is low, then this factor will be low. This may or may not be a problem. Running a machine just to keep it running is a key "waste" as defined by Ohno, the waste of overproduction. However, if demand exceeds capacity or if extra shifts are required to meet demand, then tracking the OEE of the *bottleneck* can be very useful. Nonetheless, tracking the OEE of nonbottlenecks does not appear to have much utility.

Another problem is that OEE does not provide any information about the utilization of capacity or help to identify the bottleneck. Consider the two machines shown in Table 4-8. Which machine should be addressed first for improvement? Which machine is the bottleneck? The OEE of the first machine is 73 percent, whereas the that of the second machine is only 48 percent. However, if utilization is computed using the actual run rate as the demand, then the first machine has a utilization of 98.7 percent, whereas the second machine is at 86.2 percent. Clearly, the first machine is the bottleneck and about to run out of capacity, whereas the second machine is operating with a healthy but not overly wasteful capacity buffer.

If a manager really wants to see how much capacity is wasted on such things as yield, downtime, and the like, then we define a new OEE, call it OEE_{FP}, as

$$OEE_{FP} = \frac{\text{effective capacity}}{\text{capacity without detractors}}$$

$$= \frac{QY}{\dfrac{S}{T} + \dfrac{Q}{A}}$$

Effective capacity $= QY/(S + QT/A)$ and capacity without detractors $= 1/T$. Using the OEE_{FP} calculation results in an OEE value of 74.1 percent for the first machine and 74.3 percent for the second. These percentages show how much of the theoretical run rate $1/T$ is actually available for use. Such a measure would be useful to identify areas where a machine could be improved and could also be used, in the same way as OEE, to improve bottlenecks.

Best-Case Performance

In Chapter 3, graphs were introduced that depicted the best performance and what was called *marginal* performance. Here we show where these come from and give the user a bit of intuition as to how flow systems behave.

The best performance will be one with minimal waiting or queuing. Consider the top line in Figure 4-8. The minimum cycle time will occur if we release one job at a time (to avoid queuing) and will be 14 minutes. We call this the *raw process time* (RPT). The maximum throughput will be the bottleneck rate (BNR). In the preceding discussion on capacity, the bottleneck rate was $1/7$. Little's law shows that the WIP for such performance will be:

$$\text{WIP}_{critical} = \text{BNR} \times \text{RPT}$$

$$= \frac{1}{7} \times 14 = 2$$

and designates it as the *critical WIP*. So let's see what would happen if two jobs are maintained in the system. In other words, start with two jobs, and whenever one finishes, start another one to always keep WIP at two.

After a while, maximum output occurs with no queuing. This is as good as it gets. After a brief 10-minute "transient" period, the line is loaded at the critical WIP level and one job will be starting at workstation 2 while the second starts at workstation 3. After four minutes, the second job will depart, and a third job starts at workstation 1. Three minutes later, the third job finishes at exactly the same time (seven minutes from when we started) as the first job. Both then move at the same time, job one to workstation 3 and job three to workstation 2, and the cycle repeats. Note that machine 2, the bottleneck, both never starves and never has a queue—a remarkable feat. Recall that a stock operating with zero variability would require *zero* inventory to achieve maximum performance, indicated by a 100 percent fill rate. However, for a flow to have ideal performance (maximum throughput with minimum cycle time), *some WIP is required*. For the flow, the ideal is not zero, but the critical WIP. Under such conditions, a job arrives *exactly when the previous job leaves and not before.* Consequently, a production flow should not be run at this low level of WIP. Why? Because, with any variability, the throughput will fall substantially below the BNR. So now let us examine the impact of variability on a flow.

EFFECT OF VARIABILITY

Variability is all around us. Everywhere there are effects of variation and randomness. Variability in demand and in replenishment times was discussed previously. But there is also variability in processing as well. How does this affect a production line?

A manager might think, "Okay, so there is variability. I will just use the mean process time and get the mean performance." Unfortunately, it does not work this way.

Consider a two-stage system with one-piece flow and process times that half the time are fast (three units per minute) and the other half are slow (two units per minute). The average rate is 2.5 units per minute. But this is not what results. If both machines are fast, then the output is fast. But if the first machine is fast but the other is slow, then the output is slow (the first machine is "blocked" by the second machine). Likewise, if the first machine is slow but the second is fast, then the output is also slow (the second machine is "starved" by the first). And, of course, if both machines are slow, the output is slow. Any one of these four scenarios is equally likely with a probability of ¼. Thus three-quarters of the time the machine puts out two units per minute, and one-quarter of the time it puts out three units per minute. Then, the average production rate is $(0.75 \times 2) + (0.25 \times 3) = 2.25$ units per minute. Indeed, whenever there is variability, the performance of a production line will always decrease.

In Chapter 3 we discussed the presence of *buffers* whenever there is variability. The natural behavior of operations is such that if there

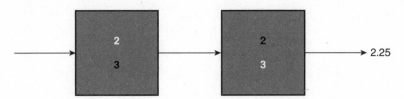

FIGURE 4-10. A two-state system with random process rates

is plenty of extra capacity, wait times should not be long. Suppose that the system shown in Figure 4-10 faced a demand of only one part per hour (remember that the capacity is 2.5 units per minute). There would never be a queue because every part would arrive to an empty system. Obviously, if parts arrived at a rate of one per *minute*, the system would develop a longer and longer queue as time went on. Such a system is said to be *unstable* because, eventually, the system will fail. In fact, even systems in which the demand is equal to the capacity are, in the long term, unstable. The cause is variability.

Now consider a version of our preceding three-machine line that allows queuing and where demand is equal to capacity. Jobs arrive, on average, every 3.5 minutes. But the time between arrivals is the roll of a die: 1, 2, 3, . . . , 6, with an average of 3.5. In this case, there are three machines, and the process times are also die rolls. The first job sees the system empty, so its cycle time should be, on average, 10.5. If there were no variability, each of the next jobs would all have the same cycle times. But this is not what happens when variability is added.

Table 4-9 shows one sequence of the die rolls for 15 jobs. The process times are in the far right columns and are random die rolls, the first job having 4, 5, and 1 at machines 1, 2, and 3. The column called "Arrival Time" has a die roll of 6 for the first job, 3 for the second (arriving at 6 + 3 = 9), 2 for job 3 (arriving at 11), and so on. The arrival time at the second machine is simply the completion time at the first machine. But the job may not be able to start when it arrives if the machine is still busy with the previous job. This is clear in the figure. Look at the third job on the second machine. Job 3 finishes on machine 1 at time 15, but job 2 finishes on machine 2 at time 19, so job 3 cannot start on machine 2 until time 19, the larger of the two. The process time for job 3 on machine 2 is 3; this is shown in the third row under the "M2" column of "Process Times." Job 3 starts on machine 2 at time 19 and finishes finishes on machine 2 at time 22.

TABLE 4-9. Cycle Times Using a Die Roll

Job	Arrival Time	Completion Times			Cycle Time	Process Times		
		M1	M2	M3		M1	M2	M3
1	6	10	15	16	10	4	5	1
2	9	14	19	23	14	4	4	4
3	11	15	22	25	14	1	3	2
4	16	21	27	29	13	5	5	2
5	20	25	29	33	13	4	2	4
6	26	30	31	36	10	4	1	3
7	32	36	42	47	15	4	6	5
8	34	38	44	51	17	2	2	4
9	37	39	45	55	18	1	1	4
10	38	41	50	58	20	2	5	3
11	43	46	56	61	18	3	6	3
12	45	48	62	63	18	2	6	1
13	49	51	66	68	19	2	4	2
14	52	53	72	78	26	1	6	6
15	54	56	74	80	26	2	2	2

So any job cannot start until it arrives *and* until the job before it departs, whichever is later. Once it gets started, it completes after a random process time. Therefore, the completion time at a machine will be the larger of the time when the job arrives to the station and the time when the previous job departs plus the process time.

This can be confusing in prose, so let's see if a little notation makes it easier. Let $C_{i,j}$ be the time the jth job completes at the ith machine, and let $P_{i,j}$ be the process time for this job at this machine. Then

$$C_{i,j} = \max\{C_{i,j-1}, C_{i-1,j}\} + P_{i,j}$$

This is an intuitive explanation. Mathematically, the reason for queuing is that

$$E[\max\{X,Y\}] \geq \max\{E[X], E[Y]\}$$

This means that the expected value (the average) of the maximum of two random numbers will not be less than the maximum of the expected values (and more often than not will be more). This is clear with a roll of two dice. The expected value of a roll of a single die is 3.5, but when two dice are rolled, the expected value of the maximum of the two will be greater than 3.5 and is around 4.5.

Not only are the cycle times in our three-machine line longer than what you would see with no variability, but they also appear to be increasing in time. This is what we would expect because the system has an arrival rate equal to its capacity and so has 100 percent utilization, as we see below.

Measures of Variability

In statistics, the average of a set of random numbers is calculated to indicate its *central tendency*, and the standard deviation or variance indicates the amount of *dispersion* in the data. Previously, when discussing demand, we computed the mean d and the variance σ_d^2 to characterize the demand and also computed a *variance-to-mean ratio* (VMR) = σ_d^2/d to provide information relative to inherent randomness. It turns out that VMR can be inflated due to batch arrivals. For instance, if there are Poisson demands (i.e., the variance in the number of demands is equal to the average number of demands) but each demand is for 100 units, the VMR would not be 1 but would be 100. Because actual demand is often for more than one unit, the VMR is often much larger than 1, even though the number of demands could be Poisson.

When discussing process time variability, we do something similar. Compute the mean process time, and denote it either as T or t_e depending on the context. We use the subscript e to indicate the *effective process time*. *Effective* means that all the components of process time are taken into account, including the actual time doing the processing, setup time, downtime, rework, and so on (see Chapter 8 of *Factory Physics* for a complete discussion). Likewise, the variance is σ^2 or σ_e^2. Finally, the squared coefficient of variation

TABLE 4-10. Three Classes of Variability

Variability Class	Coefficient of Variation	Example
Low variability	$0 \leq CV \leq 3/4$	Task/process times with no interruptions
Moderate variability	$3/4 < CV \leq 4/3$	Task/process times with short interruptions
High variability	$CV > 4/3$	Task/process times with long interruptions

$SCV_e = \sigma_e^2/t_e^2$ is computed to characterize inherent randomness for effective process times. The raw process time for the line then becomes the sum of all the effective mean process times.

We divide variability into three classes based on the CV, as shown in Table 4-10.

Note that low variability has SCV values that are significantly less than 1, whereas high variability has SCV values that are significantly above 1. Moderate variability has SCV values that are close to 1.

The rate of either machine in Figure 4-10 was two, with a probability of ½ and 3 with a probability of ½. This corresponds to process times of 1/2 and 1/3 each with a probability of ½. Thus the mean will be $T = 5/12$ and the variance $\sigma_e^2 = 1/144$, so the $SCV_e = 1/25$, making the $CV_e = 1/5$, which would indicate a low level of process time variability.

Queuing Effects

With no variability, queuing theory gets really easy. If the utilization is below 100 percent, the queue time will be 0. If utilization is above 100 percent, the queue becomes unbounded (no limit) as time goes to infinity, as we saw in the dice example.

However, with variability, there can be a queue even when the utilization is less than 100 percent. Figure 4-11 represents a production line with variability (indicated by the cloud). The x-axis represents the cycle time; in this case, it is equal to the process time T. The y-axis represents the demand, with the mean equal to d and the demand variance indicated by V. Note that the average production must be equal to the average demand over the long term. If production exceeded demand, inventory would continue to increase, whereas if

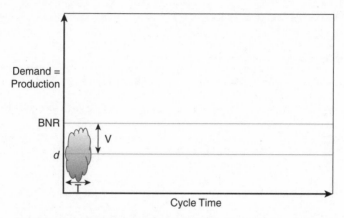

FIGURE 4-11. Representation of a production system with variability

production were less than demand, backorders would grow without limit. In this case, the bottleneck rate (BNR) is set significantly higher than the average demand so that the demand (almost) never exceeds the capacity. Consequently, there is never any queuing, so the cycle time is equal to the process time T.

Figure 4-12 shows what happens when capacity is reduced. Because production cannot exceed capacity, the cloud becomes flattened but remains somewhat symmetrical around the average demand. Because the variability must "go" somewhere, it can be thought of as being transferred out of *capacity* variability and into *time* variability. This *derivation* is not rigorous but helps to illustrate this natural behavior.

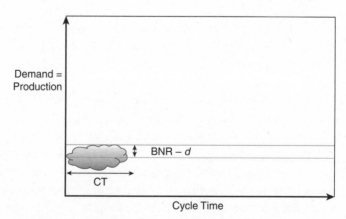

FIGURE 4-12. Production system with variability having less capacity

If the amount of variability stays constant, then the area denoted by $V \times T$ should equal that given by $CT(BNR - d)$. This provides an intuitive way to estimate the cycle time (CT):

$$V \times T = CT(BNR - d)$$

$$CT = \frac{V \times T}{BNR - d}$$

$$= \frac{V \times T^2}{1 - u}$$

$$= \left(\frac{V}{d}\right)\frac{u}{1 - u}T$$

$$= VMR\frac{u}{1 - u}T$$

where VMR is the variance-to-mean ratio of all the variation. This would be the sum of the demand and production variances divided by the average demand (which is also the average production). Also, for a single-machine station, $BNR = 1/T$. This provides a fairly good approximation for the cycle time, especially for relatively high values of utilization u. However, a somewhat better approximation is:

$$CT_q = \frac{VMR_d + SCV_e}{2}\frac{u}{1 - u}T$$

where CT_q = average cycle time in queue, VMR_d = variance-to-mean ratio of demand, and SCV_e = squared coefficient of variation (i.e., the variance divided by the mean squared) of the process times. Then the approximation for the total cycle time is simply $CT = CT_q + T$.

With batch arrivals, the queue time of the *batches* is typically computed rather than the queue time of individual units. In this case, the VMR_d is for the arrival of batches. Likewise, the parameters SCV_e and T are for a batch, not for a single unit. Similar to the relationship between VMR for batch arrivals and unit arrivals, the SCV for a batch of Q parts and the SCV for individual units are related as:

$$SCV_Q = \frac{SCV_1}{Q}$$

A simplified way to write this is:

$$CT_q = VUT$$

This *VUT* equation tells an interesting story. It says that the waiting time in queue is equal to a dimensionless variability coefficient multiplied by a dimensionless utilization constant (not the utilization but a function of the utilization) multiplied by the average process time. The coefficients are *multiplied*, not added. Thus the *VUT* equation is a representation of the tradeoff between the time and the capacity buffers. If a manager wants to keep the time buffer low (i.e., keep CT_q low), then either variability must be kept to a minimum or the utilization factor must be kept low. A low utilization factor implies a large capacity buffer, as seen in the next example.

Suppose, for example, that a manager decides that all cycle times should be no longer than two times the process time (i.e., CT_q is equal to average process time), and suppose that variability was at the moderate level (i.e., $V \approx 1$). Then the *VUT* equation would tell us that:

$$VUT = T$$

Therefore, $VU = 1$. But because $V = 1$, $U = 1$. Because $U = u/(1 - u)$, $u = 0.5$, meaning that there is 50 percent utilization of the resource. However, if $V = 0.1$, then the resource could have $u = 10/11$ and keep total cycle time equal to twice the process time.

Another interesting application of the *VUT* equation comes into play for those companies that have time-stamp information on their process times at workstations and for cycle times through a routing. This is common in the semiconductor industry. Having that data means that the company has the CT and T information for its process. In determining where to look for improvements in cycle time, a manager can use the CT and T information to determine the *VU* factor for various parts of a plant. The areas with high *VU* values usually offer target-rich opportunities for improvement.

TOTAL CYCLE TIME

We have mentioned the tautology found in the statement, "Cycle time is value-added time plus non-value-added time." Of course, everything is in category A or not in category A, but such a statement has no content because it is not telling us anything. This is why, in this section, we wish to divide cycle time into some *useful* categories. These are:

1. Raw process time
2. Move time
3. Shift-differential time
4. Batch time
5. Queue time

The two largest components are usually batch time and queue time. We have already discussed queue time. Meanwhile, raw process time is composed of process time, transfer-batch time, downtime, and setup time. The raw process time is the average time it will take a single transfer batch to go through a routing when released one transfer batch at a time. The release stipulation forces queue and batch times to be zero.

Raw Process Time

The raw process time (RPT) for a routing is simply the sum of the RPTs for each step on the routing. The RPT for a given step is the average time to produce one transfer batch of parts, including random downtime and setup times. We will use the notation we had before and define Q_t to be the transfer batch and Q to be the process batch, which must be an integer number of transfer batches. Then RPT is given by

$$\mathrm{RPT} = Q_t \left(\frac{T}{A} + \frac{S}{Q} \right)$$

The T/A term is average time to produce one part, including downtime, whereas S/Q is the average setup time allocated for each part. To obtain the RPT, we multiply by the size of the transfer batch Q_t. Note that the capacity for a process center is given by

$$\mathrm{Capacity} = \frac{Q_t}{\mathrm{RPT}}$$

$$= \frac{1}{\dfrac{T}{A} + \dfrac{S}{Q}}$$

$$= \frac{Q}{\dfrac{QT}{A} + S}$$

That this is the capacity can be seen from the last expression. The denominator represents the time required to make Q parts, so the ratio is simply the number of parts per time, the capacity.

Move Time

Move time is the simplest to describe. It is merely the time it takes to move a part from one point to another. It is separated out because very often the resources needed to move the part are not considered. If the move resources were considered, it would be modeled as another type of process time with its associated queuing and effective process time. By just saying that it takes a certain amount of time to go from here to there, the extra calculations are avoided without giving up anything important (unless the move resources are scarce). Move times are very useful in describing the use of outside resources— those not under a manager's control. For instance, if a manager were to send metal parts out to be plated, the whole transportation and plating process might be modeled as a single move time.

Shift–Differential Time

Shift-differential time is when different resources work different amounts of time. For instance, if the first process center works 24 hours per day and feeds a second process center that, because of its faster product rate, works only 8 hours per day, WIP will accumulate between the two during the 16 hours when the second process center is off. Then, for the next 8 hours, the second process center would work down the WIP buildup.

From Little's law, WIP buildup is merely "visible cycle time." So how much time would this add? The worst case would be that the second process takes the entire 8-hour shift to burn off all the WIP. So WIP would build up at a rate equal to the TH for 16 hours and then be worked down in the next 8 hours. A bit of geometry would show that the average WIP is ½ (16 × TH). To get the added cycle time, Little's law is applied: divide by TH, yielding an 8-hour shift-differential time.

Thus, if the first process works t_1 hours and the second works t_2, and $t_1 > t_2$, then:

$$\text{Shift-differential time} = \frac{t_1 - t_2}{2}$$

And if $t_1 \leq t_2$, then shift-differential time = 0.

Batch Time

Batch time is a bit more complex. Consider the two kinds of batches—*transfer batches* Q_t and *process batches* Q. A transfer batch is how many parts are moved between workstations (or process centers). The process batch is how many parts are made between changeovers (or setups). Typically, a process batch is an integer multiple of the transfer batch.

The transfer-batch time is the time added due to the fact that the transfer batch is greater than 1. Thus, by definition, if the transfer batch is equal to 1, the transfer-batch time is 0. Otherwise, the transfer batch time is $(Q_t - 1)T$, which is simply the time it takes to process more than one part.

Batch time is the time added when releasing more than one transfer batch at a time. For instance, suppose that a machine takes five minutes to process a part, and the transfer batch is one. If one transfer batch at a time (i.e., one part at a time) is released every 10 minutes or so, the cycle time will be 5 minutes—no queuing, no batching, only process time. However, if a batch of 6 parts were released every hour, there would still be no queuing, but there would be batching effects.

The first part would be finished after 5 minutes, the second after 10, the third after 15, and so on, as shown in Table 4-11. The average batch cycle time per part would be 17.5 minutes.

TABLE 4-11. Batch Times

	Raw Process Time	**Batch Cycle Time**	**Batch Time**
Part 1	5	5	0
Part 2	5	10	5
Part 3	5	15	10
Part 4	5	20	15
Part 5	5	25	20
Part 6	5	30	25
Total	**30**	**105**	**75**
Average	**5**	**17.5**	**12.5**

Because this includes the process time, the *batch* time per part would be 17.5 − 5 = 12.5. A formula for this would be:

$$\text{Batch time} = \frac{Q_p - Q_t}{2} t_e$$

If there were a setup of 50 minutes, the first part would take 55 minutes, whereas the others take 5 minutes, as before. As shown in Table 4-12, the total time would be 80 minutes with an average of batch cycle time of 67.5 minutes.

Recall that the raw process time includes setups and is an average. So averaging 55, 5, 5, 5, 5, and 5 yields 13.3 as the average raw process time. Subtracting this from the average batch cycle time of 67.5 yields 54.2 for the batch time.

However, this "simple" analysis *does not work* in a serial line because parts do not arrive in a batch except at the first workstation. There might not be any batching affects at subsequent workstations if the earlier workstation is significantly slower. Consider the process and setup times (in hours) for a set of machines in Table 4-13 on the next page. If we release a batch with four units, the cycle times depend on the order of the machines.

Figure 4-13 on the next page shows the completion times for the four units on the three machines. At the top of the figure, the bottleneck is first, whereas at the bottom it is last. The first unit of the batch triggers a setup at each station and so takes 8 hours at machine 1

TABLE 4-12. Batch Times When There Is a Setup

	Setup Time	Process Time	Raw Process Time	Batch Cycle Time	Batch Time
Part 1	50	5	55	55	0
Part 2	0	5	5	60	55
Part 3	0	5	5	65	60
Part 4	0	5	5	70	65
Part 5	0	5	5	75	70
Part 6	0	5	5	80	75
Total	50	30	80	405	325
Average	8.3	5.0	13.3	67.5	54.2

TABLE 4-13. Setup and Process Times for a Three-Machine Line

Machine	Setup Time	Process Time
1	4	4
2	3	1
3	3	1

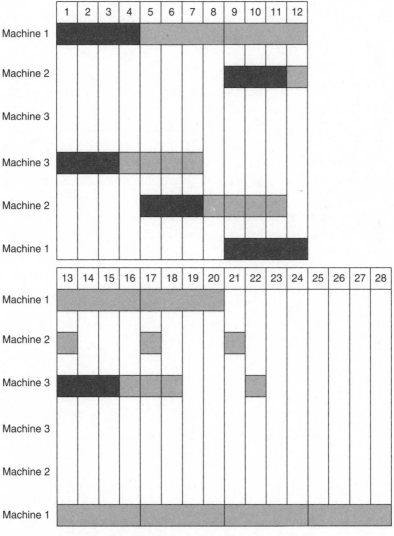

FIGURE 4-13. Completion times for a three-machine line

(4 for setup and 4 for processing). It then goes to machine 2, where it takes 3 hours to set up and 1 hour for processing; likewise with machine 3. The second unit cannot start until the first unit finishes on machine 1 but only takes 4 hours on machine 1 because it is already set up. It finishes at hour 12, the same time the first unit finishes on machine 2. Likewise, it finishes at hour 13 on machine 2 and moves to machine 3, where it has to wait for 3 hours for the first unit to finish at hour 16. The third unit must, of course, wait for the first two on machine 1 but then is able to start immediately on machine 2, which has been idle for 3 hours. When it finishes on machine 2, it finds that machine 3 has just become idle and starts immediately. More idle machines are encountered by the forth unit, which, on arrival, finds both machine 2 and machine 3 idle and waiting. All units are finished at the end of the twenty-second hour.

The situation is quite different if we reverse the order of the machines. In this case, each unit (after the first) must wait in queue at machines 2 and 3. The result is that all units are not completed until the end of hour 28, 6 hours later than in the preceding example.

This is remarkable because we are using the exact same machines, and there is no randomness. The only difference is the order of the machines. We can compute this *batch time* by comparing how long it takes a set of parts released as a batch to traverse the routing against how long it takes one transfer batch to traverse the line, released one at a time (i.e., the RPT). If we look at the first case, the cycle times are 16, 17, 21, and 25 minutes for an average of 19.75 minutes. Meanwhile, the RPT is 8.5 hours, obtained from the following equation (which also appeared earlier in the discussion):

$$RPT = Q_t \left(\frac{T}{A} + \frac{S}{Q} \right)$$

where Q_t is 1, *and* Q is 4. The difference is the batch time = 19.75 − 8.5 = 11.25. In the second case, there was more time due to batching with a batch time of 13.5. Note that in both cases the batch time was greater than the RPT for the entire routing.

Pull Systems

One way to reduce cycle times is to use a pull system. However, as we mentioned in Chapter 1, there is a great deal of confusion as to what makes a pull system.

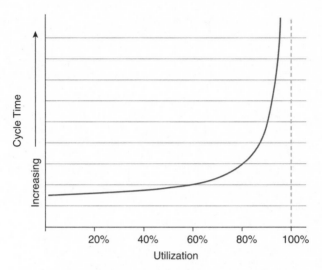

FIGURE 4-14. Cycle time versus utilization

We submit that the essence of a pull system is its control of WIP and measuring throughput instead of the other way around. MRP, the quintessential push system, computes release dates and then "pushes" the job onto the shop floor on that date. Some authors have suggested looking at WIP to see whether things have gotten out of control. However, we believe that this is too little too late.

It is apparent that it is easier to control WIP and measure throughput than to do the opposite from a few of graphs presented in Chapter 3. The first of these, repeated in Figure 4-14, shows the relationship between cycle time and utilization. Because throughput and utilization are proportional, the same result would be seen if the x-axis were throughput instead of utilization. Now consider what would happen to cycle time if the planner made a small error in setting the throughput, say, 10 percent. If the target utilization were 95 percent and the release rate were really now 105 percent, the system cycle time would blow up. Consequently, cycle time is *extremely* sensitive to small changes in throughput at high levels of utilization.

Now consider what happens if WIP is controlled. Figure 4-15 shows how cycle time and throughput vary with WIP. Once the WIP level is sufficient, small errors in setting WIP do not have much effect. Suppose that the "best" WIP level is 10,000 (these are small parts) and the actual WIP level was set to 12,000, a 20 percent error. In this case, cycle time would increase 20 percent, and throughput

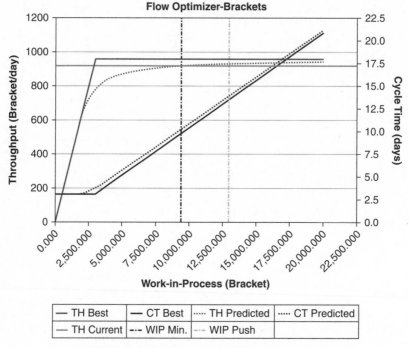

Flow Optimizer-Brackets

— TH Best	— CT Best	····· TH Predicted	····· CT Predicted
— TH Current	--- WIP Min.	--- WIP Push	

FIGURE 4-15. Cycle time and throughput versus WIP

would go up slightly. This is much better than blowing up cycle times and line performance!

While *kanban* provides one way to accomplish WIP control, it is by no means the simplest. If control of WIP is the secret to pull, then why not control WIP in the easiest way possible? This is done using a method called by various names including *CONWIP* and *FIFO Lane*. The method is characterized by maintaining a certain level of WIP in the product flow (a collection of routings). Whenever the WIP level falls below a set maximum, another work order may be released. The released work order does not have to be the same as the one that was just completed but should be whatever is next to be released according to the production-control system. This method is discussed in more detail in Chapter 7. The advantage to this system over *kanban* is *simplicity*. Instead of maintaining a card count for every item at every *kanban* square, one need maintain only one "count," the CONWIP limit itself. Obviously, such a system will be much more suitable for a high and changing product-mix environment. It has been applied with great success, as we describe in Chapter 9.

COMBINING STOCKS AND FLOWS_____

This chapter has demonstrated how to model stocks and flows. Now we would like to model processes that involve both stocks and flows together, as shown in Figure 4-16.

Modeling raw materials inventory is relatively easy because it is provided by a supplier whose replenishment times are independent of the company's production. However, modeling finished stocks in enough detail to help a manager understand production drivers of finished-goods stock requires the use of a production-flow model to represent internal replenishment times (i.e., the plant cycle time plus shipping times). The results of this production model become input for a stochastic inventory model. The combination production model and inventory model provides an integrated model that shows the effects of process times, setup times, and lot sizes on WIP and finished stocks.

This integrated model reveals the importance of lot sizing and its impact on WIP and inventory. Figure 4-17 shows the relation between lot size and cycle times for a single machine with process times of 10 minutes and setups that take one hour on average subject to a demand of 2.4 jobs per hour. The graph reveals much about the production system. First, the smallest allowable lot size is 5. Anything below 5 will result in a utilization that is greater than 100 percent,

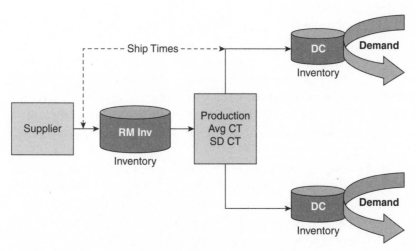

FIGURE 4-16. A production-inventory system

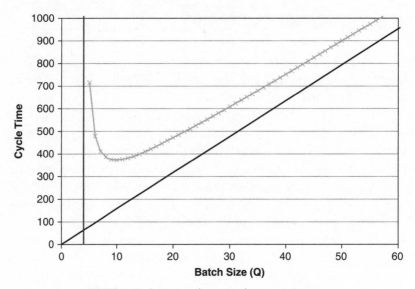

FIGURE 4-17. Cycle time (in minutes) versus batch size

and the system blows up. The best lot size is 10, which results in the shortest average cycle time of 6.2 hours. After that, the cycle times increase as the lot size increases. The standard deviation of the cycle time follows a similar curve.

Thus lot size is a key driver of both the average cycle time and the cycle-time variance. When these are added to the ship times, the results are the ℓ and σ_ℓ^2 values that are used to compute the variance of replenishment-time demand:

$$\sigma_{\text{RTD}}^2 = \ell\sigma_d^2 + \lambda^2\sigma_\ell^2$$

As covered in the discussion of inventory, the variance of replenishment-time demand is key to determining both the average on-hand inventory and the fill rate in an inventory system. If a manager wants complete control of inventory, the following is needed:

- For raw materials, an optimal policy *given* the mean and standard deviation of replenishment times from suppliers.
- For finished goods, an optimal policy for lot sizing and safety stocks that *computes* the replenishment-time parameters by taking into account internal production performance.

Cash-Flow Optimization

We will now take the concepts developed and use them to optimize all three of the Factory Physics buffers. The first buffer, capacity, is directly linked to cost; the second, (lead) time, is associated with the service we offer our customers; and inventory represents a highly controllable (balance-sheet) asset. We *could* attempt to assign a "cost" to each buffer, but this is unrealistic. How much does it cost per day per piece for an order to be late? Unless the firm is under contract to deliver with specified penalties for being late (such as in the case of some automotive suppliers), attempting to specify such a cost is a waste of management time. Likewise, the cost of capacity is unrealistic except over the very long term. When looking at capacity-expansion projects, which typically are long-term projects, managers can and should consider the depreciated capital cost and expense associated with running a plant to obtain an annual cost of the capacity. But in the short term (e.g., next month), the capacity is essentially fixed. And if a manager is not going to hire or fire any employees, even the labor cost is fixed.

So it makes much more sense to simply *fix* the demand (set by the market, not by the company), the capacity, and the customer service and then to *maximize cash flow*. To do this requires minimizing any controllable assets that change over the short term and minimizing any other real out-of-pocket costs. The one asset that quickly changes is inventory.

Out-of-pocket costs include anything that decreases cash flow over the time period being considered. An example would be scrap loss that occurs whenever a changeover occurs. Such scrap loss represents a real change in cash flow for the period because additional raw material must be purchased. However, the labor cost of performing the changeover is *not* an out-of-pocket cost because it costs the same to run the factory whether one more changeover is done or not (i.e., labor is fixed). Another example of an out-of-pocket cost could be the cost associated with outsourcing a batch of product. A more interesting example is the cost of the reagents used when testing a pharmaceutical batch. Most examples of out-of-pocket costs are the result of changeovers or setups. Outsourcing cost is a function of how demand is specified and how capacity is set and can be computed as part of planning for both demand and capacity. A case study of this is provided in Chapter 5.

The problem to be solved is to find optimal lot sizes and safety stocks that will maximize cash flow for a given capacity and service situation. In other words, minimize inventory carrying cost plus out-of-pocket costs subject to

- Capacity constraints
- Service constraints
- Lot-size constraints

Examples of Cash-Flow Optimization

We begin with a simple example, as seen in Figure 4-18. There is demand for two items: 30,000 units of item 1 and 18,000 units of item 2. Twenty percent of the item 1 units will undergo rework. The run rates for both range between 9 and 20 units per hour. There are significant setups (changeovers) at machine 1 that last between three and five hours. Moreover, each setup results in $10 worth of product lost as scrap (i.e., out-of-pocket cost). To avoid setups, the lot sizes are set at 4,000 for item 1 and 4,932 for item 2.

These policies result in cycle times of between 70 and 83 days, with $257,000 in WIP and $133,500 in finished inventory, and a fill rate of only 75 percent. The total scrap cost, however, is only $171.50 per year.

If the optimization procedure described earlier is applied, the cycle times drop to 24 and 15 days with WIP reducing proportionally to $62,000. Finished inventory goes down only slightly to $130,000, but the fill rate rises to 95 percent. Moreover, the scrap cost goes up to $1,600 per year.

A manager has to decide whether this is better or not in determining a company's course of action. Clearly, there is better service with much less WIP and slightly less finished inventory. But the scrap cost has increased by almost tenfold. So the question is whether the reduced inventory investment and better service is worth the increased out-of-pocket cost.

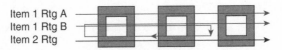

FIGURE 4-18. Routings for the simple example

One way to do this is to require both scenarios to have the same level of customer service (i.e., fill rate). This can be done by systematically increasing the safety-stock levels for the first scenario until achieving a 95 percent fill rate (and keeping the lot sizes the same). If this is done, the result is the same level of WIP but $575,000 in finished inventory.

So now the manager's comparison is $257,000 in WIP, $575,000 in finished goods, and $171.50 in out-of-pocket cost against $62,000 in WIP, $130,000 in finished goods, and $1,600 in out-of-pocket cost, with both scenarios having the same fill rate. It is pretty clear that the optimized system is better despite the increase in out-of-pocket cost. To see this, suppose that WIP is worth half what a finished product is worth. The *inventory carrying-cost ratio i* can be computed that will make both scenarios equal and provide insight as to whether this is reasonable.

$$(575,000 + 0.5 \times 257,000)i + 171.5$$
$$= (130,000 + 0.5 \times 62,000) + 1,600$$

If i is solved for, the result is an inventory carrying-cost ratio of 0.0025, or 0.25 percent. Typical inventory carrying-cost ratios are between 5 and 25 percent, so a 0.25 percent inventory carrying cost would be extremely low. Thus the optimized strategy would be better in almost any situation.

While this is a rather contrived example to illustrate some important points, we will describe a very real-world example in Chapter 9.

CONCLUSIONS

In developing a science of operations, as was our original objective, we have now completed both the scientific theories and a vast body of evidence supporting the theories. The fundamental concepts of tradeoffs, demand-stock-production, buffers, and variability were stated in great detail. The theories were further shown to be highly predictive through the use of performance graphs and efficient frontiers. In this chapter, we have provided the tip of the iceberg of the vast body of evidence supporting Factory Physics science, as seen in the mathematics describing the Factory Physics science of operations behavior. The remainder of this book will:

- Describe how managers can tie Factory Physics science directly to a business' financial statements.
- Incorporate the science into company planning to tie executive strategy to daily execution *using whatever IT a company currently uses.*
- Provide specific examples of control-of-operations performance guided by Factory Physics science.
- Provide guidance and examples for managers in applying Factory Physics science to their organizations.

CHAPTER 5

Profit, Cash Flow, and Factory Physics Science

The ultimate measures for business are profit and cash. The Factory Physics approach has a direct impact on profit and cash, as reflected in traditional financial statements. While Factory Physics is primarily a theory of operations behavior, it can also be viewed in one sense as a theory of cash flow, profit, and return on assets. The buffers of inventory, capacity, and time and the demand-stock-production (DSP) framework essentially correspond to the financial resources of a company. Consequently, the key elements of the Factory Physics framework tie into the income statement, balance sheet, and cash-flow statement. Those ties are the topic of discussion of this chapter. For example, the policy choices generated by selecting a position on the fill-rate-versus-inventory efficient frontier result in the inventory shown on the balance sheet. The policy choices for capacity utilization result in equipment assets listed on the balance sheet, as well as the equipment and labor expenses listed on the income statement.

The Factory Physics approach embodies a fundamentally different take on achieving profit, cash flow, and return-on-asset performance. The classic approach is to allocate revenue to expenses and then provide some unit cost as a way to guide decisions about what product portfolio will produce the highest profitability. Using Factory Physics science to understand the best portfolio of buffers and variability provides a more powerful angle than using standard cost accounting using the following steps:

1. Determine the range of demand (product portfolio) revenue that is feasible.
2. Evaluate the cost required for the capacity and inventory to meet the desired response time for the product portfolio.

3. Iterate revenue ranges and cost until a suitable configuration is found.
4. If no suitable revenue/cost configuration can be found, the initial analysis process provides targets for improvement. The fact that the planning is based on a quantified description of the company's demand and transformation enables high precision on what types of improvements need to be made to get the desired results. This provides clear direction for the company's continuous-improvement resources.

These steps are the essence of the Factory Physics operations strategy and execution, and we will detail them much more in the next couple of chapters. The Factory Physics approach manages cost and revenue drivers based on the underlying natural behavior of those drivers. It is putting the cart before the horse to make extensive, detailed allocations of cost to products and then, using the resulting *product-cost avatar*, to drive organizational behavior. As discussed in Chapter 3, cost avatars (unit costs from the standard cost model) can drive counterproductive behavior in the real world because their behavior does not accurately describe real-world behavior. Additionally, use of variances based on product-cost avatars just perpetuates an organization's move away from dynamic management of the natural behavior of demand and transformation. With the concepts of performance boundaries of production and stocks, managers should determine how well their processes are working compared with best-possible performance. The financial measures correspond to how well demand is within the planned range and how well the cost and buffer configuration is performing compared with best-possible performance. This works in concert with standard financial reporting requirements rather than proposing different accounting approaches. The focus of the Factory Physics approach is to drive highest possible cash flow by optimally managing the natural behavior of the drivers of cash flow. As mentioned earlier, if a solid cash flow is maintained, then profitability results, and allocation of revenue to expenses using the standard cost model for financial reporting is not a particularly controversial process.

The Factory Physics approach is in contrast to the hodgepodge of measurements often used to connect operations to a business's financial statements through initiatives such as Lean, Six Sigma, and enterprise resources planning (ERP) implementations. We provided a number of examples illustrating how misaligned measures and poor intuition can drive a high level of activity with, at best, uneven results. The quest to quantify the value of operations and continuous-improvement initiatives is as timeless as the initiatives themselves. An example comes from a plant where one of us worked during the total quality management (TQM) era of the 1980s and early 1990s. The plant manager was frustrated because the amount of dollars claimed as having been saved by TQM was not showing up in the financial statements. He said something akin to, "The next time someone tells me about labor cost saved by a TQM project, I want the name of the person who isn't working here anymore because of that project." Similar sentiments are expressed today; just replace TQM with Lean or Six Sigma initiatives. Use of *Factory Physics* science to choose strategies, tactics, and controls leads to successful management of predicted levels of capacity, inventory, and response time. This predictive control, in turn, leads to success in attaining targeted profitability.

Profit equals revenue minus costs. Later in this chapter we will show in detail how cost elements on the financial statements are driven by capacity and inventory choices that drive cost. We now consider a simple model of revenue:

$$\text{Revenue} = \text{unit price} \times \text{units sold}$$

The only way to change revenue is to change the price or change the quantity of units sold. Units sold increase or decrease based on marketing decisions. In addition, performance of sales and operations functions can affect how many units are sold. Some examples of marketing decisions might include the introduction of new products, offering quicker delivery with shorter lead times, and increasing the number of salespeople. Raising or lowering price can affect both elements of revenue if a market is price elastic. However, outstanding, predictive performance of sales and operations can provide a competitive advantage and actually reduce the elasticity of price—customers are usually willing to pay more for superior products and services. Consider the Apple iPod. These decisions will affect not only the quantities demanded but also the variability in demand. Variability can increase because of an increase in the number of products offered. Variability also can increase because pricing strategies for coupons or channel incentives artificially increase and lower demand over different time periods. For chosen marketing and business plans, it is imperative that operations strategies and tactics align with realistic revenue plans to ensure that customer demand can be met at desired profit levels.

Ultimately, company supply chains and operations are charged with delivering the units demanded by the market. As discussed in Chapters 3 and 4, increasing the number of units sold (demand) and the variability of demand will require more inventory and capacity. This will increase cost. In this scenario, executives and managers must decide whether the added cost drives enough revenue to generate desired profit. The science of the Factory Physics framework quantifies the levels of inventory and capacity needed for given market scenarios. Scenarios can be evaluated based on potential financial outcomes. If units don't match plan, managers can make choices to adjust levels of capacity and inventory with a scientific, quantified knowledge of financial impact and how that impact will be reflected in financial statements. In this chapter we will detail some common misperceptions about the connections between operations behavior and financial performance, describe the direction connections, and provide detailed discussions on some key areas of connection. We begin with a common misperception about how customers perceive value.

THE VALUE-ADDED FANTASY

Attempts to quantify benefits with slogans as opposed to science can lead to poor decision making by executives and managers, no matter how well-intended. Just as when inaccurate models are used to represent production behavior (see Figure 3-13), well-meaning inaccurate slogans can lead efforts astray because they don't connect directly to bottom-line financials. The value-added philosophy is one of these. Performance-improvement strategies that revolve around the notion of reducing non-value-added activities are quite popular these days. Unfortunately for the multitudes of businesses relying on them, these strategies are flawed and lead to what we call the *value-added fantasy*.

Consider the following companies:

- A European semiconductor manufacturer that uses hundreds of steps in the course of its manufacturing process has spent years reducing its cycle time. At last, it has achieved a ratio of average cycle time (CT) to value-added time (VAT) of nearly 3:1—a very respectable number indeed.
- A U.S. automotive supplier of stamped metal parts (with an average cycle time of 4 days) discovers that its CT/VAT ratio is over 100:1.
- A U.S. printer of magazines and catalogs develops a value-stream map and measures its CT/VAT ratio at around 3,000:1.

Which of these three companies is the most productive? Which is the most profitable? As it turns out, the ratio of total cycle time to value-added time is *not* going to provide the answers to these questions. In point of fact, the printer—with the "worst" ratio—is the best financial performer, whereas the semiconductor company—with apparently the "best" performance—is in big trouble. What is missing from this picture? Of course, the three companies are in three very different businesses. However, even if we narrow the field to semiconductor companies making similar products, there are examples in which a company with a smaller VAT/total-CT ratio has been much less profitable than a company with a larger ratio.

In particular, *the value-added fantasy is the perception that concentrating on value-added activities and eliminating non-value-added activities will provide the most profitable performance for a production or service process or supply chain.* A value-added strategy may or may not lead to improved profitability. Let's first look at some typical definitions of value added:

- Any step in the production process that improves the product for the customer
- Any activity that
  - The customer cares about
  - Changes the product
  - Is done right the first time

Some good things can result from a value-added analysis. The value-added concept is a simple concept. It is essentially "eliminate waste, and focus only on activities that provide value." Simplicity in direction does help to drive behavior. For instance, value-added analysis causes a search for product that is waiting instead of being acted on; it typically shows that most of the time a product spends in a process is spent waiting. Many companies, especially those where little process improvement has been done, have gotten great initial benefit from the revelations of this type of analysis. However, there are problems with the value-added fantasy. One acute problem is the notion that the value-add approach addresses things that drive customers to buy a company's products—the value in value added.

In the vast majority of cases, assuming that a company is not using unethical practices, the customer does not care what a company does in its processes. The customer makes a value statement with an exchange of money for goods or services at the time of purchase of a product or service. When purchasing a television set, most, if not all, customers do not consider the value-added versus non-value-added activities that might be taking place in its production. Because setup time is a classic non-value-added step, how would most customers respond if asked to provide one of the following survey responses?

1. "I prefer televisions from companies that have long setup times."
2. "I prefer televisions from companies that have short setup times."
3. "I am not concerned about companies' setup times."

We believe that answer 3 would win hands down.

Because most customers are not concerned about the activities that go on within a company's production or service processes, having internal decisions about what customers consider to be value-added or non-value-added activities is an extremely subjective and often dysfunctional exercise. Actually, because *value-added* is typically defined as a process step that changes form, fit, or function, the value-added steps are the ones that a company would need to do most effectively whether a customer knows about them or not. Calling these steps *value-added* is just a confounding classification and frequently leads to nonproductive discussions. For example, is the work of highly skilled quality inspectors a value-added or non-value-added activity? We submit that investment in highly skilled inspectors is highly valuable to companies that require their services to ensure that standards are being maintained and to identify opportunities for improvement of quality. The use of vague terms such as *non-value-added* leads to the creation of more vague terms. Evidence invention of the term *necessary non-value-added*—still not an inspirational label for people who are necessary but non-value-added.

If the value-added approach struggles to directly connect activity to customer revenue and thereby to the income statement, perhaps it can address the cost side of the statements? In some cases, value-added activities have been used to model cycle time and drivers of efficiency. But we would argue that even using value-added activities in this context is a flawed exercise. Let's review a couple of common operational statements often cited as fundamental in the Lean literature:

1. Cycle time = value-added time + non-value-added time.
2. Decreased non-value-added time results in increased efficiency and decreased cost.

The Lean literature proposes that these statements work in alignment to drive a relentless focus on reducing non-value-added time and that this activity reduces cost. We have suggested focusing on a practical, scientific approach to cycle time rather than using the value-added approach as a more powerful means of achieving consistent performance improvement. Recall the Toyota Production System (TPS) discussion from Chapter 1 as well as the discussion of the fundamental relationships between work in process (WIP), throughput, and cycle time in Chapters 3 and 4. Cycle time is governed by the relationships described in the *VUT* equation and Little's law. Toyota exploited its understanding of the science of operations by using a 30 percent capacity buffer to support its strategy to drive consistent, low cycle times. Most Lean practitioners would label such a capacity buffer as non-value-added and try to eliminate it because statements 1 and 2 above suggest that reducing non-value-added activity reduces cycle time and improves efficiency. In fact, the opposite is often true. Toyota chose to pay for inventory reduction, low cycle times, and continuous-improvement efforts with its capacity buffer. The cost of the capacity buffer was outweighed by the ability it provided Toyota for buffering against variability to achieve lower inventories, reduced scrap, and better response time. This was the right business choice for Toyota and was reflected in its financial statements. As we pointed out in Chapter 1, companies that just imitate the TPS without understanding why it works and where it works best do so at their own peril. Using the value-added approach might provide good results, but then again, it might not. Companies should not depend on the subjective value-added description of performance to drive financial performance. Instead, companies should drive financial health through a solid understanding of the practical science governing manufacturing supply-chain logistics. We turn now to a discussion of the direct links between Factory Physics science and financial statements.

FINANCIAL STATEMENTS AND THE SCIENCE OF OPERATIONS

As discussed in Chapter 2, the primary goals for business are positive cash flow and long-term profitability. We will build on the concept of "managing the portfolio of buffers" introduced in Chapter 3 to help managers and executives drive profit and cash flow. As Figure 5-1 demonstrates, profitability is accomplished by increasing sales while reducing cost. A key takeaway from this statement is that cost is only one part of the equation. Focus should be on increased profit, not cost reduction alone.

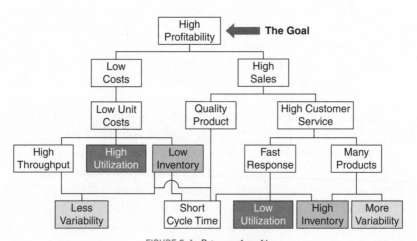

FIGURE 5-1. Drivers of profit

Ultimately, it is the *bottom line* that matters. The fundamental bottom line relationships are:

$$\text{Profit} = \text{revenue} - \text{expenses}$$
$$\text{Return on assets} = \text{profit/assets}$$

Recall the DSP framework we introduced in Chapter 3. Its key elements of demand and transformation connect directly to the financial statements. Capacity is needed to satisfy demand and thereby exerts a strong influence on revenue. Response time is tied to customer service; that also affects revenue. The cost of capacity, in terms of labor and fixed production costs, directly affects expenses. Cycle time affects expenses as well because the longer a part remains in the factory, the more likely it is to be damaged, lost, or scrapped. Additionally, there is a financial cost of the cash tied up in slow or nonmoving assets. The quicker a part moves through transformation, the quicker defects will be detected. The quicker defects can be detected, the better the chance of determining and eliminating the cause of the defect. Thus, reducing cycle time is a good way to reduce internal quality-related costs. Finally, inventory is crucial because it represents the most controllable of business assets. While it is difficult to reduce a fixed-asset base in the short term (you cannot easily sell machines and buildings only to have them back on short notice when you need them), inventory represents an asset that *can* be reduced and managed in the short term. We should also note that another important financial measure is *inventory turns*, computed as annual revenue (at cost of goods sold) divided by average inventory (at cost of goods sold).

We've discussed how Toyota chose to spend more money on capacity to achieve its business goals for consistent, shorter cycle times, lower inventories, and long-term process improvement. The elements of profit driven by strategic tradeoffs such as these are captured in the basic financial statements. Strategies, tactics, and controls based on *Factory Physics* science will predictably affect the income statement. Table 5-1 shows the links between *Factory Physics* theory and the income statement. Of course, it is not the links themselves that drive profit. It is how a leader employs Factory Physics science to drive profit and cash flow. So Table 5-1 also lists goals for managing the science to drive profit.

TABLE 5-1. Drivers of Profit

Factory Physics Elements	Direct Impact on Income Statement	Goals for Managing
Demand	Revenue	Maximize revenue. Provide minimum response time and product offering to drive best possible cash flow.
Inventory	Cost of Goods Sold	Minimize inventory while providing desired service.
Capacity	Cost of Goods Sold and Fixed Expense	Minimize salaries and equipment costs by optimizing capacity buffer.
Time	Revenue and Cost of Goods Sold	Minimize response time with lowest cost capacity and inventory strategies.

Table 5-2 shows the direct link between the core elements of the Factory Physics framework and the balance sheet. Different organizations have different goals for managing the elements of the balance sheet depending on their capital structure and business situation. That said, general balance-sheet goals linked to the *Factory Physics* framework are likely to be:

- **Assets.** Minimize cash tied up in the fixed assets of capacity and current assets of inventory.
- **Liabilities.** Minimize payables and equipment liabilities by minimizing the cost of capacity and inventory (raw materials inventory in particular).

Finally, cash flow is driven by the timing of events captured on the income statement and balance sheet. Thus the *Factory Physics* elements affecting those financial statements drive cash flow in

TABLE 5-2. Balance Sheet and the Factory Physics Framework

Factory Physics Elements	Balance Sheet Impact Line
Demand	Accounts Receivable
Inventory	Inventory and Accounts Payable
Capacity	Fixed Assets
Time	Accounts Receivable, Accounts Payable, and Inventory

conjunction with the realities of the timing of customer payments received and strategic decisions about when to pay suppliers. The cash-flow statement also shows the cash increase resulting from reduced inventory and reduced capacity financing costs.

Financial Statements and the Factory Physics Framework

1. The core elements of the Factory Physics framework directly link to the traditional financial statements.
2. Leaders can develop operations strategy for inventory, capacity, and response time based on quantified impact on the financial statements.

FINANCIAL PERFORMANCE DRIVEN BY THE SCIENCE OF OPERATIONS

In this section we highlight a few examples of how leaders can leverage the insights of the Factory Physics framework to drive profit and cash. We will analyze:

- Contribution margin at the bottleneck
- The impact of Lean manufacturing on capacity costs
- Inventory optimization
- Managing the portfolio of buffers in assemble-to-order environments

Contribution Margin at the Bottleneck

Chapters 3 and 4 described how the rate of the bottleneck controls the throughput of a production flow. To get the most profit out of a production flow, one should produce the products that are the most profitable at the bottleneck. As an example, consider the following exercise: suppose that stacks of 5, 10, and 20 dollar bills are laid on a table. Each stack contains only one type of bill, and all stacks are the same height. The table could contain any mix of stacks of currency. The first person who walks up to the table is told to take as much money as possible off the table within a five second time period. However, the stacks of bills must be picked up independently of each other. The person can't just sweep money off the table. What does your intuition say about the predicted result? Naturally, the participant is going to pick up the stacks of twenties first and pick those up until the twenties are all gone. The participant will then pick up whatever the next-highest denomination of bill is lying on the table until time's up. Why? Because this provides the most cash to the participant given the constraints of the operation. This is exactly the same idea as maximizing cash flow at the constraint in production.

The bottleneck (we use *bottleneck* and *constraint* interchangeably, as is common) of a production flow is determined by the resource with the highest long-term utilization—yet another very important reason for managers to make sure that they calculate utilization correctly. This is the same utilization that drives cycle time, as described in the discussion on the *VUT* equation in Chapter 3. The constraint limits the amount of cash a company can receive into its organization as accounts receivable because it limits the number and quantity of revenue-producing products or services that can be produced. So how do we determine the most profitable mix of products to produce at the bottleneck? We use contribution margin:

$$\text{Contribution margin} = \text{revenue} - \text{variable costs}$$
$$\text{Profit} = \text{contribution margin} - \text{fixed costs}$$

As discussed in Chapter 4 on cash-flow optimization, variable costs depend on the time frame considered. For a 20-year time frame, whole production facilities are variable costs. If a manager is only planning for the next month or the next six months and is not planning on major numbers of new hires or layoffs or new equipment acquisitions, capacity and all the indirect costs associated with it are *fixed*. *Variable costs* are those out-of-pockets cost tied directly to the production of the product or service. For instance, raw materials are often the primary variable cost. Or if a company is making pharmaceuticals and every time a batch of product is made batch quality is tested with expensive reagents, the cost of the reagent is a variable cost because it depends on the number of batches made.

Contribution margin ties directly to the income statement in terms of revenue and the variable costs found in the cost of goods sold. Ultimately, maximizing contribution margin at the constraint increases profit, as expressed in net income. Contribution margin at the constraint directly affects the return on assets on the balance

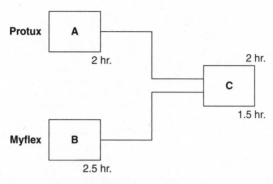

FIGURE 5-2. Protux and Myflex routings

sheet by increasing the return on the asset of capacity. As is the original intent of driving performance with contribution margin at the constraint, more cash is generated from operations, less cash is tied up in investment in capacity, and the results also show up in the cash-flow statement.

Now consider the more operations-oriented example of a pharmaceutical company with two products, Protux and Myflex. The routings for both products are shown in Figure 5-2. A unit of Protux requires 2 hours of process time at process center A and 2 hours at process center C. A unit of Myflex requires 2.5 hours of process time at process center B and 1.5 hours at process center C.

The cost elements of the two products are shown in Figure 5-3. A manager might evaluate the profitability of potential product-mix strategies by looking at the standard costing marginal profit without

Product	Price	Raw Matl. Cost	Tot. Lab or Hrs.	Unit Cost	Min. Demand	Max. Demand
Protux	$625	$50	4	$130	75	140
Myflex	$600	$100	4	$180	0	140

$20.00/hr.

21	days per month
16	hours per day
336	hours per month

(hours avail. at each process center)

$100,000 overhead (includes labor)

	Marginal Profit	Marginal Profit/Labor Hr.
Protux	$575	$144
Myflex	$500	$125

FIGURE 5-3. Protux and Myflex cost elements

	Amount (Units)	Margin	
Protux	140	$575	$80,500
Myflex	37	$500	$18,500
			$99,000
			($100,000)
			($1,000) Profit

FIGURE 5-4. Maximize Protux

regard to how much throughput can be produced by the bottleneck. In this scenario, it would seem that a manager should maximize the amount of Protux produced because it has the highest standard cost marginal profit. Note that in the "Min. Demand" and "Max. Demand" columns, the marketing and sales department has placed limits on the amount of each product that can be produced per period based on its sales forecast. The department naturally wants to make as much Protux as possible because the standard costing marginal profit calculation shows it to be the most profitable product.

Thus, if we produce the maximum amount (140 per period) of the high standard margin product Protux, we have only enough capacity left over to produce 37 units of Myflex. The results are shown in Figure 5-4.

The results are not good; the manager loses $1,000 per period. However, because the manager is aware of the Factory Physics science describing operations and thereby the importance of utilization of the constraint in controlling output, focus is shifted to contribution margin at the constraint. First, the manager has to figure out which process center is the constraint. Looking at Figure 5-2, the initial reaction might be that process center B is the constraint because it has the longest process time (2.5 hours). However, as a factory physicist in training, the manger knows that the process center with the highest utilization is the constraint. Looking again at Figure 5-2 and the data, it is obvious that process center C is in fact the constraint because both products pass through it. Given the demand mix of Protux and Myflex, process center C will run out of capacity before any of the other process centers do.

So now the manager does a simple calculation, divides the contribution margin of each product by its time on the constraint, and gets the following:

Protux = (625 − 50)/2 = $287.50 per hour on the bottleneck
Myflex = (600 − 100)/1.5 = $333.33 per hour on the bottleneck

	Amount (Units)	Margin	
Protux	75	$575	$43,125
Myflex	124	$500	$62,000
			$105,125
			($100,000)
			$5,125 Profit

FIGURE 5-5. Maximize Myflex

This is an eye opener. It turns out that Myflex is just like those stacks of $20 bills in the example at the beginning of this section. If the manager wants to generate the most cash possible for the company, he will make the minimum allowed amount of Protux because that is what marketing and sales directed and dedicate all remaining capacity to Myflex. The result of this strategy is shown in Figure 5-5, and the results are good. The company makes a profit.

It turns out that it is more profitable to minimize the amount of Protux and maximize the amount of Myflex because this product mix generates the most cash possible to cover fixed expenses.

There will naturally arise counterarguments to this example. For instance, "Oh, that's too theoretical. An operations manager can't tell the marketing and sales department what to make!" Granted. However, we didn't say that we could tell companies what to do. We are only explaining how the natural behavior of operations works as companies try to do whatever they do. In practice, the theory is a good theory because it predicts behavior. One of our clients was a company with multiple parallel-capacity production plants. Our contact was an executive vice president of manufacturing who had been a plant manager at the company earlier in his career. The plant managers of each plant could influence which products were made at their plants, and our vice president said that when he was a plant manager, he used this concept of contribution margin at the constraint as his "secret weapon." Whenever he reviewed products that could be produced at his plant, he would always lobby for those that would provide the highest contribution margin at his plant's constraint operations. It provided him with a financial performance advantage, and his plant regularly showed higher cash flow than the other plants, where the plant managers evidently were not aware of the concept. An interesting twist to this story is that the vice president as plant manager would often end up with unfavorable variances on some products, but he caught no flak for that because his overall plant financial performance was so strong. This is one answer to the "It's too theoretical" argument. Another answer is that it is operation's job in any decent sales and operations planning process to let marketing and sales know that these types of options are available for increasing cash flow.

Another client was able to exploit this concept across the supply chain with its outsourcing policies. The client was a food-manufacturing company that processed multiple products through a bottleneck blender. It could outsource to a food-processing supplier that charged by the pound of product produced. The price charged per pound by the food-processing supplier differed by product. Prior to understanding the concept of maximizing contribution margin through the bottleneck, our client chose to outsource product for which the food-processing supplier charged it the lowest price per pound. This was the approach used to maintain target utilization levels at the bottleneck, thereby managing cost and response time. After understanding contribution margin concept, the company chose to outsource based on "time at the bottleneck." As shown in Figure 5-6, the client saved 15 percent on outsourcing costs. The left combination of items shows a $56,593 cost from the first policy to outsource based on lowest price per pound. The right combination of items shows a $47,774 cost using a policy to outsource based on time at the bottleneck. Either combination would provide the required utilization level of the bottleneck.

Note that only one product (item 3) overlapped between the different methods to choose which products should be outsourced. The new strategy minimized the dollar amount outsourced because it

	Lb.	$/Lb.	$
Item 4	7,033.333	0.1975	$1,389
Item 5	24,125	0.17	$4,101
Item 3	175,020.8	0.15	$26,253
Item 6	71,025	0.18	$12,785
Item 7	11,000	0.155	$1,705
Item 8	7,003.333	0.22	$1,541
			$47,774

	Lb.	$/Lb.	$
Item 1	295.5417	0.1475	$43,592
Item 2	66.65	0.1500	$9,998
Item 3	20.02	0.1500	$3,003
			$56,593

Outsource by Lowest Price   Outsource Based on Bottleneck

FIGURE 5-6. Outsourcing at a food-manufacturing company

maximized the internal throughput at the bottleneck. Understanding this Factory Physics concept and applying it showed up directly on the outsourcing line in the cost-of-goods-sold section of the company's income statement.

When Lean Manufacturing Adds Cost

Sometimes companies misinterpret a fundamental financial relationship in their quest to drive Lean initiatives. This relationship is:

$$\text{Profit} = \text{contribution margin} - \text{fixed costs}$$

As was stated in Chapters 3 and 4, too little WIP can be as bad as too much WIP. This is because too little WIP can starve the bottleneck, increasing the need for capacity and adding fixed cost. Actually, WIP itself doesn't affect contribution margin directly. Each piece of WIP corresponds to a unit sold, and companies don't intentionally buy and then not use material (WIP) needed to meet demand. Therefore raw materials (WIP) are not part of fixed costs. The cost of WIP is part of variable cost, but having more or less WIP doesn't affect variable cost over the long term. Let's review a case encountered in industry.

In an attempt to achieve Lean performance, this company designed and built a production line designed to achieve one-piece flow. The company attempted to limit WIP and cycle times to minimal levels without understanding the impact on capacity, utilization, and fixed costs. A schematic of the line is shown in Figure 5-7. Component lines fed pieces into the main assembly line, where they were assembled into a final product.

The process was highly automated, and whenever any section of the line went down, the entire line stopped. The line had been designed for an output of 26,000 pieces per day but had only achieved an average of 22,000 pieces per day after 15 years and constant engineering attempts at modifying the line to increase output. On arriving at the client site, we performed a Factory Physics production-flow graph analysis in the first couple of days to determine how well the line was performing versus how well it could have been performing. Figure 5-8 shows the result. The gray diamonds show the throughput performance curve for the line with moderate variability (exponential) in processing times. The white triangle marks where

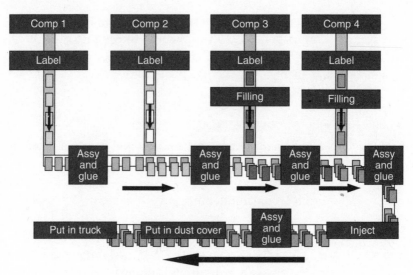

FIGURE 5-7. Single-piece-flow line

the line was performing based on data collected during the first day at the site. Only four pieces of data are required for this version of the performance-flow graph analysis, so it can be done very quickly:

- Current WIP
- Current throughput
- Bottleneck rate
- Raw process time

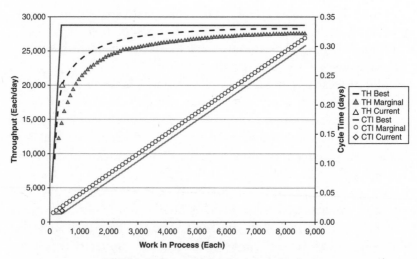

FIGURE 5-8. Flow graph for client production line

The graph shows that WIP in the line was about 300 to 400 pieces, and the throughput was 22,000 pieces per day. The fact that current throughput (white triangle) was above the marginal throughput line indicated that the production flow was operating with low variability in process times, a good thing and a useful pursuit of Lean efforts in general. The white diamond in the bottom left corner of the graph shows that the line had very low cycle times, nearly at raw process time and therefore close to the value-added time goal of the Lean effort. The CT/VAT ratio for the line was close to 1.

However, the company had traded short cycle times for a significantly lower throughput rate. The black dashed line shows an estimate of the line's throughput performance if a full-scale software model had been put together. The quick conclusion from an intuition well informed by Factory Physics science is that the line could achieve about 30 percent more throughput with more WIP in the line. This was somewhat of a surprise to the plant staff. They had been working on the line for 15 years, and a stranger walks in, does a quick analysis, and suggests that they can increase throughput by 30 percent. As always, there were tradeoffs. Increasing the WIP to about 3,000 pieces in the line would mean a huge increase in cycle time. But look at the cycle-time scale. The current cycle time for a unit was on the order of minutes—about 15 minutes. Increasing the WIP to 3,000 pieces would increase the average cycle time for a unit to about an hour and 15 minutes. However, the production output was shipped to a distribution center, and shipping was only done once a day.

In this case, there was no question that adding the extra WIP to the line was worth the extra average cycle time per piece. To their credit, the plant's staff members jumped on the opportunity. The solution was to decouple the component feeder lines from the main assembly lines and add WIP buffers between each feeder line and the main line. As a result, whenever a component line went down, the main line did not stop, and vice versa. After a few trials to validate the theory, the line was running at the increased output of 26,000 pieces per day. After 15 years of using a very large capacity buffer, the plant traded WIP for capacity and was much better off financially.

The company switched to a strategy that provided much better financial performance. Table 5-3 summarizes the choices the company had faced and their effects on the financial statements.

TABLE 5-3. Impact of Choices on Financial Statements

Business Choice	Impact on Financial Statements	Comment
Run "as is" failing to meet market demand	Revenue not maximized; capacity not achieving desire output	Management decided this was not an option
Increase capacity by adding another production line	Capacity costs on income statement and balance sheet—additional people and equipment	Capacity was expensive; costs were significant for this option
Increase WIP	Increased inventory on the balance sheet	Heresy to the zeal of the Lean culture but actually lower cost, and the added cycle time was not seen by the customer
Projects to increase the speed of the bottleneck	Cost of engineers working on project increases expenses on income statement	15 years into engineering projects to improve speed of the bottleneck

As detailed in the table, the company had multiple strategic choices that would ultimately have an impact on the financial statements. A better understanding of Factory Physics science at the outset of the line design project would have provided 30 percent more throughput for 15 years and greatly increased the financial performance of the plant. This company has now been applying Factory Physics science in operations for nearly a decade and uses the approach both for continuous improvement and as an integral part of any new capacity expansion evaluations.

Inventory Optimization

As discussed in Chapters 3 and 4, there is an efficient frontier for stocks that minimizes the amount of inventory needed for a desired fill rate. We present an example that demonstrates how using this science improved return on assets for one client. At this particular client, it was strategically important to have very high fill rates. This is common in industries such as medical devices or pharmaceuticals. The cost of being out of a product was significant. At a minimum, frustration experienced by healthcare providers when they are missing a critical instrument or pharmaceutical drug can lead to a choice to switch suppliers. In the worst case, absence of an instrument or pharmaceutical can lead to patient suffering or even death. Thus it is no surprise that companies in industries where a high fill rate is demanded often choose to keep high levels of inventory. In these industries, it is not uncommon to see inventory turns of only two or three and policies stated in such terms as "Keep six months of stock on hand."

Even in industries with high service requirements, return on assets can be improved by optimizing inventory because inventory shows up on the balance sheet as an asset. By using the efficient frontier for inventory optimization, one can ensure desired service and minimize inventory. Recall that:

$$\text{Return on assets} = \text{profit/assets}$$

If desired service (and revenue) does not change but inventory is reduced, return on assets increases. Figure 5-9 illustrates the story we described.

The company was meeting its goal for high service but had $1.2 million in inventory to support that service. The efficient frontier showed opportunities to maintain high service while reducing inventory by 75 percent (to $400,000). The company, wanting to be conservative in protecting service, chose a 50 percent reduction and wanted to be able to track progress. As will be shown in Chapter 7, Factory Physics science enables management to accurately predict

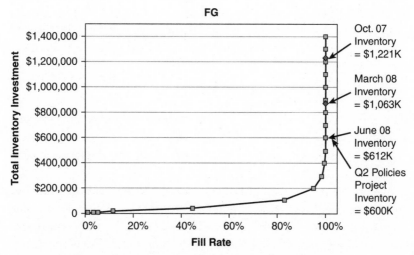

FIGURE 5-9. Inventory at a company with high service requirements

inventory levels as optimal policies are implemented and followed. The prediction at this company suggested that inventory would be reduced to $600,000 by June. Starting at $1.2 million inventory in October, the actual inventory number when June came was $612,00. Inventory reductions depend on demand, the "burn-off" rate, and the lead time of the parts in inventory.

A word of caution for aspiring factory physicists: when initially implementing optimal inventory policies, the inventory level may go up before it goes down. Alex Siegel of Emerson, during early Factory Physics inventory-optimization efforts, coined the perfectly descriptive term *inventory bloom* for the phenomenon. The reason for the inventory bloom is easy to understand. Switching to optimal policies that reduce inventory (keep in mind that *increasing* inventory also might be an optimal solution) means that the parts that have too much inventory on hand will not be ordered for a while. At the same time, parts that don't have enough inventory will need to be ordered and put in stock as soon as possible. The initial effect is for inventory to increase—the inventory bloom. When a manager briefs company leadership on anticipated inventory reductions from moving to policies that are on the efficient frontier, good management of expectations will include an analysis of the initial inventory bloom, its magnitude, and its expected duration. Likewise, the bloom can be managed by careful timing of inventory purchases, if needed.

Using Factory Physics science, leadership at the company described in this section (not Emerson) was able to project the impact on financial statements to both internal and external audiences with confidence. The company increased its return on assets and improved its inventory turns in a controlled, predicted manner.

Managing the Portfolio of Buffers

The concept of *managing the portfolio of buffers* helps managers and executives to drive profit and cash flow. Assemble-to-order environments demonstrate a great application of the Factory Physics approach with a focus on the portfolio of buffers.

We present the example of one company that, before learning the science of the Factory Physics approach, controlled each order of make-to-stock assemblies from the beginning of the component production process. The original DSP diagram for this company's process is shown in Figure 5-10. The stock point shown with dashed

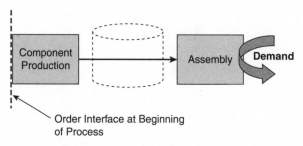

Order Interface at Beginning
of Process

FIGURE 5-10. Assembly production release starts at the beginning of the process

lines was the parts crib before assembly, but it was essentially a wait-for-match location. When all the parts needed before assemblies were in the crib, kits of parts were released to assembly. Actually, many times, if assembly was slow, incomplete kits were released to assembly to keep assembly people busy. As we mentioned earlier, there are few things worse than a manager seeing people standing around with nothing to work on. Managers will often give people work whether or not there is demand for the work. Some of this type of activity as a "work-ahead" is okay, but using work-ahead as a standard practice points to deeper problems.

The results were poor in an environment marked by high variability in demand. The company had to maintain a costly capacity buffer to deal with customer demand variability passed all the way through component production. The inventory at the crib stock was often waiting for other parts in the assembly and didn't turn very quickly. These capacity and inventory issues were compounded because component production was measured on earned hours, so the department had an incentive to run "extras." These extra components put additional demands on capacity and caused other components to wait in line to get started, and the extras ended up waiting in inventory. Finally, customer service suffered because the failure of production to sequence parts properly caused assembly to wait often for all the needed components to arrive in the crib to be assembled. Except as mentioned, assembly often did not wait and worked on whatever was available, which included cannibalizing parts from incomplete kits to get product out the door. This further exacerbated the problem of parts availability. These operational issues had a negative impact on financial statements because revenue was lower when orders didn't ship on time, and costs of capacity were higher because of the extra

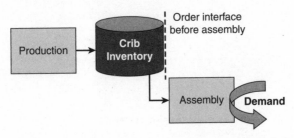

FIGURE 5-11. Assemble-to-order process with planned crib stock

labor and equipment needed to handle the variability in the operation. Finally, return on assets suffered because cash was tied up in excess equipment and inventory.

The company used the Factory Physics framework to strategically restructure its portfolio of buffers, as shown in Figure 5-11. In applying Factory Physics science, management designed an assemble-to-order production process with a planned crib inventory both to ensure that components were available for assembly and to level load-component production.

The company experienced the financial benefits typically observed when a company strategically manages its portfolio of buffers in an assemble-to-order environment. Strategic crib inventory for components enables the assemble-to-order process, which reduces the cycle time seen by the customer. The customer only sees a lead time for assembly, not the entire production lead time of all the components. Shorter lead times often result in increased revenue because of increased orders or increased pricing for quick delivery. This results in an increase in the revenue line on the income statement.

The strategic inventory-component buffer also decouples production of components from the variability in end-item demand so that the component production capacity buffer can be minimized to reduce cost. This results in decreased capacity costs on the income statement as a result of lower labor and equipment costs. This also results in lower amounts of cash tied up in equipment on the balance sheet. In addition, the extra capacity freed up by reducing variability in demand on production can delay the outlay of cash for additional capacity resources, be they extra equipment, extra people, or overtime.

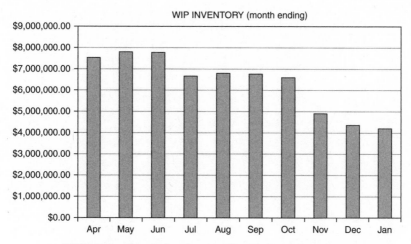

FIGURE 5-12. WIP reduction through optimal buffer portfolio design

A strategic inventory-component buffer often reduces inventory costs because pooled component inventory to serve many products is less expensive than finished-goods inventory for each end product. This also results in lower amounts of cash tied up in inventory on the balance sheet.

The net result on the financial statements is higher profit and better return on assets. For this client, the results in WIP reduction were excellent (Figure 5-12).

Original WIP inventory was about $10 million at the beginning of the project, so there was a massive reduction in WIP inventory. Interestingly, overall inventory reduction didn't go down by $6 million. Much of the inventory that was stuffed into production was ultimately maintained in the assembly crib to ensure that assembly could respond smoothly to demand. How did this affect delivery? See Figure 5-13.

There was an interesting turn of events in this particular project. Notice that on-time delivery dropped to 33 percent at one point after implementation. This understandably caused much consternation. Having a good Factory Physics model enabled quick resolution. It turned out that final inspection in assembly became a bottleneck. As directed by management, this part of the process was not considered in the initial design process. However, when the on-time delivery problem surfaced, the Factory Physics analysis was expanded and immediately pointed to inspection capacity as the culprit. That was

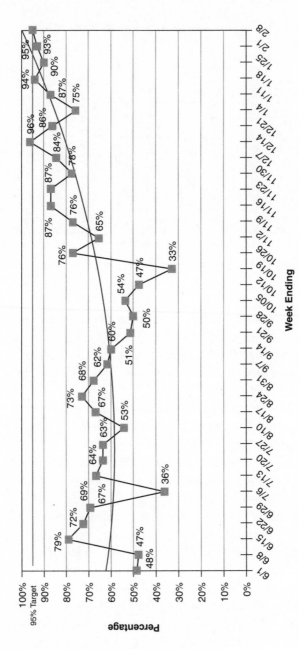

FIGURE 5-13. On-time delivery improvement thorough optimal buffer portfolio design

quickly remedied, and on-time delivery performance improved rapidly.

Financial Performance Driven by the Science of Operations

1. Maximize contribution margin at bottlenecks.
2. Check to make sure that Lean initiatives don't unintentionally starve bottlenecks.
3. Optimize inventory.
4. Manage the portfolio of buffers.

MARKETING AND OPERATIONS STRATEGIES DRIVE FINANCIAL RESULTS

The fact that marketing and operations strategies drive financial results may seem self-evident. Unfortunately, many companies fail to make quantitative links based on this obvious connection to select and manage initiatives that achieve desired financial results. Companies implement initiatives without scientifically quantifying the impact to the financial statements. In essence, they experiment with their operations, hoping that good results are achieved. This can be an expensive approach when the experiment requires capacity and inventory investments that fail to predictably produce financial results.

The Factory Physics framework provides a comprehensive, practical, and scientific approach to managing manufacturing and supply-chain operations that ties directly to the common financial statements. Companies can use the science of the framework to evaluate and select proposed strategies based on the quantitative impact to the financial statement of different levels of capacity, inventory, response time, and demand. Chapter 6 addresses how leaders can use the science as a practical planning hierarchy based on strategies, tactics, and controls to drive financial results. At a high level, the iterative planning process tied to financials is shown in Figure 5-14.

The Factory Physics approach works for executives and managers because it directly and predictably affects profit and cash flow. This

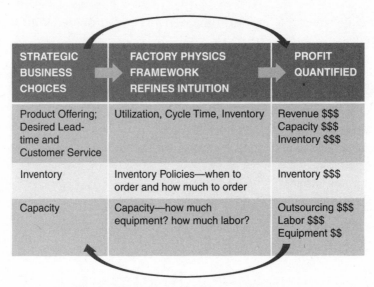

FIGURE 5-14. Planning with the Factory Physics approach

impact can be tracked directly to traditional financial statements. We very often see managers use accounting methods for allocating revenue to expenses as a way to understand and drive performance initiatives. As we hope we have demonstrated by now, *accounting models for cost allocation do not make good models for understanding and controlling the natural behavior of operations.* However, we do not propose that managers come up with different models for accounting. In other words, lay off criticism of the standard cost model of allocation of revenue to expenses. It works very well for accountant reporting purposes. A better approach is to work with the natural behavior of operations to optimally (for each company's unique competitive strategy) minimize costs while providing the best possible service to support increases in revenue. This provides best possible cash flow, which then can be allocated for reporting purposes as best suits reporting requirements.

CHAPTER 6

Operations Strategy and Planning

As promised, we now have a structure that can be used strategically and quantitatively to determine the most productive operations plan for a business.

OPERATIONS STRATEGY

That structure involves the following:

1. A value stream/supply chain is composed of demand and transformation.
2. Performance components of transformation are stock and production.
3. Buffers of inventory, capacity, and time are required to synchronize demand and transformation in the presence of variability.
4. Performance boundaries can be determined for stock and production given a mean and variance of replenishment time and demand.
5. Buffer portfolio design provides predictable performance of a stock, production, and service (response-time) configuration even in the presence of variability.
6. Stock, production, and service performance are tied directly to the financial statements.

Now we will consider how to incorporate these concepts into the operations planning process. An *operations plan* is composed of four primary elements:

1. Strategy
2. Tactics
3. Controls
4. Measures

The strength of this description of an operations plan is that it sets up managers to successfully lead their organizations through a fundamentally different approach from what is commonly practiced. The difference is that the Factory Physics approach plans and executes working with the natural behavior of demand and transformation while using dynamic controls to predictably manage variability in the environment.

Strategy

Strategies are often "blue sky" exercises that are created, put in a book, and then put on a shelf to sit. We want to avoid that. With the concepts introduced thus far, we define *operations strategy* as *the design, implementation, and control of the portfolio of demand, inventory, time, capacity, variability, and cost to best achieve a company's financial and marketing goals.* Notice that there is a design component. Business managers should lead the design of a buffer portfolio to achieve their company's business goals. Any technical design job should be guided by the science of the technology being designed. For operations plan design, the fundamental science is Factory Physics science.

Defining operations strategy as *design*, *implementation*, and *control* of demand, buffers, variability, and cost is a very powerful concept. It allows executives to think in terms of creative options to structure the tradeoffs we talked about earlier—more or less inventory, more or less capacity, and more or less response time—and to then explore the effects of increasing or decreasing variability while focused on increasing revenue and profit.

A good operations strategy process supports the overall business strategy process. A good operations strategy process provides scenario analysis for making overall business decisions. For instance, what capacity is needed for market-leading lead times? What ranges of demand can be handled with existing or planned capacity? What is the optimal level of inventory (raw materials and finished goods) required, and what are the possible tradeoffs among inventory, fill rate, and lead time? Finally, the operations strategy provides projections about operating cash flow, which is the life blood of any company.

Tactics

Tactics are policies or actions implemented to accomplish a task or objective. A *policy* is a statement of intent and is implemented as a procedure.[1] In the context of an operations plan, policies are such things as capacity resource levels (people and machines), target capacity utilization levels, days of supply, safety stock, lead times, work-in-process (WIP) levels, batch sizes, work-ahead period, inventory investment, work hours, and overtime levels. Policies, in the Factory Physics approach, are essentially design parameters. There are a myriad of operations strategies, and each yields a particular portfolio of inventory, time, capacity, and variability. Each portfolio, in turn, determines a set of policies. If the policies are put into action correctly and the environmental assumptions hold (e.g., range of demand, capacity performance, and range of supplier lead time), expected cash flow and customer service will be achieved.

Controls

Controls in an operations world are methods or systems used to implement tactics for achieving desired performance, for instance, a manufacturing requirements planning (MRP) system, upper and lower limits on inventory position, CONstant work in progress (CONWIP) control of WIP, or the use of a virtual queue with a capacity trigger. A sales and operations planning (S&OP) process is a control for overall business management performance. The most effective controls provide some sort of feedback mechanism to indicate the status of the performance being controlled.

Measures

For an operations plan, *measures* are quantities used to report performance characteristics of a process, for instance, on-time delivery, capacity utilization, or number of parts within policy compliance.

Execution

Execution is the use of tactics, controls, and measures in support of a strategy. What we often see is that companies set goals as part of the overall business strategy, and then it's controlled chaos as managers try to herd individual efforts to achieve the goals. Managers often execute with tactics and controls that work against the natural behavior of demand and transformation. Also, actions are taken with a view to achieve goals often in spite of the IT systems and other controls in place rather than using the existing controls effectively. The enterprise resources planning (ERP) system or IT system is typically used only as a transaction tracker and database (*financial ERP*). Another typical approach we see in execution involves starting performance-improvement efforts at execution. "Going to *gemba*" is a prominent Lean practice. It refers to walking around the production or planning area observing activity. The idea is to identify and implement opportunities for waste reduction by careful observation at the point of action. We think going to *gemba* is not the first place to start, although it is a highly valuable tactic. If the planning environment (demand and replenishment time ranges) is infeasible, focusing on waste reduction at the *gemba* is mostly futile. Good design makes planning easier; good planning makes execution easier. Starting on the plant floor or, for supply-chain efforts, in the supply base or distribution network in trying to improve or achieve desired performance is a ready, fire, aim approach. Managers should start with a design approach to strategy supported by options for tactics, controls, and measures that are grounded in Factory Physics science. Finally, a manager should not underestimate the cultural change effort involved in converting an organization from a reactive-execution approach to the Factory Physics approach.

INFORMATION TECHNOLOGY CONTROL AND CONTROL LIMITS

Note that the type of IT a manager uses to help execute a strategy is also an important decision. However, IT is an enabler of execution; it is not a determinant of which buffer and variability tradeoffs work best for a manager's business. Although IT is pretty much indispensable these days, many contemporary IT offerings provide ways to do more effectively what is already being done rather than providing business solutions for problems of operations science.

It is widely documented that many ERP implementations, after many billions of dollars of investment across industry, do not provide the benefits anticipated prior to implementation. The final result is often *financial ERP*. That is to say, the ERP system is used for tracking accounting transactions such as WIP to finished goods, purchase orders released, and the other chart-of-accounts transactions necessary for financial reporting. This is definitely a benefit for managers trying to standardize financial controls across an organization. However, when it comes to such things as scheduling the day's work on the production floor or service calls for the day for a service business, spreadsheets are almost always used. We have queried well over a thousand people over the years as part of our seminars and educational training on Factory Physics concepts. When asked if their ERP system provided complete planning and control capability, every person said that they use spreadsheets to manage scheduling and planning activities rather than relying solely on ERP systems.

Another indicator of the weak theory behind common ERP systems is the fact that none of the ERP systems we know of offer a control-limit approach to help leaders manage business performance. The control standard for ERP, APO, and APS systems is detailed scheduling. The real world is one of constant variability. A well-known quality tool for managing product performance is *statistical process control* (SPC). The SPC concept is that product characteristics, for example, outer diameter or acid concentration or formulation impurity, will vary between upper and lower control limits. As long as the characteristic is within the limits, nothing needs to be done because the performance is deemed to be acceptable a priori. In contrast, *all* ERP systems we have seen take the complexity and variability inherent in running businesses and attempt to attain required performance by putting all the detail in the system and varying the details (e.g., pull-in, push-out, release, cancel) as changes occur—detailed scheduling. Nowadays, many MRP systems replan on a daily basis, so the massive detail also changes daily. It is unreasonable to think that managers can optimally manage planning and scheduling with this approach.

An analysis of computational complexity (see Section 15.2.4 of *Factory Physics*, 3rd ed.) shows that it is impossible to compute an optimal schedule for a production process of anything more than

50 jobs and 10 process centers because of the number of possible schedule permutations that must be analyzed. Furthermore, ERP information overload overwhelms planners and managers, and as a result, many spreadsheets are created in the hope of building an approach that will enable management of performance without having to manage all the detail. Another effect of this detail overload is that planners often end up becoming expediters. Because the detail in the IT system and the constant change recommendations are overwhelming for managers and planners, the IT system is used primarily to track high-priority jobs, and those are the ones that get worked on. Meanwhile, the low-priority jobs eventually become high-priority jobs as a result of inattention, which leads to many high-priority jobs because scheduling and delivery to customers become unpredictable. The presence of many high-priority jobs leads to "hot lists" of jobs, "hot hot lists," and so on. Managers who have been in operations for any number of years have almost certainly seen the drill. Applying Factory Physics science to the natural behavior of buffers and variability provides a control-limit approach for optimally managing all the complexity of operations and supply-chain management. The result is a standard operating procedure (SOP) for a planning hierarchy that connects strategy directly to control and enables leaders to more easily manage all the complexity and variability than with the classic detail planning and scheduling approach. The SOP is realized as part of a company's sales and operations planning process.

FACTORY PHYSICS SALES AND OPERATIONS PLANNING

The sales and operations planning (S&OP) process is a series of tasks and meetings that operates continuously and repeats every month. The S&OP process is designed to ensure tight coordination of the manager's organization's efforts in achieving its financial and marketing goals. Typically, these goals are part of a business's annual operating plan.

The S&OP+ process developed in this chapter is based on the Factory Physics practical, scientific approach to understanding and managing the natural behavior of demand and transformation. For example, managing demand successfully requires understanding and planning for the variability of demand. This is fundamentally different from trying to exactly predict demand each month and then reacting when the exactly predicted demand doesn't materialize. We'll provide a brief description of the organizational process, participants, and practices of the standard S&OP process and then describe the Factory Physics S&OP+ version that provides the benefits of:

1. Determining the optimal combination of buffers to use for achieving best-possible profitability and cash flow
2. Quantifying performance boundaries of stock and production flows for predictive decision making and identification of improvement opportunities
3. Enabling use of the IT system as a control system to ensure that executive strategy can be tracked and monitored to get predictable results

S&OP Event Sequence and Participants

The S&OP sequence of events is illustrated in Figure 6-1. The S&OP structure and process are owned by the S&OP process owner. The S&OP process owner may be the director of materials or

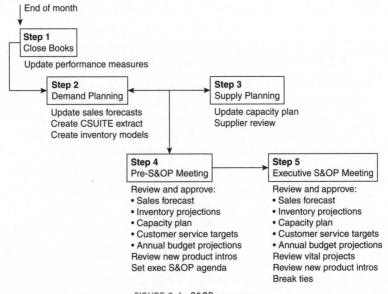

FIGURE 6-1. S&OP sequence

planning, but the S&OP process owner's role within the organization varies by organization. The S&OP process owner is responsible for scheduling S&OP activities throughout the month, coordinating the pre-S&OP and executive S&OP meetings, distributing the agenda and materials before each meeting, and distributing minutes after the executive S&OP meeting. The S&OP process champion has ultimate responsibility for the S&OP process, although the execution details are handled by the S&OP process owner. The S&OP process champion is usually in the role of senior vice president of operations or a similar role that is responsible for operations. There is another school of thought that says that the ultimate owner/champion of the process is the most senior officer of the company, that is, the president or CEO. We agree that the most senior manager *must* own the process as far as making sure that it happens every month, attending and actively leading executive S&OP meetings, and breaking ties for final decisions. This doesn't mean that the senior officer of the company has to monitor and manage the process month to month, though. It's really a judgment call, and the champion is different from company to company. One thing is for certain: if the senior officer does not actively support the process, it is much less effective than otherwise.

Step 1: Close Books. The S&OP process reloads each month with the closing of the financial books from the previous month so that the previous month's results can be used for the S&OP process's historical data. Sometimes this is not the start point because closing the books for the previous month lasts well into the current month. Again, when to start a new month's S&OP process is a judgment call based on each company's situation. Sometimes the process proceeds at the beginning of the month with whatever data are available, perhaps even with data from the month before last. The tradeoffs are obviously whatever disadvantages occur from working with old data. If significant changes in demand and transformation are a regular monthly occurrence, the disadvantages of using two-month-old data can seriously degrade S&OP effectiveness.

Step 2: Demand Planning. Product families must be defined for management of demand planning. For any parts that are going to be managed using the efficient-frontier approach for optimization, forecasts must be made at the *part* level. Many times managers will report forecast accuracy by product family. This is not very useful. Production or service capacity does not produce product families; it produces parts or jobs. Forecasting software packages are very helpful in managing this type of detail. Forecasts can be made at the product-family level and then blown down through the hierarchy to calculate the part-level forecast. As terrible as the forecast accuracy may be by part, only part-level forecasts are useful for planning inventory optimally. See Chapter 4's section "Forecast Error and Lead Time" for a review of the issues surrounding forecast accuracy and guidance on how to use forecast accuracy properly.

Forecast accuracy must be measured as mean square error (MSE) to correspond to the use of demand variance in managing demand variability. Part-level forecasts nowadays are relatively easy to make using forecasting software. However, the forecasting software packages that we have seen are very heavily concentrated on using the so-called most accurate algorithms for forecasting, for example, exponential smoothing or the Box-Jenkins method. The state of the art is for the software to pick which model fits the data best when making a forecast. Additionally, forecast software usually allows extensive customization of the forecast by a planner. As we have described before, more complexity in handling data is not necessarily better. The problem with the contemporary forecast-software approach is that it is in pursuit of an impossible goal—forecasting cannot predict the future. Getting tied up in complex discussions of which mathematical method best predicts the future is splitting hairs and can suck up tremendous amounts of time. Forecasts are always wrong and always change. Pick a method, track the error, and plan according to the variability encountered from demand variability or forecast error.

Unfortunately, we haven't seen any forecasting software that facilitates the Factory Physics approach very well. If a manager is going to forecast properly, the forecast for each part should be at the part's replenishment time horizon. The forecast packages we have seen require a manager to pick a forecast horizon for all parts and then forecast at that horizon. It may not be very reflective of the natural behavior of a part with a 3-month replenishment time to constantly be looking at demand over a 12-month horizon. This can be mitigated somewhat by grouping parts by replenishment time, but forecast software structure typically makes this a cumbersome process. In addition, the use of MSE at lead time and comparing that with the variance-to-mean ratio, as discussed in Chapter 4 under the heading "Forecast Error and Lead Time," is nonexistent in any packages we have seen. This would be an excellent function of forecast software because the computer handles high levels of detail very well. The lack of this type of functionality supports our conjecture that software vendors do not build software that provides good control over the natural behavior of demand. We do not claim to be forecasting-software experts, but we have worked with many companies on demand management. We have not seen a good application that handles forecasting at lead times and the use of forecast error in a way that facilitates optimal analysis and control of demand. That being said, forecasting software is very useful in providing a structured approach for an organization to improve demand planning. Just the act of looking at demand on all parts on a regular basis in an organized fashion can be very beneficial.

Step 3: Supply Planning. Manufacturing updates a capacity profile. Planning uses this capacity profile to determine demand loading in the MRP or ERP system. Planning *must* ensure that the requirements proposed for loading into the planning system are capacity feasible. It is not uncommon for planning groups to load a demand forecast without checking for capacity feasibility. This is a counterproductive practice. Even if capacity is managed in production to ensure a feasible schedule no matter the forecast, if overcapacity demand is loaded into the planning system, it will drive purchased material requirements that do not align with production. For instance, we have seen situations where demand requirements of 400 units per week were entered into the ERP system, but manufacturing had never produced more than 200 units per week. While this excess production was damped down by manufacturing during production scheduling, the purchasing organization was overwhelmed with purchase orders for double the amount of material the company could ever possibly use.

The purchasing organization will review supplier performance to determine whether there are any issues with suppliers meeting projected demand. Problem suppliers are set up with corrective actions. Additionally, in manufacturing, the previous month's performance will be reviewed and corrective actions taken. New-product introductions and upcoming promotions are reviewed to ensure that they are being addressed as needed to ensure success.

Step 4: Pre-S&OP Meeting. Using the work described in steps 2 and 3, the objectives of this meeting are to:

- Review progress against the annual operating plan, and direct business activities so that the plan is achieved, exceeded, or adjusted. Based on meeting conclusions, document options for updating the financial plan to present at the executive S&OP meeting.
- Resolve issues in demand and supply, including new-product introduction and sales promotions, so that a single set of recommendations can be made at the executive S&OP meeting.
- Identify areas where consensus cannot be reached, and determine dispute resolution options for presentation at the executive S&OP meeting.
- Set the agenda for the executive S&OP meeting.

In large corporations, there may be a series of pre-S&OP meetings in the various departments associated with demand and supply, respectively.

Step 5: Executive S&OP Meeting. The objectives of this meeting are to:

- Review progress against annual operating plan, and direct business activities so that the plan is achieved, exceeded, or adjusted. Based on meeting conclusions, decide on and document updates to operating plan.

- Review issues in supply and demand, and determine the appropriate courses of action where the current situation deviates from the plan.
- Review new-product introductions, sales promotions, and pricing to ensure successful implementations.
- Review product discontinuations and inventory burnoff.
- "Break the ties" on unresolved decisions from the pre-S&OP meeting.
- Review customer-service issues, and take appropriate action to implement corrective actions where needed.

Table 6-1 provides a list of typical tasks and responsibilities for the S&OP process. The inventory models mentioned provide efficient frontiers, predicted backorder days, inventory turns, service levels, and variability drivers for inventory stock points. The production models provide production flow graphs for production flows and additional capacity performance information such as utilization levels, cycle times, and throughput rates.

S&OP Meeting Practices

Both the pre-S&OP and executive S&OP meetings should incorporate good meeting practices. The point is to ensure that the meetings are run efficiently to produce the best decisions possible for the business. The need for efficient meetings would seem to be obvious, but companies' meeting practices run the gamut from concise and controlled to ineffective chat sessions. Poor meeting control is arguably one of the biggest forms of waste in companies today. If managers would drive to improve meeting practices as seriously as they drive to improve production or service processes, the benefits would be huge in most companies. The best meetings are not sterile, mechanical affairs. The best S&OP meetings are those where people are respectfully but passionately expressing differences of opinion (conjecture and refutation). The discussion should have some fire to it because participants are discussing issues that directly affect organizational performance—and their own individual performance and compensation.

If one takes a Factory Physics view of meetings, the capacity is obviously people—a manager's most valuable resource. The product of meetings varies but should be well defined going into the meeting

TABLE 6-1. Sample List of S&OP Tasks and Owners

Task	Owner
Ultimate Responsibility for S&OP	S&OP Champion: Senior VP of Operations
Run the S&OP Process	S&OP Owner: Director of Materials
Financial Results Reporting	Financial Analyst
Demand Forecast: Product Family 1	Sales Analyst
Demand Forecast: Product Family 2	Sales Analyst
Demand Forecast: Product Family 3	Sales Analyst
Inventory Model: Product Family 1 units	Master Scheduler
Inventory Model: Product Family 2 units	Master Scheduler
Inventory Model: Product Family 3	Master Scheduler
Inventory Model: Raw Material Components	Procurement Manager
New Products Introductions: Product Family 1	Product Management
New Products Introductions: Product Family 2	Product Management
Sales Promotions: Product Family 1	National Accounts
Sales Promotions: Product Family 2	VP Sales
Manufacturing Capacity Plan	Director of Manufacturing
Production Model	Manufacturing Engineer
Supplier Capacity and Performance	Procurement Manager
Loading Demand and Policies in ERP: Product Family 1	Master Scheduler
Loading Demand and Policies in ERP: Product Family 2	Master Scheduler
Loading Demand and Policies in ERP: Product Family 3	Master Scheduler
Loading Policies in ERP: Raw Material Components	Procurement Manager
Plan Approval	President

so that the meeting capacity is employed as efficiently as possible. The products of meetings include new ideas or an approved plan of action, as with the S&OP meetings. Action items *should be written down*, along with the following information:

1. What the expected action is
2. Who is responsible for completing the action
3. What the result of completing the action will be
4. When the action is due to be completed

If at all possible, avoid assigning an action to a team. There should be one name beside an action that a leader can go to for an update or questions about the action. With S&OP meetings, actions are published as part of the meeting minutes and reviewed at the beginning of each subsequent meeting. It is almost a complete waste of time to hold an S&OP meeting and not capture action items. There are few to no people who can keep all the actions or issues from an S&OP meeting in memory. From a Factory Physics view of meetings, managers who do not capture issues discussed and action items assigned are generating high amounts of rework and scrap from their most valuable capacity.

The following items should be standard practice for the S&OP meetings:

1. Agenda and any relevant material distributed a couple of days ahead of each meeting.
2. Roles defined and used for each meeting:
   a. **Leader.** Responsible for directing the flow of the meeting and ensuring that the agenda is followed and that the objectives of the meeting are met.
   b. **Recorder.** Responsible for taking notes during the meeting, capturing action items, and publishing minutes afterwards.
   c. **Timekeeper.** Responsible for making sure that the meeting stays on schedule. An effective practice for finding a timekeeper is to ask, "Who wants to get out of this meeting quickest?" The first respondent becomes the timekeeper.
   d. **Facilitator (optional).** Makes sure that the roles are being used appropriately and that good meeting practices are used in the meeting.

3. Code of conduct should be defined and observed for each meeting, for example:
    a. Stick to the agenda.
    b. Be on time.
    c. Only one conversation at a time.
    d. Use conjecture and refutation (testing ideas is a good idea).
    e. Use a "parking lot" for issues that drag on in discussion.
    f. No personal attacks.

The code of conduct does not need to be re-created for every meeting. Adapt a company policy for a meeting code of conduct, and standardize it.

S&OP+

We will describe the S&OP+ ("S&OP plus") process as a framework to get predictable results even in the face of variability. As you may have guessed, the "plus" in S&OP+ is application of Factory Physics science to the standard S&OP process. The changes to the standard S&OP process are not drastic, but they can make a major difference in how well managers meet business goals. Additionally, a manager does not have to run an S&OP+ process to apply the concepts of Factory Physics science. We hope that managers reading this book have already thought of applications of Factory Physics science for their daily jobs. That option was readily available after completing Chapter 3. The S&OP+ process is primarily for executive managers coordinating the activities of entire organizations or divisions of large corporations.

The advantage of S&OP+ proceeds from exploiting the natural behavior of demand and transformation in a structured, scientific framework. We have described that behavior at some length already, so the question becomes, "How is a manager to manage that natural behavior for a business to achieve desired results?" The answer is a combination of scientifically structured processes, controls, and measures. The base process is the S&OP+ process. In Chapter 7, we describe the measures and controls for stocks and production flows as required to translate strategy into day-to-day execution.

Financial measures are the ultimate measures of the success of the S&OP+ process. As stated in Chapter 5, financial goals and measures should be focused on profit and cash flow. In pursuit of these goals, the Factory Physics approach focuses on financial measures that are:

1. Tied to the natural behavior of operations
2. Recognized as generally accepted accounting principles (GAAP)
3. Useful in supporting the goal

Contrary to many efforts to come up with approaches such as Lean accounting, throughput accounting, and activity-based costing, we think that the current GAAP principles work fine in managing a business. Thus the primary financial measures of Factory Physics S&OP+ are:

- **Cash flow.** Movement of money into or out of a business.
- **Profit.** Revenue – expenses.
- **Return on assets.** Profit/assets.
- **Marginal contribution at the constraint.** Revenue – variable costs (at the constraint).

S&OP+ Process

There are a myriad of guides on standard S&OP procedures and many S&OP software offerings. The S&OP+ process steps that we describe here add Factory Physics science to the S&OP process to provide optimal and predictive control for executives managers. How the details of each step get worked out will vary from company to company. A huge benefit provided in the Factory Physics approach is the use of control limits for execution. This ensures that the goals that executives set as part of high-level strategic decisions are translated into day-to-day execution by the organization. Even better, managers can manage the status of execution *using the existing ERP system* to ensure that stated policies are being followed. In our experience, getting data for the control limits of inventory position or WIP levels or the capacity trigger is not difficult. We have done so at many clients using Excel spreadsheets. Unfortunately, we have not seen a software company that offers a good IT system based on Factory Physics science, controls, and measures, but as the saying goes, "Never say never." Fortunately, good science can be used no matter

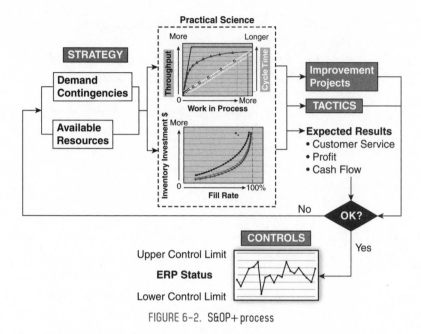

FIGURE 6-2. S&OP+ process

the IT platform. The Factory Physics S&OP+ process is illustrated in Figure 6-2 and is outlined below:

1. Demand and supply planning:
   a. Determine target limits for the mean and variance of demand rates for items. This can be accomplished by starting out at the product family level but must be translated to the stock-keeping unit (SKU) level, as discussed previously.
   b. By stock point and production flow, determine the performance boundaries and where to operate within those performance boundaries to accomplish the company's business goals. The process of configuring product families, stock points, and production flows is one of experimentation. Sometimes the configurations are obvious. For instance, a business has a consumer product line, an industrial product line, and spare parts. This pretty well sets the product-family definitions for the S&OP process. Once the stock points and production flows are specified for product families, the efficient frontier (for stocks) and the production flow graph

(for production) can be used to set expected performance targets. This step sets a company's configuration of buffers and variability. It is formulated in the pre-S&OP+ meeting and finalized in the executive S&OP+ meeting. These performance targets then translate into goals for financial performance and service (lead time and fill rate).

c. The distributions (mean and variance) of targeted demand and replenishment time characterize the environment for the plan. The wider the range accounted for in the plan, the more likely it is that actual performance will meet planned performance. However, Factory Physics science shows that planning for larger amounts of variability will require larger buffers (e.g., larger investments in labor and capacity or a willingness to have customers wait longer). If ranges of demand and replenishment time are too narrow, frequent replanning will be required, although the required financial investment may be smaller. Setting the required planning environment for a company is a key success factor for executive leaders. Finally, if the desired results cannot be predictably achieved in the existing environment, a gap analysis will lead to target areas for improvement projects. Even if desired results can be achieved, managers should push organizations and employees to constantly improve. As illustrated in Figure 6-2, an output of the scientific, quantitative nature of the S&OP+ process is identification of improvement projects. S&OP+ provides a company's continuous-improvement resources with a focused approach on where to improve and what to expect from improvements. See the Chapter 3 sections on the flow-performance graph and visual management of stock point performance for more detail on the connection between S&OP+ and identification of improvement opportunities. The discussion there shows how varying demand, or variability, or some other factor will change performance of production or stocks. These "what if" capabilities provide excellent direction for continuous-improvement efforts.

2. Generate policies to achieve planned performance: Given the initial design of a manager's planning environment and buffer configuration, there will be optimal policies to load

into the ERP system, for example, when to order, how much to order (lot sizes), WIP levels, and lead times, that will enable the business to achieve cash-flow and profit targets. As described in Chapters 3 and 4, these policies are created using mathematical models that accurately reflect the natural behavior of operations and supply-chain performance.

3. Implement appropriate feedback controls and monitor performance within control limits

   a. Install and maintain feedback controls that allow measurement of system status. Monitor system-status measures such as WIP levels, inventory position, and virtual queue length to make sure that they remain between upper and lower control limits. React *only* when the indicators are out of control—that is, above the upper control limit or below the lower control limit. Reacting to every change in system status is just reacting to noise. As basic control theory shows, feeding back noise into a system only increases the variability of the system. However, we see this reaction to noise on a regular basis. The semiconductor fabrication industry comes to mind. Semiconductor fabs are extremely expensive and complex environments. They are also data-rich environments, and the number of cassettes (WIP) can be tracked to the minute and machine. There are typically production meetings tracking WIP "bubbles" (accumulations of WIP) and reacting to reduce the bubbles. This activity primarily feeds noise into the system. WIP bubbles are a natural result of variability. Constantly tracking and working down random WIP bubbles are not going to make much, if any, difference in overall throughput, but it will increase production flow variability.

   b. Set up the IT system using optimal policies generated from selection of the buffer configuration. For stocks, this refers to when to order and how much to order— universally common options in ERP systems. The initial optimization of stocks often takes some time, even extending over a few planning periods. However, once the process is in place, subsequent planning periods typically generate updates to policies for only the relatively few parts that require changes from period to period. We have even had clients update hundreds of parts by hand for the first round because, after the initial update, the management effort was minimal, and there was no need to establish extensive IT support. ERP systems don't typically present production-flow policies such as WIP level or capacity triggers as parameters to be set. However, the information on amount of WIP and number of production work orders is readily available, so the controls can usually be established and monitored without much trouble.

c. Monitor IT system on a daily or weekly basis to make sure that planners and managers are using the system as the policies were designed to be used—system indicators are within control limits. Figure 6-3 shows an example of this from a client tracking inventory position on parts.

d. If system indicators are out of control limits, ask why. Often there are very good reasons for the system indicators to be out of control. For example, inventory position is too high because demand just dropped out of the system owing to a canceled order. In Figure 6-3,

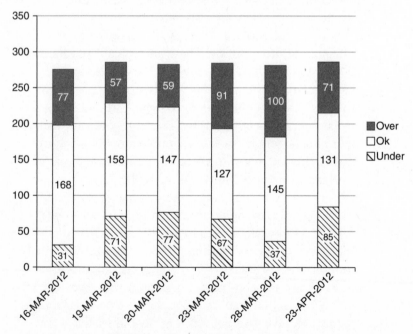

FIGURE 6-3. Number of parts by policy range

a manager would first want to understand why there are parts with inventory positions that are under the lower control limit. These pose immediate threats to planned customer-service levels. For the parts that are over the upper control limit, investigation is required to see whether these inventory positions can be adjusted before excess on-hand inventory results.

e. Provide corrective actions for the planners, buyers, and managers that are consistently maintaining their system indicators out of control. Reward those who consistently maintain their system indicators within control.

This control-limit approach provides a very powerful connection between a leader's strategy and day-to-day execution. If demand and transformation remain within the expected ranges of performance and system performance is maintained within control limits, then cost, cash-flow, and customer targets will be achieved as predicted. We look forward to the day when IT systems will facilitate a convenient control-limit approach for managers.

This is not to say that employees should park their brains at the door. On the contrary, employees should be monitoring the environment and the IT system to make sure that exceptions are managed. Employees and managers need to determine when a decision must be made to either replan for environmental changes outside the planned ranges, take temporary corrective actions such as expediting, or accept less than the desired results. In the end, the control-limit approach greatly reduces firefighting. One of our clients saw his expediting activity reduced by 90 percent by using the Factory Physics approach. Following the operations and performance design approach of S&OP+, employees are freed up to work on real performance enhancers, such as improved production performance or training for broader skills.

Give Michelangelo a sculptor's tools and a block of marble, and *David* emerges. Give the average operations executive a sculptor's tools and a block of marble, and the result is a smaller block of marble. Hopefully, by now you are starting to look at operations planning, design, and execution with the eye and intuition of a master designer and craftsman.

After all, though, the process of formulating and leading a powerful operations strategy is a design process. We once had an executive tell us, "Executives don't design supply chains." Our response was, "That is exactly the problem." Executives and managers often thrash around with buzzword initiatives or pay for publicity analysts or "thought leading " consultants because they have no good grasp of the science required to design their operations effectively. This, in turn, hobbles a manager's ability to lead. While there are many different areas of application for Factory Physics science, the S&OP+ process provides the ability to apply the science at a very high level and thereby more effectively set a path for a company, determine whether the path is being followed correctly, and make course corrections should the path need to be adjusted.

CHAPTER 7

Implementing Tactics, Controls, and Measures for Optimal Results

In operations, *execution* is the ultimate buzzword. Everyone talks about execution, but few companies consistently achieve planned results. The tactics, controls, and measures presented in this chapter are used to drive execution of chosen strategies to achieve planned goals. As discussed throughout this book, executives and managers must first develop an operations strategy that supports the business strategy. The next step is to deploy tactics and controls to execute the chosen strategy. Finally, appropriate measures must be monitored to ensure that execution is proceeding as planned. A scientific understanding of operations enables the implementation of control and measurement processes to achieve predictable business results. In addition, the ability to quantify the impact of operations tactics enables one to choose when and how to appropriately use Lean, Six Sigma, or Theory of Constraints (TOC) tools and enterprise resources planning (ERP) processes. As illustrated in Figure 7-1, Factory Physics science enables a leader to synchronize various operations initiatives to achieve business goals.

Armed with knowledge of Factory Physics science, leaders can choose the right tactics and controls for their businesses. In this chapter we discuss deployment of tactics, controls, and measures in the context of the Factory Physics framework. Along with all the concepts covered so far, Figure 7-2 provides a simple illustration for thinking about the concepts of Factory Physics science and what fits where.

When describing tactics, controls, and measures, we will use the fundamental model that this book has covered all

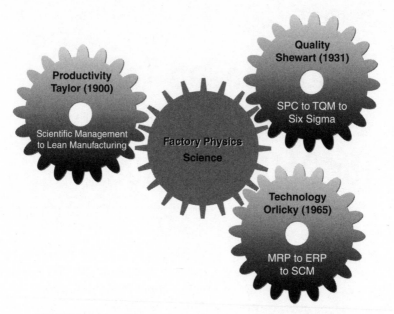

FIGURE 7-1. Factory Physics science integrates popular operations tactics

along—*demand-stock-production* (DSP). This simple framework is powerful because the concepts used to control the elements of DSP can be used to cover simple DSP configurations or highly complex configurations. We have applied it in simple environments, such as a one-product production line in a make-to-stock (MTS) environment. We have also applied the concepts successfully in semiconductor fabrication, one of the most complex manufacturing processes in the world. The purpose of this chapter on tactics, controls, and measures is to provide more detail on how Factory Physics science, using the concepts and underlying behavior of DSP, buffers, and variability, can be employed in practice. We begin our discussion of tactics and controls with demand.

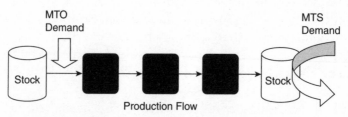

FIGURE 7-2: The basic elements of demand and transformation

DEMAND TACTICS AND CONTROLS_____

The scope of this book is primarily limited to operations, and in operations customer demand is a given. In this respect, there are no controls for customer demand. Topics such as pricing or demand "shaping" are outside the scope of this book. However, an operations manager's interpretation of customer demand and subsequent scheduling of operations are most definitely a control and should be considered carefully. Those considerations of how to schedule demand are influenced first by how demand is described.

Describing and Forecasting Demand

This topic has been covered in great detail in Chapter 4, but to reiterate, statistical mean and variance are used to describe demand. Even if considering make-to-order (MTO) production, where no stock is held, a demand mean and variance can be calculated for hours of demand expected. This is then used to plan capacity for MTO production. Attempting to describe demand deterministically (e.g., part A will have a demand of 4 this month, 14 next month, and 12 the following month) is also known as "predicting the future." It is a laborious and futile approach. Even if the part in question is a low-demand part of only one or two per year, the best tactic is to figure out how much inventory investment a company is willing to invest and for how long. For example, part Z has a demand of two per year. If part Z is relatively low cost, it makes sense to build the two parts at the first available capacity slot in the beginning of the year and then forget about them until it's time to replenish. Yes, the days-of-supply (DOS) value will be high, but it doesn't matter because the cost investment is low. We commonly see managers look at DOS values and get worked up because there are, for example, 540 days of supply in stock even though the inventory value is less than $200. Further investigation often reveals that the reason there are so many DOS is that the supplier has a minimum order quantity on the part.

Demand management software will forecast *mean* demand but often does not provide information about future variance of demand. As mentioned earlier, parts with a demand of fewer than about 10 per period do not provide a very good statistical basis for using the variance-to-mean ratio (VMR) to convert historical variance to future

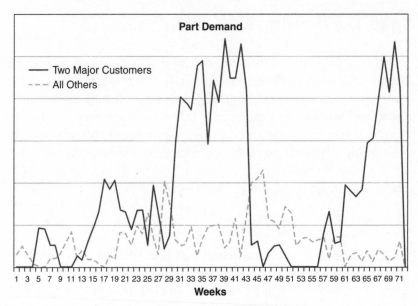

FIGURE 7-3. Lumpy demand

variance. However, mean square error (MSE) of the forecast can still be used for a variance estimate.

Lumpy Demand

One of the issues we run into almost invariably is how to handle lumpy demand. For instance, Figure 7-3 shows a demand profile for one finished goods assembly. As is immediately apparent from the graph, there are two customers that drive huge spikes in demand. How a manager handles this type of demand can make a major difference in the inventory or capacity investment required.

There are only a few choices:

1. Hold enough inventory and/or invest in enough capacity to handle this variability year round.
2. Remove the two large spikes in demand from the demand calculations when deciding how much inventory or capacity to maintain year round. At the same time, ensure that there is enough peak capacity to handle the spikes. Peak capacity considerations:
   a. Have access to enough peak capacity, such as overtime, temporary personnel, or outsourcing to handle all demand.

  b. Get advance notice from the customer or build ahead in anticipation of spike orders (a risk-management decision).

  This approach means that the manager is trading a time buffer for capacity and inventory buffers. If the manager does not get enough advance notice from the major customers or guess right as to when the spike orders are going to arrive, the orders will be late. However, the investment required will be much lower including the spikes when planning for year-round demand.

3. Put in some sort of demand clipping filter when deciding on how much demand to plan for. For example, any demand within a week that is more than three standard deviations above the average year-round demand is taken out of the demand calculations. The advantages to this are:

  a. Lower overall investment than for option 1.

  b. When the spikes do come, at least some of the demand will be covered by the planned demand.

  The disadvantage, of course, is that as in option 2, sufficient notice needs to be provided in advance of the spikes to ensure that material and capacity are available to meet the spike demand.

One problem we have seen with options 2 and 3 is that in an attempt to please the customer, the due dates of the spike demand will be flexible. In other words, sales will accept the spike demand order and put sales orders in the ERP system with enough advance notice to ensure timely delivery. However, as the due date gets near, the customer will be allowed to push out the order a month or months. Operations is now left with essentially wasted capacity (making parts in advance that weren't needed) and stacks of unneeded raw material.

This type of issue must be addressed in some kind of sales and operations planning (S&OP) forum. There are two diametrically opposed dynamics at work in a company if it trains its customers to expect this type of service. On the one hand, the company wants to give customers free rein to move orders around. On the other hand, the company wants to reduce inventory and expenses to increase profit. Allowing customers this type of leeway, even if choosing option 1, creates tremendous self-induced variability in demand. As Factory Physics science shows, tremendous increases in variability lead to tremendous increases in buffering requirements, which usually translates into both increased cost and poor service. These tradeoffs should be quantified and a value established so that, at least, if a company is going to allow customers to move orders around, it will know how much it is paying to be able to provide the service.

INVENTORY TACTICS

It is a strategic decision for managers to decide where they want to be on an efficient frontier for inventory. Once this decision is made, there are many tactical issues to be addressed to make sure that the manager's plan for fill rate and inventory investment is realized. We move now to a discussion of considerations that a manager will make to determine where to be on the efficient frontier and then to the tactics and controls used to ensure achievement of the desired results. As illustrated in Figure 7-4, we now add more detail to our control of the demand and transformation elements.

With consideration of stock control, additional information is needed for our DSP diagram. As described in the discussion of variance of replenishment-time demand in Chapter 3, controlling the behavior of stocks requires information about the mean and variance of demand (just discussed) and the mean and variance of replenishment time. The planned lead time shown in Figure 7-4 is what is used in ERP systems for replenishment time (see "Modeling Stocks, Replenishment Times" in Chapter 4 of this book for a review of replenishment times).

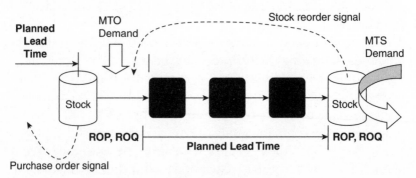

FIGURE 7-4. Demand and stock considerations

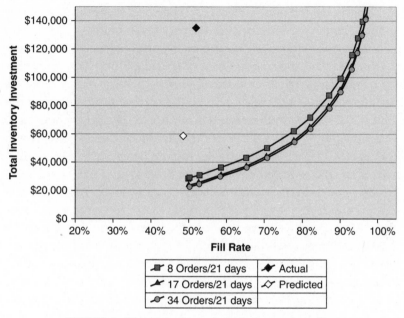

FIGURE 7-5. Efficient-frontier analysis: three capacity profiles

Inventory Strategy Considerations

Many advantages are gained from application of Factory Physics science to inventory analysis. Here we'll cover some of those strategic considerations for inventory. Part of the strategic decision of what point to pick on the efficient-frontier curve involves consideration of which tactics to use to set optimal inventory policy. For example, Figure 7-5 shows an efficient-frontier analysis for a sample set of 11 parts from a company that uses a make-to-stock approach for finished goods.

Capacity Considerations

The first thing to note is that all three curves in Figure 7-5 are nearly on top of each other. As the key at the bottom of the figure shows, the different curves represent different numbers of orders per period. In this case, the period is 21 days, or a work month. These parts are purchased raw materials, so the curves represent purchase-order capacity. Obviously, buying 11 parts does not use the full capacity of a purchasing department, but the example is illustrative nonetheless. The current number of orders per month is 17. This means that there will be 17 orders per month generated on average over all 11 parts. Stated another way, each part will be ordered 17/11 or about 1.5 times a month or 3 times every two months.

Simply observing the close proximity of the curves tells a manager that there is an opportunity to *reduce* utilization in the purchasing department. In other words, selecting a point on the 8 orders per period curve will yield optimal polices that produce about the same combination of fill rate and inventory as the current options at 17 orders per month. Of course, calculation of these tradeoffs will have to take into account any order requirements, such as minimum, maximum, and required increments of order size. If these parts were finished-goods items and the supplier was a company's own internal processes, the orders per month would correspond to number of setups in production per month. Such news would generally be quite welcome in production, where fewer setups are much preferred over more setups. However, in purchasing, the opportunity to reduce the number of purchase orders (POs) per month is not to be ignored. Fewer POs means fewer opportunities for error and less work for buyers.

Less work for buyers does not necessarily mean less cost. The stratagem of assigning some cost to POs is another cost avatar that does not represent reality. Purchasing capacity (i.e., buyers and managers) is not a variable cost by PO. If the purchasing department originates, for example, 10 fewer POs on average per month, this is most likely not going to result in one less buyer needed. Purchasing capacity comes in step-function increments corresponding to the people and systems required to place and manage POs. Freeing up extra capacity does not necessarily mean reducing capacity cost. The result of this type of capacity analysis is usually not that buyer jobs are eliminated but that buyers are freed up to work on things that will really make a difference, such as supplier performance improvement and strategic sourcing decisions.

Current Performance versus Predicted Performance

Figure 7-5 also shows two diamonds that relate to current performance. The black diamond is actual inventory dollars and fill rate as reported by the company. The white diamond is the predicted fill rate that the company should see if the polices in the company's ERP system are being followed. Actual fill rate is much lower than expected, and inventory is much more than needed. When first asked, the company estimated the fill rate on these parts to be 87 percent. After an initial efficient-frontier analysis and the disconnect between the company's estimated 87 percent fill rate and predicted fill rate of about 49 percent, the company went back and looked at detailed fill-rate performance data. The actual fill rate turned out to be 52 percent—a real eye-opener for the company.

Another big discovery was that the company had about twice as much inventory ($134,656) as needed to achieve the 49 percent fill rate ($58,378). Thus the initial analysis revealed a double whammy. Not only was the fill rate much lower than thought, but the on-hand inventory was double what was needed at the lower fill rate. Therefore a manager with a trained Factory Physics eye would conclude the following:

1. The policies in the ERP system are not very good. The amount of inventory required for the current policies is low, but the policies also result in a low fill rate.
2. Buyers are not following the policy in the system for whatever reason and are stocking enough inventory for a 96 percent fill rate but are getting nowhere near that fill rate.
3. This calls for some quick root-cause and corrective-action analysis. Even if optimal policies are selected and put into the system, based on current practice, they won't be followed very well. Moving to the efficient frontier requires determining optimal policies, entering optimal policies into the ERP system, *and* following those policies. An inventory-position compliance monitor would provide a good control to get inventory management practices heading in the right direction.

Strategic Options

Strategic options for managers working on optimal inventory policy include the following:

1. Move to the efficient-frontier curve.
2. Use a balance of inventory and time to drastically reduce inventory and achieve 100 percent customer service (reposition on the curve).
3. Change the environment: reduce replenishment time and demand variability (move the curve).

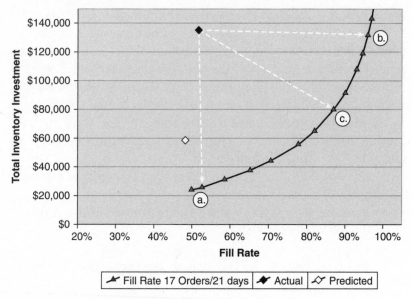

FIGURE 7-6. Options for moving to the efficient frontier

We will illustrate these options using the sample analysis of Figure 7-5.
The first decision is to pick which curve to use. This example will
use the current capacity profile curve of 17 orders per month.

1. **Move to the efficient-frontier curve.** Moving to the efficient-
   frontier curve will provide major benefit in this analysis.
   Figure 7-6 illustrates the range of options a manager has in
   determining where on the curve to be.
   Table 7-1 quantitatively summarizes the benefits of moving
   to the efficient frontier, but the tradeoff plot in Figure 7-6

TABLE 7-1. Strategic Options for the Efficient Frontier

	Strategy	Inventory Effect	Fill Rate Effect
a.	Reduce inventory $$, maintain current fill rate	$134,665 to ~$24,500 (82% reduction)	No change, still 52%
b.	Maintain inventory $$, improve fill rate	$134,665 to $129,814 (slight decrease)	Increase from 52% to 96%
c.	Reduce inventory $$, improve fill rate	$134,665 to $91,513 (32% reduction)	Increase from 52% to 90%

provides a quick visual for the manager trained in Factory Physics applications. As mentioned in Chapter 3, perfect performance is at 100 percent fill rate and $0 of inventory. From the current performance (black diamond), moving anywhere below and to the right is going to get this set of parts closer to perfect performance and provide improved performance. What would you do? This is a real-world decision, so there's no one correct answer. It depends on a manager's unique business considerations. However, most managers would probably rule out option a in the table because a 52 percent fill rate is pretty abysmal, that is, unless the manager is working with marketing and sales to exploit knowledge of backorder time, as described by the next option.

2. **Use a balance of inventory and time to drastically reduce inventory and achieve 100 percent customer service (reposition on the curve).** An infrequently considered strategic opportunity involves a deliberate increase in the time buffer to decrease the inventory buffer while still providing 100 percent customer service. This type of opportunity requires good tactical coordination among marketing, sales, and operations, but the rewards can be handsome. The key is in understanding and leveraging backorder time.

   For example, Figure 7-7 shows that moving from point b on the curve to a point with a 71 percent fill rate reduces the required inventory investment to $43,712—a 67 percent reduction. This means that inventory will not be available 29 percent of the time when a demand occurs—not a great delivery policy. However, a backorder-time calculation also shows that the average backorder time for the 71 percent fill-rate policy is approximately 12 days. Technically, the term is *backorder time when backordered*. We will use the term *backorder time* a little loosely to refer only to backorder time when backordered because managers are not concerned about the backorder time when they are not backordered (it's zero).

   A smart strategic option (provided that the market will tolerate it) is to set customer expectations to a 14-day lead time. If this is acceptable, the customer will see on-time delivery effectively 100 percent of the time. Actually, 71 percent of the time the customer will receive delivery in the

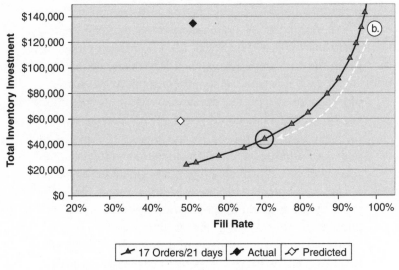

FIGURE 7-7. Trading an inventory buffer for a time buffer

time it takes to pick and ship the product. Only 29 percent of the time will the full 14-day lead time be needed.

While a 14-day lead time will not be tolerated in many businesses, the example still points to a very powerful buffer design option for managers to consider. A variant of this option is to determine how much inventory investment a company is willing to maintain, determine the resulting backorder time, and set market expectations for lead time to ensure 100 percent customer service all the time. Executing this option requires operations to know its capabilities and requires marketing and sales to know what the market will tolerate—another natural discussion for an S&OP+ process. This efficient-frontier analysis option provides a combination of very powerful strategic and tactical capabilities for a manager.

3. **Change the environment: reduce replenishment time and demand variability (move the curve).** The final, typically more resource-intensive option is to move the curve or change the environment. As we showed in Figure 3-30, there are environmental changes that will move the efficient frontier. Operations strategy design efforts should consider the options of changing policy, as discussed earlier, or changing the environment. Once a policy is optimized, at its simplest, implementation of policy changes involves

uploading the new policy into the information technology (IT) system and then managing the orders generated. Usually policy changes are not so simple because training is required for planners and managers to understand why the new policies are being used and how they were derived. Additionally, management needs to ensure that planners and managers are using the policy as it is designed to be used. This can be a cultural change effort requiring a fair amount of effort on the part of those involved. Even so, changing policy is typically much simpler than changing environment.

Changing the environment means doing such things as reducing demand variability or replenishment-time variability. These are not always straightforward tasks and generally involve extensive effort. Given the fact that environment changes are not easy, it makes sense to be able to gauge whether or not the effort is even worthwhile before investing resources in the effort to make a change.

In Figure 7-8, the solid black line shows the results of reducing demand variance to Poisson levels (mean = variance) and reducing replenishment-time standard deviation to zero. Granted, these are both very high hurdles

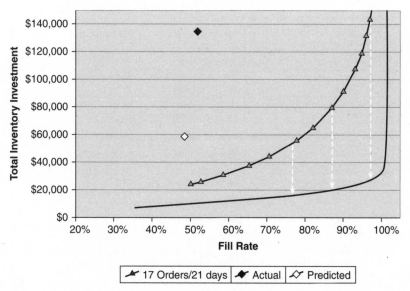

FIGURE 7-8. Effects of improving the environment

to actually achieve in managing the environment, but the results are great. Another way to use this analysis is to examine environmental effects based on what a manager thinks is possible, for example, reducing the variance of demand by 20 percent and reducing replenishment-time variance by 50 percent or including a reduction in average replenishment time. When these types of options are examined, the manager will be better prepared to determine where resources (typically, continuous-improvement efforts) should be focused and what the expected return should be from the improvement efforts.

As we wrote way back in Chapter 2, *strategy* is plan of action designed to achieve a specific end. Figure 7-9 provides summary tables for this example illustrating actions available to a manager when making plans for managing stocks.

Tactics for Inventory Management

Now that a strategy has been selected, it needs to be implemented. Because we defined tactics as actions or policies implemented to accomplish a task or objective, the tactics for stock management in

1. Implement optimal policy (move to the efficient frontier).

	Strategy	Inventory Effect	Fill Rate Effect
a.	Reduce inventory $$, maintain current fill rate	$134,665 to ~$24,500 (82% reduction)	No change, still 52%
b.	Maintain inventory $$, improve fill rate	$134,665 to $129,814 (slight decrease)	Increase from 52% to 96%
c.	Reduce inventory $$, improve fill rate	$134,665 to $91,513 (32% reduction)	Increase from 52% to 90%

2. Redesign buffer portfolio—trade inventory for time (reposition on the efficient frontier).

Strategy	Inventory Effect	Fill Rate Effect
Leverage use of backorder time (comparision is moving from 96% fill rate on curve to 71% fill rate)	$134,665 to ~$44,000 (67% reduction)	Decrease from 96% to 71% Customer service ~ 100%

3. Change the environment (move the efficient frontier).

Strategy	Inventory Effect	Fill Rate Effect
Reduce demand variability and reduce replenishment time variability	$134,665 to ~$30,000 (78% reduction)	Increase from 52% to 96%

FIGURE 7-9. Summary results from example

TABLE 7-2. Polices for Execution of Selected Strategy

	Avg. Demand in Period (units)	Order Timing			Order Quantity	
		Reorder Point (units)	Planned Lead Time (days)	Safety Stock (units)	Reorder Quantity (units)	Days of Supply
Part 01	5,738.15	4,839.00	15	740	1,794.00	7.00
Part 02	5,311.50	4,683.00	15	889	1,848.00	7.00
Part 03	4,923.73	14,416.00	50	2,693	2,184.00	9.00
Part 04	4,705.81	21,168.00	58	8,171	3,588.00	16.00
Part 05	4,549.08	18,861.00	60	5,864	3,213.00	15.00
Part 06	879.62	6,729.00	60	4,216	2,054.00	49.00
Part 07	571.35	1,795.00	60	163	561.00	21.00
Part 08	343.96	1,041.00	55	140	418.00	26.00
Part 09	303.69	868.00	60	0	245.00	17.00
Part 10	291.96	748.00	31	317	576.00	41.00
Part 11	107.96	170.00	33	0	105.00	20.00

this case are when to order and how much to order when ordering. Table 7-2 shows the optimal reorder points and reorder quantities that result from the choice to execute option c in Figure 7-6. This is a best-of-both-worlds strategy. From current performance, improve fill rate *and* reduce inventory.

Note that there are two configurations of order timing and order quantity as summarized in Table 7-3. As will be shown in the discussion of MRP for Inventory Control later in this chapter, this input can be stated in either configuration as required by the ERP system.

TABLE 7-3. Two Configurations of Order Timing and Order Quantity

	Order Timing (Quantity)	Order Quantity
Classics reorder point	Reorder Point	Reorder Quantity
Time-phased reorder point (MRP)	Lead Time Demand + Safety Stock	Days of Supply

TABLE 7-4. Current versus Optimal Policy Comparison

	Avg. Demand in Period (units)	Current Reorder Quantity (units)	Optimal Reorder Quantity (units)	ROQ Change (Opt.-Cur.)	Current Reorder Point (units)	Optimal Reorder Point (units)	ROP Change (Opt.-Cur.)
Part 01	5,738.15	5,390.00	1,794.00	–3,596.00	7,950.40	4,839.00	–3,111.40
Part 02	5,311.50	5,081.00	1,848.00	–3,233.00	6,730.32	4,683.00	–2,047.32
Part 03	4,923.73	1,905.00	2,184.00	279.00	3,682.89	14,416.00	10,733.11
Part 04	4,705.81	3,465.00	3,588.00	123.00	8,632.23	21,168.00	12,535.78
Part 05	4,549.08	4,117.00	3,213 00	–904.00	4,693.50	18,861.00	14,167.50
Part 06	879.62	258.00	2,054.00	1,796.00	257.16	6,729.00	6,471.84
Part 07	571.35	408.00	561.00	153.00	1,088.30	1,795.00	706.70
Part 08	343.96	229.00	418.00	189.00	171.05	1,041.00	869.96
Part 09	303.69	268.00	245.00	–23.00	504.73	868.00	363.28
Part 10	291.96	290.00	576.00	286.00	289.66	748.00	458.34
Part 11	107.96	95.00	105.00	10.00	70.70	170.00	99.31

For now, we will continue the discussion in terms of reorder points and reorder quantities.

The optimal reorder point (ROP) and reorder quantity (ROQ) policies from the efficient-frontier analysis are transferred to the ERP system to begin implementation of optimal inventory management. A comparison of optimal versus current ROPs and ROQs is shown in Table 7-4. Note that in optimizing ROPs and ROQs, some items increased and some items decreased. As discussed in Chapter 4 of this book, the policies for each item should be individualized based on the demand and replenishment profile of that item. This is further reinforcement of the idea that forecasting must be done at the part level. Parts are controlled individually at the part level. Forecasting and forecast accuracy at a product family level may make the forecast numbers look better, but they don't help much with managing performance.

This is a far different approach from what we often see. Many companies deploy a fixed-order-period tactic for setting inventory policies, such as "Keep three months of inventory on hand." This tactic ignores the realities of the demand and replenishment profiles of individual items. As a result, such inventory-control tactics are nearly always suboptimal.

Inventory Control

As stated in Chapter 4, if a company is executing planned tactics, the inventory position (i.e., on hand + on order − backorders) for individual items will always be between $r + 1$ and $r + Q$, where r is the reorder point and Q is the reorder quantity.

Inventory Compliance Monitor

Adherence to policy can be easily tracked with a *compliance monitor*. For daily or weekly execution, a compliance monitor is created and used to determine whether parts are being managed to the optimal tactics. This is a very powerful tool because it provides:

- Management with the ability to see whether the policies are being used as directed in support of chosen strategies.
- A management-by-exception capability for buyers and planners to ascertain day-to-day which parts require attention without having to review all parts every day.

An example of a compliance monitor is shown in Figure 7-10. Parts that are listed as "OK" on the far right "Order Status" column are compliant with policy limits—inventory position is greater than r and less than or equal to $r + Q$. No action is needed. Parts with "Order" in the "Order Status" column are below policy limits, less than or equal to r, and need to have orders placed. Parts with "Over" in the "Order Status" column have too much on hand and/or on order—inventory position is greater than $r + Q$. In this case, actions must be taken to reduce the excess inventory position. If demand will not reduce the inventory position through part consumption, the remaining choices are to cancel existing orders for parts or write excess inventory off as obsolete. What often occurs is that the excess inventory just sits around until it becomes obsolete. Even after it becomes obsolete, often the inventory is not written off because no one wants to take the hit to the income statement and balance sheet.

Part ID	Planner	Buyer	Supplier No.	On Hand	On Order	$ on Order	Current BO	Reorder Point	Reorder Quantity	ROP + ROQ	Current Inventory Position	Delta	Order Status
Part9	Dax	Yeldon	Tiger Co.	15	0	$ -	12	32	12	44	3	-29	Order
Part2	Dax	Fowler	Messier Precision	11	0	$ -	0	25	10	35	11	-14	Order
Part110	Leia	Norwood	Bytheway Parts	0	0	$ -	0	12	7	19	0	-12	Order
Part96	Leia	Norwood	Bytheway Parts	0	0	$ -	0	11	6	17	0	-11	Order
Part97	Leia	Norwood	Bytheway Parts	0	0	$ -	0	4	3	7	0	-4	Order
Part112	Leia	Norwood	Aggie Inc.	0	0	$ -	0	4	4	8	0	-4	Order
Part20	Leia	Norwood	Bytheway Parts	0	0	$ -	1	2	2	4	-1	-3	Order
Part53	Leia	Lacy	Gamecock Inc.	1	0	$ -	0	4	4	8	1	-3	Order
Part11	Dax	Yeldon	Bear Mfg.	6	0	$ -	0	2	4	6	6	InRange	OK
Part13	Dax	Yeldon	Gamecock Inc.	5	0	$ -	0	3	2	5	5	InRange	OK
Part10	Leia	Lacy	Bytheway Parts	12	0	$ -	2	7	5	12	10	InRange	OK
Part15	Leia	Lacy	Wildcat Applications	4	0	$ -	0	1	3	4	4	InRange	OK
Part26	Leia	Lacy	Gamecock Inc.	0	0	$ -	0	-1	1	0	0	InRange	OK
Part39	Leia	Lacy	Wildcat Applications	2	0	$ -	0	1	2	3	2	InRange	OK
Part40	Leia	Lacy	Gamecock Inc.	4	5	$9,258	2	4	3	7	7	InRange	OK
Part22	Dax	Fowler	Einstein Mfg.	0	0	$ -	0	-1	1	0	0	InRange	OK
Part23	Dax	Fowler	Einstein Mfg.	1	3	$7,069	0	2	2	4	4	InRange	OK
Part24	Dax	Fowler	Gamecock Inc.	0	0	$ -	0	-1	1	0	0	InRange	OK
Part25	Dax	Fowler	Gamecock Inc.	0	0	$ -	0	-1	1	0	0	InRange	OK
Part36	Dax	Yeldon	Bulldog Mfg.	10	0	$ -	0	2	2	4	10	6	Over
Part38	Leia	Lacy	Wildcat Applications	5	0	$ -	0	-1	1	0	5	5	Over
Part31	Dax	Yeldon	Bytheway Parts	6	1	$2,573	0	1	2	3	7	4	Over
Part48	Dax	Fowler	Bear Mfg.	4	0	$ -	0	-1	1	0	4	4	Over
Part82	Dax	Yeldon	Bytheway Parts	1	0	$ -	0	-1	1	0	1	1	Over
Part16	Leia	Lacy	Bytheway Parts	5	0	$ -	0	1	3	4	5	1	Over
Part69	Dax	Fowler	Bear Mfg.	4	0	$ -	0	1	2	3	4	1	Over

FIGURE 7-10. Inventory compliance monitor example

Policy compliance also can be shown graphically as in Figure 7-11. In this case, the process was brought in control by following the policies in the system. Easier said than done, implementing this approach with buyers and planners requires a significant amount of coaching. Like anyone, planners and buyers have their own habits and practices. Modifying their work practices to these types of standard procedures is an adjustment. There may be good reasons why part numbers are out of compliance. The point is not to let the few "war stories" serve as a reason to abandon the entire approach. Actually, many planners and buyers like the system once they get used to it. It provides an easy way for them to prioritize their efforts.

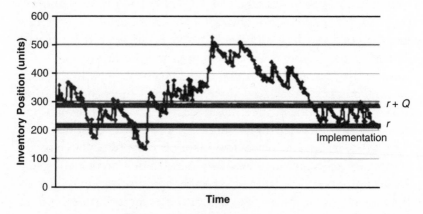

FIGURE 7-11. Inventory position progress

Cycle Counting and Inventory Accuracy

Another common control issue we see is inventory accuracy problems in a planning or control system. If managers aren't measuring inventory accuracy, they absolutely must start doing so. Inventory accuracy means the accuracy of both part location and part quantity at any one time. If inventory accuracy in a planning system isn't at least 95 percent, managers are whistling past the graveyard if they think that they are going to be able to achieve the desired results for use of their inventory buffers. Companies actually should have 99+ percent inventory accuracy, although that can be tough to do without bar coding or electronic tracking. It's actually surprising how often this measure is out of control. If managers can't control something as straightforward as storing and counting parts, there are likely to be more serious problems when it comes to trying to achieve high performance in planning, scheduling, and production.

The control for inventory accuracy is *cycle counting*. This involves a periodic—weekly is good—generation of a list of parts and a check of those parts for inventory accuracy. A cycle-count error is treated as a defect, and standard quality-control practices are used to analyze root causes and implement corrective actions. Today's MRP/ERP systems typically provide some sort of cycle-counting functionality to generate the cycle-count lists and track results. As with action items in S&OP meetings, assigning inventory accuracy to a team or department is often an exercise in frustration. If at all possible, a single person should be assigned a zone corresponding to physical location of parts and be held responsible for inventory accuracy in that zone. This approach works to prevent diffusion of focus on and control of inventory accuracy.

Inventory Dollars

Commonly, a manager's primary concern for measuring the performance of stocks is to determine average on-hand inventory dollars. This measure gets distorted when managers are measured against month-end or some period-ending inventory balance. Period-ending measures of inventory value are highly counterproductive. They provide another classic example of financial models that do not reflect the natural behavior of operations. This practice acts directly *against* the natural behavior of operations. Given standard demand for products, there may be seasonality, but there is rarely a natural monthly drop in demand. However, on many occasions, though, our analysis of daily inventory levels over a year showed some apparently magical drop in inventory at the end of each month. This type of behavior only serves to whipsaw production behavior, which increases variability, which, as you now know, drives a need for more buffers. On-hand inventory levels should be measured as a rolling-average value to truly understand how well a company is managing inventory.

A New Paradigm for Inventory Classifications

A manager can realize great benefit from analyzing and implementing inventory policies based on accurate science. Today's powerful computer technology enables this to be done with relative ease for thousands of parts at a time. Consider this approach in the context of assemble-to-order (ATO) environments. Fill rate on raw materials is critical for ATO operations. An aircraft engine could have on the order of 20,000 individual parts. Granted, the final assembly operations for an aircraft engine won't have nearly as many individual part numbers to track because many of the individual parts are in subassemblies. However, it's not unusual for an ATO company to have thousands of parts to manage.

ABC inventory classification tactics were used historically before computers as a way to manage the large volume of parts in complex assembly environments. An obvious flaw with ABC analysis is apparent in the fill-rate results that it provides *by design* in assembly environments. Assemblies can be problematic because to assemble a 10-part device, you need all 10 parts on hand to assemble. Thus, if each individual component had a 95 percent service level, the assembly at best would have a 60 percent service level:

$$\text{Prob \{All components arrive on time\}} = (0.95)^{10} = 0.5987$$

To achieve a 95 percent service level on the assembly, *all* components would need a service level of 99.5 percent:

$$P^{10} = 0.95$$
$$p = 0.95 1/10 = 0.9949$$

ABC classifications, by definition, ensure a different range of fill rates on components in an assembly, setting an operation up for less than desired performance. With the science of inventory optimization and the computing prowess that exists today, inventory policies can be individually tailored to ensure that components are available for assembly when it is time to assemble them.

Another obvious flaw in ABC classifications is the use of part cost in determining ABC classification category. As discussed in Chapters 3 and 4 regarding the components of variance of replenishment-time demand, there is no cost component. Adding cost to the formulation in trying to determine inventory policies is dysfunctional in that cost is not part of the description of the natural behavior of inventory systems. Cost certainly influences replenishment times and demand. However, once replenishment time and demand statistics are known, putting cost back into the analysis of inventory behavior just skews inventory management away from accuracy in providing parts when needed. For an example, let's look at two parts:

Part A's demand is 10,000 per period, and its cost is 10 cents.
Part B's demand is 1 per period, and its cost is $1,000.

The demand value for both parts is $1,000/period, and in an ABC approach, both parts would be in the same policy category. This approach is completely dysfunctional as it probably makes sense to hold six periods of Part A while a manager might only want to hold one period of Part B. While this is a contrived example, it illustrates the point of using a model that does not reflect the natural behavior of the system being modeled.

As we have emphasized throughout this book, managers are much better off working with the natural behavior of operations than against it. In this regard, a better classification for inventory management is shown in Figure 7-12. The random variable of interest in inventory control is replenishment-time demand, and the

Classification	High Volume	Low Volume
Short Lead Time	Low fill rate	Low fill rate
Long Lead Time	High fill rate	Low fill rate

FIGURE 7-12. A new paradigm for inventory classifications

components of replenishment-time demand are replenishment time and demand. Thus, managing parts in categories of replenishment time and demand allows managers to gain advantages in inventory management by exploiting the natural behavior of inventory systems. A case study and further discussion are provided in Chapter 9.

CAPACITY TACTICS

We now turn to a discussion of tactics, controls, and measures for capacity. With this we can complete the DSP diagram showing all the basic components and signals needed to manage performance predictively using Factory Physics science. The DSP diagram in Figure 7-13 shows all the basic components. The two new components are the CONWIP level, a form of work-in-process (WIP) control, and the virtual-queue quantity, a device for monitoring the status of a production flow and providing a capacity trigger to signal when recourse capacity options (i.e. overtime or outsourcing) are needed.

This configuration provides complete, predictive control of demand and transformation mechanics. As with most good conceptual models, it is pretty simple. The trick, as always, is in handling all the complexity of thousands of parts, tens or hundreds of processes, and demand that varies from part to part. To really do this well, a good software model is needed, but the conceptual model still provides strong insight and intuition for management control of operations performance. At the end of this chapter, we discuss

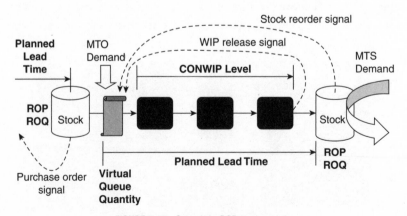

FIGURE 7-13. Complete DSP components

dynamic risk-based scheduling (DRS), a comprehensive planning and control approach that ties all these concepts together.

Utilization

Profitability and success in manufacturing hinge on choosing a target amount of utilization that achieves desired marketing and financial results from capacity investments. If there is too much open capacity cost, the business won't make money. If there is too little, the business won't be responsive enough or will be forced to carry a lot of inventory to be responsive. If it is just right, the business makes money while being responsive to market needs. How do you know what is just right?

Again, the strategic choice for operations depends on the business strategy. We discussed the *VUT* model of utilization at length in Chapters 3 and 4. Here we provide some simple examples of utilization implications for a business's performance goals. Figure 7-14 demonstrates likely utilization choices for different business strategies.

Recall the Toyota Production System (TPS) description from Chapter 1. For Toyota, implementing Lean as a tactic included a 30 percent capacity buffer. Toyota believed that this was the right operations decision to support its business strategy. Operations strategy for utilization should be considered in the context of overall

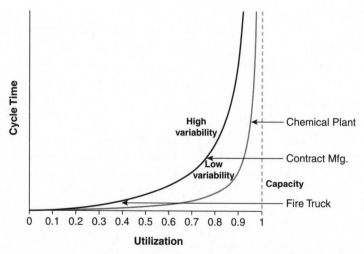

FIGURE 7-14. Strategic choices for capacity utilization

business strategy. Let's look at some of the examples displayed in Figure 7-14.

Example 1: Chemical Plant

A chemical plant has extremely high fixed costs of capacity, so the primary business driver is utilization of that capacity to get the desired return on assets. In terms of the portfolio of buffers, a capacity buffer is expensive and should be minimized. As this strategy is executed and the facility runs around the clock, an inventory buffer will be created in times of low demand, and a time buffer will result in times of high demand. In short, the strategy is to run the facility as much as possible to use expensive fixed assets.

Example 2: Contract Manufacturer

A contract manufacturer needs to be reasonably responsive. However, use of quoted lead times is common (rather than fulfilling demand from stock), so there will be some time buffer with which to trade off utilization (the capacity buffer). The contract manufacturer usually has a small inventory buffer because it doesn't know what unique product will be demanded by its customers. It may be able to have some raw-materials and even finished-goods inventory if it has repeat work for customers. With a business strategy aimed at capping time and inventory buffers, the contract manufacturer will need to have significant capacity buffer. Alternatively, the large contract manufacturers use large, flexible-labor capacity buffers as evidenced by the huge, sometimes controversial, labor recruiting efforts required to support introduction of the latest technology devices. The contract manufacturer wants to minimize the cost of the capacity buffer to achieve the highest possible profitability and return on assets. In short, the strategy is to maximize the economic return from maintaining a competitive time buffer (short lead times) to meet market demand and grow sales. In exchange for minimizing the time buffer, the companies in contract manufacturing will have to include in their capacity costs the inevitability of unutilized capacity. One way to do this is to determine planned throughput levels that provide the targeted level of utilization and measure both the throughput achieved and demand levels. Chapter 8 provides an example of how this is done at Arc Precision, a contract manufacturer of medical device components. Later in this chapter, the discussion "Virtual Queues and Due-Date Quoting" describes in detail the concepts of virtual queues and capacity triggers. One control mechanism for the contract manufacturer managing its capacity buffer closely is to set a capacity trigger. When the trigger is reached, the manufacturer responds proactively with a temporary increase in capacity, such as overtime or outsourcing. If demand causes the capacity trigger to trip on a regular basis, the manufacturer will have to add more permanent capacity with hiring or plant expansions.

Example 3: Fire Truck

A fire truck needs to respond quickly as the primary strategy. There is no ability to inventory the service of putting out a fire. In short, the strategy is to have open capacity so that fires can be put out quickly.

Perhaps capacity strategy sounds simple, but it is usually the first place to look for disconnects between stated strategy and operational reality. One Factory Physics Inc., client was a contract manufacturer of food ingredients with an entire marketing campaign built around best-in-class responsiveness. However, the dominant measures the company used in operations were capacity utilization and earned hours. The company didn't even measure lead time, service level, or average days late. Not surprisingly, utilization was very high (97+ percent), and customer service was poor—a direct disconnect from stated strategy. When confronted with the utilization-versus-cycle-time curve and an opportunity to cut lead times in half by dropping utilization targets to 92 percent for a small increase in the cost of capacity, the CEO stated, "I'm not going to do that until marketing can show me the benefit of responsiveness in terms of increased sales and/or higher pricing. Perhaps responsiveness isn't really our strategy."

In the process of diagnosing poor business results from perceived failed execution, we find it extremely helpful to check the alignment among strategies, policies/tactics, and controls for capacity. Often the issue is not execution of tactics or controls but instead the fact that managers overlook or are ignorant of the implications of utilization management. We sat in a meeting at a large company where a corporate vice president was told that his organization was regularly having to respond to schedules that were way over demonstrated capacity. He was somewhat taken aback, made a note, and said that he would check into it. Six months later, nothing had changed. This is a multibillion-dollar corporation. It has poor capacity management, though, and through brute force, it produces respectable results. Our read on it was that once poor capacity planning practices are in place, an organization just adapts to the chaotic world this creates. We like this corporate vice president; he is an excellent leader and is highly respected. For someone like him, the effort to change practices would require a massive investment of political capital to spearhead a cooperative effort across the organization outside his span of control with much uncertainty as to the conclusion. He is not nearly the first to let that type of issue slide off his desk. However, there is a gold mine of benefit waiting for leaders who can successfully steer a company from poor management of utilization to a science-based approach.

Cellular Manufacturing

We discuss cellular manufacturing here because it is a popular concept for production capacity configuration and, thereby, utilization management. Often cycle time is touted as a major benefit of cellular manufacturing. However, not so often do we hear of the capacity buffer created by many cellular manufacturing configurations. The common layout of a cell is a U shape, as shown in Figure 7-15. The idea is that workers in the cell can move back and forth across the line to run more than one machine at a time. Additionally, cellular manufacturing efforts are usually tied to some type of one-piece-flow material control.

Chapter 4 discussed the concept of move batches. The fact that move batches, in most cases, do not need to equal process batches provides a powerful tactic for reducing cycle time. Cellular manufacturing works well to reduce cycle time because it leverages the science behind batching effects—a key benefit of one-piece flow.

Many companies have adopted cellular manufacturing as part of Lean initiatives with good success. Cellular manufacturing works very well when demand and product routings result in highly utilized cells.

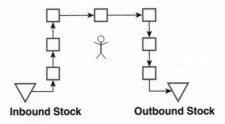

Inbound Stock   **Outbound Stock**

FIGURE 7-15. Cellular manufacturing layout

These highly utilized cells result in a portfolio of reasonably high capacity utilization to reduce cost and a relatively small time buffer. However, we have seen some companies where setting up most of the factory in cellular layouts resulted in lower utilization and higher cost because the demanded product mix didn't align with a complete cellular layout. In these cases, the companies did not always understand that the "move" batch was key to the short cycle times provided by cellular manufacturing. With this understanding, they could have just reduced move batches instead of setting up the physical cell. It would have required more material handling. Sometimes, the extra investment in material handling for reduced move batches is worth the benefit of reduced cost of capacity and reduced cycle time.

In addition, another practice we see is for an initial improvement push: the high-volume parts are all taken and put in a cellular flow. This might represent 10 or 20 percent of demand, but the success of the initial effort in reducing cycle time is given great press. Less talked about is what happens to the remaining 80 or 90 percent of the parts that are not in a cellular layout. Our point is not that cellular manufacturing is bad. As a matter of fact, if a company can buy inexpensive (maybe used) machines to support having a large capacity buffer, it may provide the best of both worlds—low cost with quick response. However, focusing on the benefits of a few showcase manufacturing cells without taking into account overall cost is not good management practice.

WIP Control and CONWIP

As stated in the Chapter 3 discussion of the production flow graph, WIP is a control parameter for determing the amount of throughput and cycle time a production flow will produce. WIP control is the secret behind the success of *kanban* systems and so-called pull systems in general. Optimal WIP levels provide maximum throughput with minimum cycle time for a given environment. As discussed in Chapter 3 and illustrated again in Figure 7-16, there are WIP control zones that serve as guidelines for WIP levels in a production flow. Too little WIP is as bad as too much WIP.

Lean manufacturing offers many mechanisms (e.g., single-piece flow, *kanbans*, etc.) to control WIP. Often companies succeed with Lean efforts without even knowing why they worked because the managers just imitated the mechanics of someone else's Lean

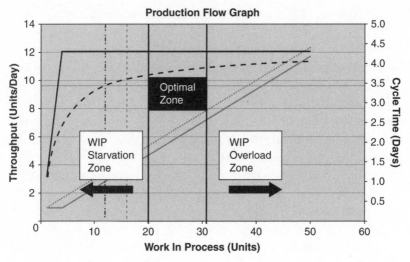

FIGURE 7-16.   WIP control zones*

*This figure originally appeared in Factory Physics, third edition.

implementation. We call this *initiative by imitation*. As we have discussed amply by now, predictive success in operations depends on
understanding the science of operations.

Controlling WIP levels is a key determinant of line performance,
but the question then becomes, "What is the best way to control
WIP?" Using a classic MRP approach, when it's time to start an
order because of the order's lead-time offset from its due date, start
the order; that is, release the WIP to the production flow. This is
commonly known as a *push approach* to controlling WIP. Classic
kanban originated with Toyota and controls WIP by only allowing
WIP to be released to one process center when that process center is
ready for a job. *Kanban* controls WIP at every process center. In the
CONWIP approach, the WIP control mechanism is more robust and
simpler to use than *kanban*.

Figure 7-17 illustrates the schematics involved in each of the three
WIP mechanisms described. MRP controls WIP by responding
directly to demand signals (ironically, a benefit most associated with
pull systems) but releases WIP without regard to the amount of
WIP in the production flow or to the utilization level of the production flow. *Kanban* is the ultimate in detailed WIP control because
it controls WIP in small line segments, often at a single station. As
discussed previously, this is very effective in controlling cycle time

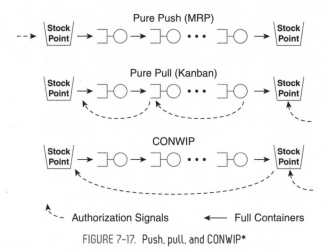

FIGURE 7-17. Push, pull, and CONWIP*

This figure originally appeared in Factory Physics, *third edition.*

but can result in starvation of the bottleneck and an accompanying reduction in throughput. Using a CONWIP mechanism, a manager would release WIP to the production flow only when the WIP level in the flow has fallen below a predetermined level—the CONWIP level of Figure 7-13. A benefit of CONWIP is that it allows the natural behavior of the production flow to move WIP to the constraint *dynamically*. In other words, if in a four-station line station 2 is the bottleneck, WIP will accumulate in front of station 2. Now suppose that product mix changes, and in the new product mix, station 4 is the bottleneck. Because CONWIP allows WIP to flow freely in the production flow, WIP will naturally accumulate in front of station 4. This dynamic response of CONWIP keeps WIP in front of the bottleneck and thereby ensures the best possible throughput from WIP control.

One tradeoff to this approach, though, is that there might not always be WIP at every station in a production flow. This has the potential to create the dreaded sight of workers standing around with no work—another example of a capacity buffer. However, as we have discussed time and again, a capacity buffer is not necessarily a bad thing. One option is to cross-train workers so that they can move from process center to process center following the WIP—a flexible capacity buffer.

As shown in Figure 7-18, strategically designing CONWIP loops enables predictive control of production throughput across complicated flow lines with shared resources. The completion of WIP at

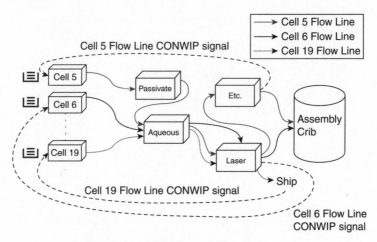

FIGURE 7-18. CONWIP in complex environments

strategically chosen points triggers a release of jobs at the beginning of the line to maximize throughput of the bottlenecks and provide predictive control of lead times. Choosing the strategic WIP level using the science of the Factory Physics framework ensures that the CONWIP loops are set up to work in the optimal WIP zone. The robustness and flexibility of CONWIP are the primary reasons that CONWIP is at the heart of many of the response-time tactics we demonstrate.

Virtual Queues and Due-Date Quoting

With predictive control of cycle times established using a WIP cap (the recommended CONWIP level) the next consideration is, "How long do I have to wait before my order enters the process?" This can be planned and measured using the concept of a virtual queue. A *virtual queue* is a list of orders (typically production work orders) waiting in sequence to enter the process. The benefits of having a virtual queue compared with a physical queue are numerous, including:

- Keeping orders in the virtual queue as opposed to releasing them to the process enables adherence to the WIP cap.
- The queue allows for *expedite slots* that enable critical orders to be moved to the front of the line, if necessary.
- One can quantify the length of the queue, so lead times can be quoted accurately and decisions can be made to add capacity to reduce these lead times, if necessary.

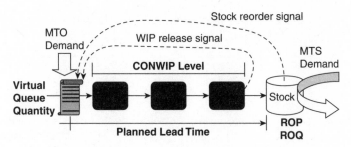

FIGURE 7-19. Virtual-queue mechanics

Figure 7-19 is a slightly decluttered DSP diagram showing the location and signals used with a virtual queue and a CONWIP line. The black lines on the virtual-queue "scroll" represent planned orders. As stock levels hit their ROPs, an ROQ is placed in the virtual queue (via the stock-reorder signal). When make-to-order (MTO) demand shows up, it goes in the virtual queue. Orders are released to the production flow as a CONWIP signal from the end of the production flow signals that the line WIP level is below the CONWIP level. The signal is authorization to release WIP into the production flow from the virtual queue (WIP release signal). The sharp-eyed reader might notice that in the virtual-queue scroll there is a blank spot right above the bottom order in the virtual queue. This is what is known as an *expedite slot* that can be used to great advantage in providing extra responsiveness to customers.

If a customer shows up and needs a job in a hurry and an expedite slot is available, it's no problem. The expedited job gets put in the expedite slot and released to the flow without having to get in line behind all the other orders. The client can be charged a premium for this type of service—sort of like the "flyby" passes one can purchase for a premium at amusement parks to avoid waiting in line. Or the expedite slot can be used to stock up on goodwill from customers. The expedite slots are planned for in the normal course of capacity planning. If no one shows up with a need for an expedited job when the slot is due for release, the adjustment is simple—release the next job in line.

With this framework in place, it is possible to give customers quoted due dates based on their needs and the status of the operation given current demand and actual throughput. To give a due date, one just needs to know where the customer order will be placed in the virtual queue and use Little's law to calculate how much time it will take to proceed through the system. We call this *due-date quoting*. The quoted due date is then:

$$l = \frac{m}{\mu} + \text{SLT}$$

where m represents the total number of items that need to go through the system to complete the order. It consists of the WIP in the system, the existing backlog (booked orders), and the size of the new job. Using Little's law with μ representing throughput enables one to determine how long it will take the new job to get through the virtual queue and the CONWIP line. Of course, variability always degrades performance, so it is wise to add safety lead time (SLT) to provide a time buffer for the variability. To help determine SLT, one can use a SWAG or a more detailed analytical approach based on statistics.

In using due-date quoting as a response-time tactic, the policies to be set are WIP levels and lead times. In general, quoted lead times will be based on a first-in, first-out (FIFO) policy. However, in special cases where you charge for an expedite or need to service a strategic customer, the lead time can be shortened by slotting those orders in the expedite slots in the virtual queue.

The remaining policy in this framework is the *capacity trigger*. When the quoted lead time starts to exceed the acceptable range because of an increase in the length of the virtual queue, this triggers a need for additional short-term capacity such as overtime or outsourcing. The length of the virtual queue could be due to increased demand or failure to execute on planned throughput levels or a combination of these issues. In either case, the timing of the signal also includes the time required to react and add capacity before the order is late.

If a manager controls WIP and achieves planned throughput, cycle time will be as planned. Therefore, in practice, control WIP, and measure throughput. To ensure policy adherence, count the WIP in the line. If WIP falls below the CONWIP level, orders can be released to the floor. Otherwise, work should not be released.

As shown in Figure 7-20, schedule-adherence charts are one of a number of ways to measure achievement of planned throughput.

Sequence Compliance

Sequence compliance means that process-center operators should run jobs as close to the planned sequence as possible. The sequence

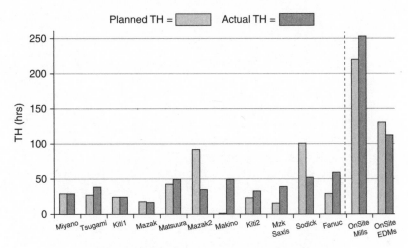

FIGURE 7-20. Example of a schedule-adherence chart

should be determined by first in the system, not earliest due date. Another way to think of this is that if two jobs show up at a process center at the same time, the one that gets worked on first is the one the was released from the virtual queue first. There is always a little art to this. For instance, depending on planned lead time, it may be okay to run two jobs together if their due dates are only three days apart. On the other hand, running jobs together that have due dates over 14 days apart probably should not be allowed.

In summary, the application of WIP control and job sequencing in a virtual queue provides a simple, robust mechanism to develop and implement strategies, tactics, and controls for minimal and predictive response time.

Rework and Scrap

A couple of causes of significant variability in a production flow are rework and scrap. Increasing variability requires increased buffering. In the cases of scrap and rework as the sources of variability, utilization also increases because capacity is needed to perform the rework or make additional parts to replace the scrap. The *VUT* equation dictates that an increase in variability and utilization will increase cycle time. Six Sigma tools for variability reduction are very powerful when focused on scrap and rework reduction and often pay big dividends.

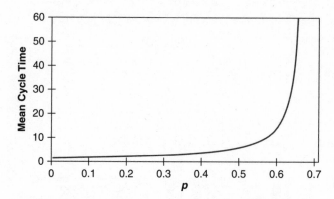

FIGURE 7-21. Cycle time and the probability of rework

First, let's look at an example of the effect of rework. Please refer to Section 12.5 of *Factory Physics*, third edition, for a detailed mathematical discussion of the effect of rework. In the scenario shown in Figure 7-21, the probability that a part is defective is *p*. Cycle time increases with rework in a nonlinear fashion.

In short, rework increases both the mean and the standard deviation of the cycle time of production. It increases the time buffer unless additional capacity, which adds cost, is installed. The rework also negatively affects the throughput obtained from installed capacity. Figure 7-22 shows the decrease in throughput *TH* as the probability of rework in the line increases.

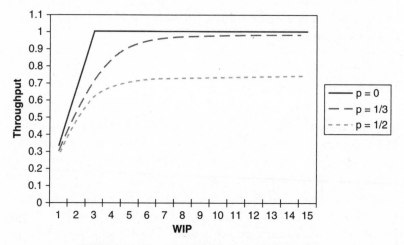

FIGURE 7-22. Throughput and the probability of rework

Factory Physics, third edition, page 420, nicely summarizes the impact of rework as follows:

1. **Throughput effects.** If the rework is high enough to cause a resource to become a bottleneck (or, even worse, the rework problem is on the bottleneck resource), it can substantially alter the capacity of the line.
2. **WIP effects.** Rework on a nonbottleneck resource, even one that has plenty of spare capacity, increases the variability in the line, thereby requiring higher WIP (and cycle time) to attain a given level of throughput.
3. **Lead-time effects.** By decreasing capacity and increasing variability, rework problems necessitate additional WIP in the line and hence lead to longer average cycle times. These problems also increase the variability of cycle times and hence lead to either longer quoted lead times or poorer service to the customer.

The reduction of rework can significantly increase revenue by increasing throughput while decreasing WIP and cycle time. Scrap can be modeled as rework that has to restart at the beginning of the line. It has the same negative impacts as rework, but the impacts are even more pronounced because scrap affects the entire line. Scrap increases the demand on a flow as extra demand because more parts must be started to recover from the scrap losses in an attempt to meet target throughput.

Use of increased starts to account for yield loss does not always provide the desired effect. In fact, it often results in the same customer service with more inventory—not the desired result. How does this happen? We often see companies inflate job size to compensate for yield loss. We will reference the example from Section 12.5 of *Factory Physics*, third edition, where the yield rate is 90 percent for 90 parts, so the release rate is 100 parts if one determines release rate by dividing the desired quantity by the yield rate. This is a fairly common approach. The issue with this approach arises from the fact that yield rate is not deterministic. The *Factory Physics* textbook considers a situation characterized by an "all-or-nothing" yield, where in 9 of 10 instances the yield is 100 percent, but in the other instance the yield is 0 percent. If this is the situation, then extra parts in the 9 of 10 instances become finished goods, driving up inventory. The complete yield loss in the tenth instance results in a shortage to the customer. Thus customer service did not improve, and inventory went up.

This is a fairly common result. We have visited over 100 machining operations in the past decade and have often seen small businesses with annual revenue of $5 million have up to $1 million in overrun inventory that had been built up over many years in business. Worst case, most of this inventory was obsolete, and even in the best case, it did not help to avoid future setups or job runs. We analyzed one shop that ran a number of the same parts every month for a customer. Despite putting a few extra parts into inventory each time, the shop never once received a small enough order where the extra inventory could be used to fill then order without having to set up and run. Thus, even in the case where the inventory was not obsolete, it did not help to avoid the cost of a setup. It did not level load capacity. Instead, it consumed capacity each time with extras that increased the cost, inventory, and cycle time of the orders waiting in line to get on the machining center as the extras finished. A better approach for repeat parts is to run to planned and optimized inventory levels so that there is enough inventory to serve customer needs and level load capacity. Of course, we don't just see this in machining operations. We often see it in component production for assemble-to-order operations at Fortune 500 companies. The repeat product nature of most of these businesses should make it even easier to run to plan and maintain optimized inventory levels. In any case, the larger point is the significant impact scrap and rework can have on cost, inventory, and customer service. The tactics of Six Sigma and other quality initiatives can pay large benefits when applied in places that generate the highest return. The Factory Physics framework and science help to identify where to apply these initiatives for the highest return.

RESPONSE-TIME STRATAGEMS

Time can be a competitive weapon for ensuring customer satisfaction and achieving best possible cash flow. We've covered all the elements of control of the DSP construct, and now we will discuss some of the strategies and tactics that can be used with the predictive control now established. In many industries, customers will accept a lead time. In these industries, one can minimize the cost of capacity and inventory buffers by maximizing the acceptable time buffer to customers. The marketing insight needed is to know what time buffer customers will accept before they give their order to the competition. In rare but highly profitable cases, a longer time buffer and often higher pricing are not only acceptable to the customer but also desired because these characteristics are expected for custom branding of high-end products. The bottom line, no matter what the industry, is to take advantage of a company's ability to use a time buffer. Companies that don't make strategic use of the time buffer leave money on the table because they carry capacity and inventory to support a response time not valued by their customers.

For example, consider a two-competitor industry where customers will often place their orders with the supplier that has the shortest lead time. If supplier A has lead times of four weeks but supplier B's Lean manufacturing enables delivery in two days, supplier B still probably should quote a three-week lead time. This enables supplier B to win the business on lead time while minimizing capacity/inventory cost and providing an opportunity to charge extra for "quick ship" when it uses its two-day delivery capability.

We have a client company that has successfully applied Factory Physics science to its research and development (R&D) process. The business is such that the company is running many new product-development projects each year. The company has established such predictable control over its R&D process that it doesn't start projects until the latest possible date. The cycle-time reduction has been huge, on the order of months. The manager we worked with told us that one time a customer called up in a panic insisting that the company immediately stop purchasing of tooling because the project in question had been delayed and could well be canceled. The industry practice was to invest capital at the beginning of the development process to ensure that it was available when needed. The manager was a bit conflicted but responded that the company would do everything it could to help the customer. The manager didn't want to say that because of the company's rapid R&D process, it hadn't even ordered any tooling for the project yet because that would have raised serious questions on the customer's part as to why the company was departing from standard industry practice.

We often see that managers who *choose not to decide have still made a choice* when they leave management of their response time to chance, and the default result is usually poor customer service as a result of late orders.

The strategic options for using a time buffer depend on customer needs and current status of operations. In contract manufacturing, lead times within an acceptable range are common. If most customers can accept a range of four- to six-week lead times, policies can be set to deliver four- to six-week lead times while maintaining the flexibility to deliver in shorter lead times for customers willing to pay an expedite fee or for strategic customers in key situations that will build long-term relationships.

If a company has some choice to use a time buffer because customers are willing to wait for a period of time prior to receipt of the product, that company can use the concept of *due-date quoting*, as discussed previously. Due-date quoting, as opposed to quoting standard lead times, suggests a due date for delivery based on the current status of the supply chain's ability to deliver the product. Here is an example of how one company strategically used this concept to improve delivery performance, restore credibility with its sales channel, and drive growth. The company made flowmeters. Delivery was critical because flowmeters fit into pipes in processing plants that produce chemicals, food, and oil. Typically, customers would time a flowmeter order so that it could be installed during a planned shutdown. If the flowmeter did not arrive on time, the customer would have to have an unplanned shutdown to install it when it did arrive. In short, without on-time delivery of the flowmeter, there will be a "hole in the pipe," and the process has to shut down. In the flowmeter business, customers with processes shut down and waiting for a flowmeter to arrive are usually soon looking for a flowmeter from the competitors. In our example, the flowmeter company had far and away the best technically performing flowmeter in the market, but late deliveries were killing the business because customers (and sales channels) did not want to risk having a "hole in their pipe."

The executives at the company came to realize that because they had the best flowmeter on the market, customers would wait for the flowmeter to come *as long as it came when promised.* The executives used Factory Physics science to establish predictive control of deliveries by quoting lead times.

The company began to track production cycle time so that it understood its average and variability. Having gained this knowledge, the company could choose a lead time that would ensure that the flowmeter arrived prior to a customer's planned shutdown. The company measured on-time delivery and average days late. It shared these measures weekly with the sales force to help restore credibility on delivery capability. As the company reduced production cycle time and its variability, it was able to reduce lead times so that it beat the competition on this dimension, too. As a result, the company grew its business because of its differentiated product and the restored confidence of its customers and sales force in the predictive control of deliveries. Ultimately, the company became the market-share leader.

PREDICTIVE CONTROL USING MRP/ERP SYSTEMS

Too often we find that companies do not understand how their ERP/MRP systems work. They don't have a practical, scientific approach for determining the inputs to the specific fields in the systems that drive messages about when to order and how much to order. On the production side, lot sizes might as well be engraved in stone because they are rarely reviewed and even less rarely changed. In some industries, such as pharmaceuticals, the *campaign size* is a parameter filed with the U.S. government and corresponds to the longest run between cleaning and/or sterilization of equipment. Thus, not only are pharmaceutical campaigns set in stone, but the term itself stimulates images of large quantities, as in, by comparison, saying, "Napoleon's Austrian campaign." However, the large campaign size in pharmaceuticals doesn't require large move batch sizes. Anyway, it is highly likely that a company's strategy is disconnected from the tactics in the ERP system. As a matter of fact, the idea that a company's ERP system could be used to control daily execution of executive strategy is probably foreign to most executives.

Common Practices

While the basic MRP planning paradigm that is at the heart of all production planning and control systems is pretty simple, many planners and buyers are regularly overwhelmed by a blizzard of messages created by the system managing massive amounts of detail in responding to changes in demand or supply. The following is an example that explains this phenomenon. Later we will talk about ways to master control of performance using an ERP system.

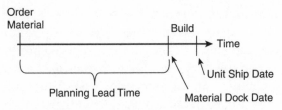

FIGURE 7-23. The ERP/MRP planning world

As shown in Figure 7-23, with a due date, lead time, and lot-size rules in the system, the ERP system calculates when the order needs to be placed and sends the buyer or planner a message to place the order. This is the same for purchased or manufactured parts.

The issues start with the inputs. For example, we often see systems where apparently suppliers only have lead times of 30, 60, or 90 days. This is a red flag that accurate lead times are not in the system, so the plan generated by the system is set up to fail. Further, supply chains and suppliers are variable in their performance. Often, even if average lead times are correct, replenishment-time variability has not been taken into account in setting up the inputs that drive the system. The impact of this variability is illustrated in Figure 7-24, which overlays the probability distributions of the planned events onto the timeline.

As things change because of either irrelevant lead times, replenishment-time variability, or changes in customer demand, the cycle of "pull-in," "push-out," and "cancel" messages begins, as shown in Figure 7-25.

Of course, buyers and planners often manage hundreds of parts, and the MRP system often runs every night to take into account any changes made during the day. Consequently, before long, this cycle

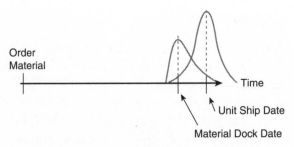

FIGURE 7-24. Real-world variability versus MRP planning

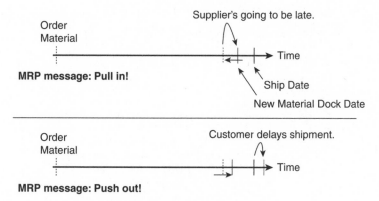

FIGURE 7-25. System change messages

crescendos into a "blizzard of messages" (Figure 7-26) that buyers often ignore because of volume, instability, and inaccuracy.

What is the buyer/planner to do in the face of this overwhelming detail? One buyer at a client told us, "That message doesn't mean I should place an order. It means that I should start thinking about placing an order." We contend that buyers and planners will do what their goals and measurements tell them to do. For example, imagine the scenario shown in Figure 7-27, where two different suppliers have the same average lead time of 10 days but different variability in their performance.

Clearly, for both suppliers, a static 10-day lead time in the system will result in late deliveries 50 percent of the time. The increased

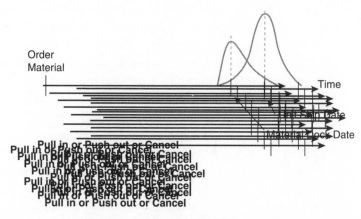

FIGURE 7-26. Blizzard of ERP/MRP messages

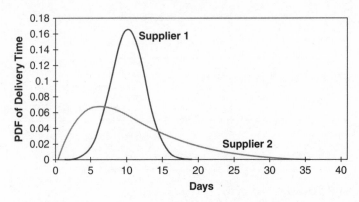

FIGURE 7-27. Two suppliers, same average lead time, but much different performance*

*This figure appeared previously in Factory Physics, third edition.

variability of supplier 2 will result in longer outages than for supplier 1. What do buyers and planners do when their intuition tells them that the 10-day lead time in the system isn't correct? Here is what we often see in companies:

- If the company has measures and incentives focused on inventory reduction, the buyers and planners "hope" that they maintain low inventory and high customer service by either reducing the lead time in the system to the "best case" or leaving the lead time in the system "as is" but then use system order messages as a reminder and order when they think they should order. This works for managing a few parts, but performance quickly degrades as larger numbers of parts are managed. Inventory and customer service drop.
- If the company has measures and incentives focused on customer service, the buyers and planners "preempt" the risk of the late scenario by putting longer lead times in the system or order larger amounts of inventory than recommended by the system. Inventory and customer service increase.
- As described in Chapter 2 of this book, the cycle of "whack-a-mole management" begins as the company alternates between these scenarios in an attempt to drive "continuous improvement." Often the management oscillation between the two approaches results in the worst of both worlds, more inventory and poorer customer service.

One company we observed demonstrated how measurements both drive behavior and create a ripple effect across the supply chain. This company had a version of the first scenario just mentioned because it measured "push-outs," with the idea that push-outs were positive events to reduce inventory. When an order came close to being due, the buyers would call the supplier with the request to "push out" the order unless it was going to be used quickly on arrival at the plant. Most suppliers, though irritated by an unplanned delay in revenue and cash flow because of the push-out, acquiesced in the name of the customer relationship. At face value, this might be seen as a win for the buyer, who reduced inventory by not taking product in the manner it had been ordered. However, the push-out often was accompanied by another "pull-in" for something needed for the buyer's production line. Consider a one-station example, where the supplier just spent last week making product A. Now the supplier is asked to push out product A and instead deliver product B, which it was not making last week. Of course, the supplier cannot deliver a product that it did not yet produce, so the customer's line shuts down. By implementing the push-out measurement system, the company we observed systemically induced variability into its supply chain, causing poor service and higher inventories as components "waited" for "match" parts to arrive to enable final assembly of finished products. For the supplier, this customer behavior results in "wasted" capacity and typically increases costs.

MRP for Inventory Control

Executives and managers can avoid this type of dysfunction by using their ERP/MRP systems as a key part of developing and executing inventory strategies, tactics, and controls using the Factory Physics framework. In Chapters 3 and 4 we established the science and math of inventory optimization. Typically, inventory policies are deployed in a company's ERP/MRP system. We provide an example of how the science of inventory optimization can integrate with ERP/MRP planning. MRP is the driver of materials planning in ERP, so we will refer to MRP in the rest of this discussion, although we mean any type of MRP/ERP system. The discussion is based on how MRP systems generally work. Any individual implementation of an MRP system will have unique features, but they can all be translated to the basic framework described here.

Frequently, MRP systems deploy policies in one of two *equivalent* formats:

- Classic (Q, r) reorder point policies: reorder quantity (ROQ), reorder point (ROP)
- Time-phased reorder policies (MRP): planned lead time, safety stock, and days of supply

Before getting into a description of how to use the two different formats, it's important to understand how the formats are equivalent. Any inventory policy must provide two different pieces of information:

- When to order
- How much to order

When to Order

In a classic (Q, r) approach, an order is placed when the ROP is reached. In a time-phased approach, an order is placed when the projected available balance at lead time reaches the safety-stock amount. Mathematically, to keep our units straight:

- *Planned lead time* (PLT) is in units of time, that is, days.
- *Average demand D* is measured as units per time, that is, pieces per day. Note that the units of time must be the same for both PLT and D.
- *Safety stock* (SS) is measured in units, for example, pieces.
- *Reorder point r* is measured in units, for example, pieces.

As stated in Chapter 4, the expression relating the time-phased quantity for "when to order" and the (Q, r) quantity for "when to order" is written as:

$$PLT \times D + SS = r$$

How Much to Order

In a classic (Q, r) approach, the amount ordered is Q. In the time-phased approach, the amount to order is *days of supply* (DOS). DOS is measured in time, but the result of using DOS in an MRP system is to specify a quantity. This typically causes confusion but will be explained. As stated in Chapter 4, the expression relating time-phased quantity for "how much to order" and the (Q, r) quantity for "how much to order" is written as:

$$\text{DOS} \times D = Q$$

As we have shown, time-phased policies are mathematically equivalent to the (Q, r) policies.

MRP Policy Mechanics

For (Q, r) policies in MRP systems, the MRP system should create a purchase order (PO) or production work order (PWO) for the amount Q (the ROQ) when the on-hand + on-order amount reaches r (the ROP). Technically, the ROP should be on hand + on order − backorders (the *inventory position*), but many MRP systems do not consider backorders in determining the inventory position. If you are using the ROP policy in your MRP system, this reorder point/quantity calculation should be confirmed.

   (Q, r) policies order Q units whenever r is reached. *This is independent of future demand.* The disadvantage here is that the ROQ will be ordered no matter what the future demand is. Thus, for instance, the ROP is 20 units, and the ROQ is 100 units. Using the ROP policy in the MRP system, 100 units will be ordered whenever the ROP of 20 is reached, even if future demand in the system is zero. Using time-phased ROPs avoids this potential pitfall.

   For time-phased policies in MRP systems, the MRP system will check the *available balance* (on hand + scheduled receipts − demand) at the part's planned lead time (PLT). If the projected available balance at planned lead time is less than or equal to safety stock, the MRP system will create a recommended replenishment order. The quantity of the recommended replenishment order is determined by the DOS value. When available balance at planned lead time hits the safety-stock level (the *trigger date*), the MRP system looks out past the trigger date for demand. This makes the time-phased approach more dynamic than using a classic (Q, r) policy—if there is no demand in the DOS period after the trigger date, the MRP system will not recommend a replenishment order. If there is demand in the DOS period after the trigger date, the MRP system sums up all the demand during the DOS period. The total demand during the DOS period plus any quantity needed to get the available balance back to the safety-stock level on the trigger date are added together and

Demand	Supply	Available	Day	Message
0	0	150	1	
17	0	133	2	Place order for 25
4	0	129	3	
9	0	120	4	
0	0	120	5	
0	0	120	6	
15	0	105	7	
7	25	123	8	
5	0	118	9	Place order for 40
2	DOS 0	116	10	
1	← Qty 0	115	11	
0	0	115	12	
5	0	110	13	
5	0	105	14	
7	40	138	15	
8	0	130	16	
12	DOS 0	118	17	
15	← Qty 0	103	18	
0	0	103	19	
3	0	100	20	

FIGURE 7-28. MRP mechanics

entered as a recommended PO or PWO, subject to order size minimum, maximum, and increment specifications. The recommended release date for the PO or PWO is the trigger date minus the PLT. A simple example is shown in Figure 7-28. Stock-keeping unit (SKU) ABC has a six-day PLT. The SS level is 100 pieces. The DOS for the part is five days, and beginning on-hand balance is 150 pieces. Minimum order quantity is 25. Given the demand shown (it could be actual demand or forecast demand), the available balance hits 98 on day 8. This triggers an order of 25 that needs to be released on day 2. The order quantity is calculated as follows:

- $100 - 98 = 2$ is the amount needed to get the available balance back to 100.
- DOS is 5, so the total demand in the five days following the trigger day (day 8) is $5 + 2 + 1 + 0 + 5 = 13$.
- Recommended order quantity $= 2 + 13 = 15$, but the minimum reorder quantity is 25, so an order for 25 pieces is scheduled.

We think that it is important that companies understand and use their ERP/MRP systems as control systems rather than merely as transaction tracking systems. We think that companies should pay great attention to the inputs to the specific fields in the MRP system that drive messages about when to order and how much to order. If managers, planners, and buyers understand this behavior and use MRP mechanics in conjunction with the inventory compliance monitor discussed earlier *and* maintain 95+ percent inventory accuracy in their system, predictable results are guaranteed. This integrates executive inventory strategy with the policies in the ERP/MRP system and enables predictable results.

MRP for Production Control

Production-control mechanics are greatly simplified with the Factory Physics approach to production. The massive simplification comes from avoiding detailed scheduling. In other words, a production planner using the Factory Physics approach will not be monitoring and trying to control the status of every job on every machine every day. The process for production control is pretty straightforward:

1. Make sure that schedule requirements are feasible. For example, ensure that planned capacity utilization is reasonable and consistent with the business strategy on capacity buffer design.
2. Periodic planning—determined by production lead times. There is no need to replan every day if lead times are three weeks. Given expected utilization levels and period demand, determine optimal lot sizes for production and CONWIP level.
3. On daily basis, monitor planned work orders (virtual queue):
   a. If the number of planned work orders exceeds the capacity trigger, schedule recourse capacity.
   b. If the CONWIP level for production flows is below target, release work orders to the line.
   c. Monitor daily production throughput to ensure it is within expected control limits.

DYNAMIC RISK-BASED SCHEDULING

In this chapter we have discussed tactics and controls for inventory, capacity, response time, and variability reduction. We now pull these together, along with a discussion of lot sizing and inventory/

order interface tactics, to introduce the concept of *dynamic risk-based scheduling* (DRS). Effective risk management is essentially a matter of effective buffer deployment. *Determining and deploying an optimal portfolio of buffers means determining how much risk to take on and, given that risk, determining how best to buffer it, whether it is extra inventory, extra time to satisfy the customer, or extra capacity to cover disruptions.*

As we have discussed throughout this book, there is no one answer to this problem. The optimal configuration of risk and buffers will be very different for different business situations. The aspirin operations of Bayer Corporation and the computer factory of Dell Corporation have very different configurations. Bayer is likely to have a considerable amount of inventory with little excess capacity (to keep costs down). Conversely, Dell's original business model included *no* finished-goods inventory and a significant amount of extra installed capacity. How else could Dell build custom computers in a timely way when there are peaks in demand at Christmas and at the beginning of the school year? As PCs became more and more of a commodity at the beginning of the twenty-first century, with an accompanying drop in price, Dell changed its buffer strategy to use external capacity (contract manufacturers) and inventory as buffers. Neither of these situations uses a significant *time buffer*, but the Moog Corporation, a supplier of custom servo valves to high-tech and aerospace customers, requires a time buffer to create a customized product. Choosing and deploying the portfolio of buffers require a confluence of strategy, execution, and risk management.

A key point in this book is that strategy must be integrated with tactics and controls. This can be difficult when day-to-day scheduling and actions are driven by deterministic planning systems. There are at least three problems that prevent the approach of using deterministic simulation and planning from being effective in managing supply-chain risk:

1. **The supply chain and plant have inherent randomness.**
   This does not allow for the complete specification of a time for each job with a given labor component at each process center. Such detailed schedules often quickly become out of date because of the intrinsic variability in the system. Moreover, detailed schedules do not manage risk, which involves random events that may or may not happen. In the

past, the disconnect between detailed schedules and the inherent randomness in all processes was addressed by using ever more detailed models requiring ever more computer power. This misses the point. Variability and risk are facts of life and are the result of not only process variation (something that one attempts to control) but also unforeseen events and variability in demand (things that cannot be controlled). At any rate, the result is the same regardless of the variability source. Detailed scheduling can only provide a very short-term solution, and in practice, the solution often becomes invalid between the time it is generated and the time that the schedule is distributed and reviewed as part of production planning meetings.

2. **The detailed scheduling system must be rerun often.** This is so because of the short-term nature of the solution. This becomes cumbersome and time-consuming. Moreover, without a method for determining whether a significant change has occurred, often the schedule is regenerated in response to random noise (e.g., a temporary lull in demand) that is then fed back into the system. Unfortunately, feeding back random noise results in an increase in the variability in the system being controlled. Because of these problems, many companies have turned off their advanced planning and scheduling systems after spending a great deal of money to install them. One of our own clients, a biopharmaceutical company, shut down its advanced planning and optimization module after trying to manage the massive data-collection efforts for "keeping it fed."

3. **It is impossible to find an optimal schedule.** The scheduling problems addressed are mathematically characterized as "NP-hard," which means that no algorithm exists that works in "polynomial" time to provide an optimal scheduling solution. The practical result is that for realistic problems faced in modern factories and in the supply chain, there has not been enough time since the beginning of the universe to find an optimal schedule regardless of the speed of the computer. Consequently, heuristics must be applied to generate a hopefully near-optimal schedule. *The effectiveness of these heuristics is typically unknown* for a broad range of applications.

The result is that a great deal of computer power is used to create a detailed schedule for a single instance that will never happen (i.e., the random "sample path" will never be what is predicted a priori), and the schedule becomes obsolete as soon as something unanticipated occurs. Effectively, detailed schedules never reflect current conditions.

The most advanced systems today offer two methods of planning for manufacturing supply chains: (1) what-if analysis using a deterministic simulation of the supply chain and (2) optimization of a set of penalties (again, using a deterministic simulation) associated with inventory, on-time delivery, setups, and wasted capacity.

In addition to the fundamental problems just listed, there are two practical problems with this approach: (1) what-if analysis is tedious and (2) optimizing a penalty function is not intuitive. The tediousness of what-if analysis comes from all the detail that must be considered. The planner can move jobs into the schedule and drill down on other items to view inventory projections. While this level of integration is impressive, it is not particularly useful, especially when there are hundreds of machines (not to mention labor) to consider, along with thousands of individual items, each with its own demand. Likewise, the use of penalties to determine an optimal schedule is not intuitive. What should the penalty be for carrying additional inventory? What is the cost of a late order? What are the savings generated by reducing the number of setups, particularly if there is no reduction in head count? What is the cost of having idle machines? Penalties such as these are, at best, an estimate and the source of endless internal wrangling between production and accounting.

Thus there is currently a huge gap between what is needed and what is offered. The Factory Physics framework addresses that gap with *a fundamental change in the way manufacturing and service supply chains are managed.* So how are the tactics and controls of the Factory Physics approach used to create a system that can (1) accommodate risk and (2) provide a method for effective planning and control. The key to creating such a system is to replace the model of a schedule as points in time when particular jobs finish at particular stations with a model of a schedule as the *flow* of jobs through the system. With a predictable flow, the schedule completion time is known from the offset to the start time. It's interesting to note that the basic MRP paradigm supports this approach with lead-time offsets and then essentially destroys the usefulness of the flow concept by attempting to manage lead-time offsets at every step in a routing for every product with changes occurring every day. If we can achieve manageable flow, then planning and controlling production become relatively easy. Then, instead of attempting to schedule hundreds of individual jobs on a Gantt chart or trying to specify artificial penalties in an advanced planning and optimization (APO) system, a planner uses a few basic measures and controls to manage the *flow*.

We can take this simple framework and create a new and more effective way to manage manufacturing and service supply chains. The key to this is to reduce the number of values that must be monitored as well as control variables in the problem. This means that *instead of providing a detailed schedule indicating where each job is scheduled in a process center during a given time slice, we determine a set of control variables that will dynamically and automatically determine the schedule as the system evolves.* We call this approach *dynamic risk-based planning and scheduling* (DRS). Under DRS, only projected inventory and projected service levels are monitored, and then a few key parameters are controlled—reorder points and/or lead times, production quantities (lot sizes), installed capacity, makeup capacity, WIP level, and the virtual queue.

A brief reflection on the design of the system will show that if the planning parameters just listed have been optimized, the entire system attains projected service and inventory levels as long as environmental assumptions stay within accepted ranges. Lot sizes have been established that minimize WIP and finished goods subject to the available capacity. Lead times (and/or reorder points) are set by considering the tradeoffs between service and inventory levels. Thus jobs can move through the flow in a *first-in-system, first-out* (FISFO) order without the need for a detailed schedule. Safety stocks are set considering the time in the virtual queue plus the time through the flow and with regard to the error in the forecast. Thus, once these parameters are set (reviewed periodically, perhaps once per month), the planner need only monitor the projected inventory and service levels. The only time action is required is when these levels exceed set trigger points. Figure 7-29 shows the integrated DRS system.

These trigger points take two forms: (1) indicating insufficient capacity and (2) indicating more capacity than is needed. If the virtual queue grows beyond what is planned for in the lead times, there is insufficient capacity, so recourse capacity (e.g., overtime, makeup shift, etc.) is applied. If the virtual queue becomes too low, one can either reduce capacity or pull in some jobs early. The result is not

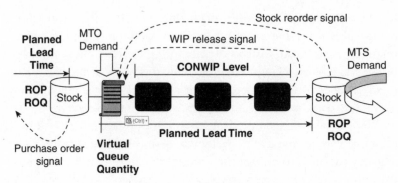

FIGURE 7-29. A DRS control system

only a much simpler supply chain management approach but one that can automatically respond to random changes in demand and supply *without the need to reschedule.* This ability to automatically adjust is a tremendous improvement and makes DRS more effective than the more complex APO system. Table 7-5 compares dynamic risk-based planning and scheduling with APO in this regard.

Once these parameters [reorder points and/or lead times, production quantities (lot sizes), installed capacity, makeup capacity, WIP level, and the virtual queue] are known, the system is ready to be implemented. Fortunately, this can be done relatively easily using the existing MRP system and CONWIP.

We have seen that neither traditional systems such as MRP nor modern systems such as APO adequately address risk issues. It is also apparent that more IT is not the solution to the problem without

TABLE 7-5. ERP Advanced Planning versus Dynamic Risk-Based Scheduling

Situation	ERP APO	DRS
Capacity greater than expected	Cannot work ahead of generated schedule	Can work ahead up to defined earliest release dates
Capacity less than expected	Schedule becomes increasingly infeasible, orders become late unless high safety lead time	"Shortfall trigger" indicates need for additional capacity; do not need high safety lead time
Demand greater than expected	Shortages unless very high safety stock	Shortfall trigger indicates need for additional capacity; no shortages, minimal safety stock
Demand less than expected	Unneeded orders released; inventory rises	No unneeded orders released; inventory stays in planned range

completely rethinking the problem. What is needed is a system that is *dynamic* to avoid rescheduling, that is *risk based* to accommodate risk factors and randomness, and that links *planning* and *execution*. It is also important to note that a *flexible buffer* is less costly than a permanent one. This is why *postponement*, the ability to delay committing a common component into the final product until the last possible moment, is effective in reducing both the inventory and time buffers. Likewise, having a flexible capacity buffer such as the makeup shift used by Toyota or temporary workers who can be called on when demand is higher than normal is less costly than employing all the workers all the time. Furthermore, quoting due dates with variable lead times is more effective than stating a constant lead time.

The steps to implement DRS are:

1. Use appropriate risk-based models to optimize MRP planning parameters: lot size, planned lead times, and safety-stock levels.
2. Use the MRP system to perform netting and bill-of-material (BOM) explosions and to generate a job release pool.
3. Quote lead times using the position in the virtual queue and cycle time in the CONWIP line.
4. Use a CONWIP system to pull from the job release pool into shop.
5. Use FISFO for prioritization in the line.
6. Monitor the virtual queue to indicate when extra capacity is needed.

Dynamic Risk–Based Scheduling in Assemble-to-Order Environments

We present an example that pulls from several assemble-to-order (ATO) clients to demonstrate some of the specific activities of DRS. Clients have improved service while reducing cost and inventory in ATO environments by deploying three of the cornerstones of the Factory Physics framework:

1. Drive profit by strategically managing the portfolio of operations buffers (i.e., response time, inventory, capacity).
2. Use Little's law (cycle time = WIP/throughput or CT = WIP/TH) to deliver best-possible (i.e., as short as possible) predictable cycle times. An understanding of Little's law

enables companies to achieve short cycle times by reducing WIP while enabling maximum throughput.
3. Optimize component inventory, enabling assemble to order: variance of replenishment-time demand drives inventory requirements:

$$\sigma^2 = \ell\sigma_d^2 + d^2\sigma_\ell^2$$

As discussed many times in this book, given that there is variability when trying to synchronize supply and demand, companies *will* have a portfolio of buffers, and there are only three buffers—inventory, capacity, and response time. A supply chain can be responsive to its customers by having a stock of *inventory* or having excess *capacity* to handle variations in demand. Alternatively, it can offer lower costs by having the customer wait a longer *time*. ATO environments demonstrate a great application of the Factory Physics approach of dynamic risk-based scheduling with a focus on the portfolio of buffers because:

1. A strategic inventory component buffer enables assemble to order, which reduces the cycle time seen by the customer. The customer only sees a lead time for assembly, not the entire production of all the components, as would be the case if the process was make to order instead of assemble to order.
2. A strategic inventory component buffer also decouples production of components from the variability in end demand so that the component production capacity buffer can be minimized to reduce cost.
3. A strategic inventory component buffer often reduces inventory costs because pooled component inventory to serve many products is less expensive than finished-goods inventory for each end product.

In short, the strategic use of a component inventory buffer reduces lead time (response-time buffer) to the customer and cost buffers (capacity and finished-goods inventory) to the manufacturer. In this context, let's detail implementation of dynamic risk-based scheduling in ATO operations. Figure 7-30 shows the elements of the Factory Physics framework as applied in ATO environments.

A key tactic for this configuration of buffers is the choice of an inventory/order interface prior to assembly. As discussed earlier, this

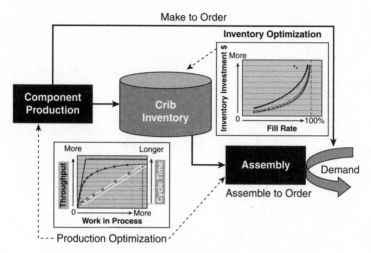

FIGURE 7-30. DRS in ATO environments

reduces the cycle time seen by the customer and decouples component production from end-customer demand variability. With the basic framework in place to support an ATO process, we can follow the steps of dynamic risk-based scheduling.

The first step in the DRS process is to use appropriate risk-based models to optimize MRP planning parameters: lot size, planned lead times, WIP levels, capacity triggers, and inventory policies. We have a lot of discussion in this chapter on tactics and controls for lead times, capacity triggers, WIP levels, and inventory policies. Please refer to Chapter 4 of this book for a detailed discussion on lot sizing. Many clients use software such as CSUITE from Factory Physics Inc., to determine these parameters to minimize the amount of resources spent on modeling. However it is done, once the parameters are specified and input into the planning system, planners can manage the system by monitoring the key parameters. In fact, this becomes the *standard work of the planner.*

There are standard control practices to be followed that will provide the most productive, predictive performance possible. These practices fall into four general categories:

1. **Capacity management.** Planner responsibility: *Always provide a feasible schedule for production.*
2. **Crib inventory management.** Planner responsibility: *Maintain proper inventory position at all times.*

TABLE 7-6. Production-Plan Options

Production Plan vs. Demand	Production Plan vs. Capacity	Comments
Production Plan < Demand	Production Plan < Capacity	Not a great situation but practical. Need more capacity.
Production Plan ≥ Demand	Production Plan < Capacity	Sweet spot. Could be building ahead to address seasonality if Production Plan > Demand—use minimal build-ahead.
Production Plan < Demand	Production Plan ≥ Capacity	Abandon all hope of controlled, predictive performance. *Enter Expediting Hell.*
Production Plan ≥ Demand	Production Plan ≥ Capacity	

3. **Flow control of shop work order (SWO) and planned work order (PWO) for assembly components and end items.** Planner responsibility: *Control the number of SWOs (WIP levels) at all times and ensure that jobs are worked on in "first in system" sequence.*

4. **Lead-time management for end items.** Planner responsibility: *Ensure that planned lead times are accurate.*

A planner's primary responsibility is *capacity management*. The planner must understand the capacity of the operations and ensure that *any* production plan is a feasible plan that can be achieved. Potential options for production-plan creation are detailed in Table 7.6.

A planner should *never* create a production plan that specifies production greater than capacity. Planners at clients that implemented policies for capacity triggers recognized when triggers were reached and worked with production management to issue flexible capacity additions such as overtime and outsourcing.

The planners also managed the interaction of crib inventory policies with component production. The planners used the planning system to monitor inventory position and manage release of component orders into the virtual queue when components reached replenishment points. Figure 7-31 provides a conceptual illustration of this process.

Planners often do not have direct responsibility for the rates at which parts are produced or for allocation of resources within

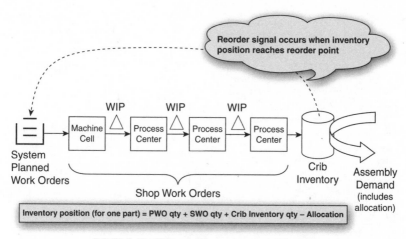

FIGURE 7-31. DRS inventory-replenishment triggers

production. Thus it is critical that they work with line-production management to:

1. Control the amount of WIP on the production floor at any one time.
2. Ensure that SWOs (shop work orders) are worked on in proper sequence: earliest first in system date.

It is a natural reaction for workers (and sometimes supervisors) on the production floor to want to have plenty of work at stations. The problem is that given the natural behavior of manufacturing systems, the only place that *should* have work all the time is the bottleneck process center. Nonbottleneck process centers will be low on work or empty from time to time—this is the natural behavior of any manufacturing system in the presence of variability. As we have discussed, too many SWOs on the floor causes two problems:

1. An increase in overall cycle time with a minimal, if any, increase in throughput
2. Wasted capacity

In many of the implementations, component production had setups. Workers and supervisors naturally wanted to group SWOs to minimize setups. The tendency is to group far too many SWOs, and

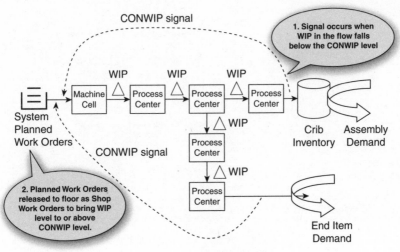

FIGURE 7-32. DRS and CONWIP

the capacity that is saved by minimizing setups is wasted in producing parts that aren't needed. Having SWOs that are more than a week overdue to start date is good evidence that this wasteful use of capacity is occurring in a cell. Having lots of SWOs that have completed early and are ready to ship is another indication of wasted capacity.

Many of our clients used CONWIP to manage the release of orders and avoid these issues. As previously discussed, the CONWIP concept is pretty simple (a big advantage). CONWIP as part of DRS is shown in Figure 7-32.

Because the CONWIP method controls WIP in the entire flow, *not at each process center*, WIP will migrate to the bottleneck. This is a very good control policy because the bottleneck should never be starved. Another benefit is that the planner doesn't have to specify the bottleneck in the face of changing product mixes and plant conditions—a very difficult task.

Finally, planners managed the planned lead times in the system for components and assembled end items. Managing the planned lead time for end items is made fairly simple for the planner if appropriate flow control is used, as described earlier. Good flow control provides the shortest practical cycle time and decreases variability of cycle times. With proper flow control, lead-time management mainly entails analyzing actual cycle times periodically to ensure that appropriate planned lead times are used.

Dynamic risk-based scheduling is a tactic to leverage the natural behavior of operations by using the Factory Physics framework to set and control planning parameters. It provides a practical technique to manage risk and achieve predictive control.

Dynamic Risk-Based Scheduling

1. Develop strategy by understanding the natural behavior of operations.
2. Define tactics with planning parameters based on the Factory Physics science for "when to order," "how much to order," "when to release," and "how much to produce."
3. Execute by staying within the control limits established for planning parameters.

MEASURES ALIGNMENT AND INSIGHT

This chapter focused on tactics and controls in the context of the Factory Physics framework. We acknowledge that things that sound great on paper only become great when they happen in actual day-to-day operations. We observe, and have discussed, that measures motivate behavior. Thus any performance measures must align and support strategies, tactics, and controls. It is also important to understand that measures should connect to goals in the context of the environment being managed. Measures should not be set as arbitrary goals. On-time delivery provides substantial potential for misleading use in practice. Exclusive focus on on-time delivery without an understanding of utilization is often an exercise in ignoring reality. We see many organizations set an on-time delivery-improvement goal because customer service is poor. An organization that attributes increased on-time delivery to efforts started in response to poor customer service may just be affirming the fallacy of the consequent. It is not unusual for poor customer service to lead to a decline in demand, which, of course, leads to a decrease in utilization. Lower utilization means faster response time, which improves on-time delivery. Improved on-time delivery is a reason to celebrate! If it turns out that the increase in on-time delivery was due to a drop in demand and an accompanying drop in utilization, the celebration is hollow. Often what happens, though, is that the celebration continues in blissful ignorance, but as demand recovers, customer service again declines as utilization rises—the whack-a-mole cycle begins anew! The tactics and controls of the Factory Physics framework drive true improvement in the context of business goals because they integrate and relate the key elements of operations—variability, time, capacity, and inventory. A manager knows that an organization has truly improved in the arena of on-time delivery when on-time delivery measures remain stable or improve in the face of increasing demand with decreasing or similar cost.

Measures not only provide insight to performance but also motivate behavior needed for consistent execution and predictable results. Without good measures, conflicting efforts between individuals occur by design. Measures should be aligned to ensure that:

1. **Individual efforts do not attempt to push the operations system in a direction it won't go.** For example, a planner can schedule production at a level above capacity when demand is above capacity, but that won't change the fact that the production can't meet demand—and doing so causes great confusion on the floor in determining what the real priorities are.
2. **Individual efforts are aligned within an organization so that conflict is minimized.** Measuring a planner on WIP reduction and a machinist on equipment utilization is guaranteed to cause conflict and the accompanying loss of productivity.
3. **Individual measures can be affected by the individual.** It is useless to hold a design engineer responsible for on-time delivery; the measure is too broad, and the engineer's span of authority does not provide him or her with the ability to directly affect on-time delivery. On the other hand, measuring an engineer on bill-of-material (BOM) accuracy provides measures that are well within the engineer's span of authority. Engineers are directly responsible for BOM accuracy, and having accurate BOMs is a critical requirement for management to successfully meet on-time delivery.

Following in Table 7-7 is a list of the measures and controls needed to ensure that an operation is planned properly and is in control during execution. It may seem like a long and involved list, except that almost any company with manufacturing, service, or supply-chain operations should be already measuring most, if not all, of these things—they are fairly common throughout industry.

Note that there are no controls for finance. There are certainly financial controls, such as audits and budgets, but the control

TABLE 7-7. Measures and Controls Needed for Operations

Operations Segment	Execution Mechanism	Item
Finance	Measures	1. Cash flow 2. Profit 3. Return on assets 4. Marginal contribution at the constraint
Stock	Controls	1. Inventory position limits • Reorder point • Reorder quantity 2. MRP/ERP system • Bills of material 3. Cycle counting
	Process measures	1. Demand mean and variance 2. Replenishment time mean and variance 3. Overtime (if applicable) 4. Shipment volume 5. Fill rate 6. Average days late 7. On-hand dollars 8. Inventory turns
	Individual measures	*Inventory planner:* 1. Inventory position 2. Replenishment orders/period 3. Inventory accuracy by zone *Engineering* (manufacturing, industrial, or design as is appropriate for individual companies. Sometimes handled by planners) 1. Bill of material accuracy

(*continued*)

TABLE 7-7. Measures and Controls Needed for Operations (Continued)

Operations Segment	Execution Mechanism	Item

Production	Controls	1. Demand mean and variance
		2. WIP
		3. Capacity trigger
		4. Lot size
		5. MRP/ERP system
		    a. Bills of material
		    b. Routings

	Process measures	1. Planned demand mean and variance 2. Throughput 3. Overtime 4. Machine availability 5. Amount of WIP in a production flow 6. Amount of work in the virtual queue 7. Cycle time of the flow (mean and standard deviation) 8. Average utilization of capacity

	Individual measures	*Process-center operators:*
		1. Scrap
		2. Rework
		3. Rate
		4. Setup time
		5. Lot size compliance
		6. Sequence compliance
		
		Production planners:
		1. Schedule feasibility
		2. WIP level
		3. Lot size compliance
		4. Sequence compliance
		Engineering (see note in "Stock" section above):
		1. Bill-of-material accuracy
		2. Router accuracy
		
		Maintenance:
		1. Machine availability
		    • Mean time to repair
		    • Mean time between failures

required to get desired financial performance from operations is optimal control of stocks and production. The individual roles assigned to each of the individual measures may vary from company to company. This is not a problem. However, it is important that all the measures are tied to behavior in the organization to ensure that a process is in control and providing expected performance. The process measures are owned by the manager in charge of the stock point or flow being measured. The manager should be using the controls and measures for a management-by-exception approach, which makes the management job easier. In other words, check the control measures often to make sure that a flow or stock is in control. React only to those that are out of control.

Of these individual measures, sequence compliance is probably the least familiar. *Sequence compliance* means that process-center operators should run jobs as close to the planned sequence as possible. The sequence is the sequence in which the jobs are released to a flow. If two jobs show up at a process center and they both have the same due date, the job that was released to the flow first is run first. There is always a little art to this. For instance, specify for the process-center operators that it is okay to run two jobs of a like part number (i.e., combine setups) together if their sequence dates are only three days apart, but jobs with sequence dates that are more than seven days apart may not be run together. What the right span is depends on the cycle time of the process. The idea in any case is that running jobs that are fairly close together in sequence is not going to cause much disruption in overall due-date performance. However, taking jobs that are far apart in sequence and running them together is sacrificing schedule adherence for capacity efficiency. Sequence compliance is also listed as a measure for production planners, and this may be questioned by some, since the production planners might say it's the operators who decide what to run when. That may or may not be the case, but it is our belief that more productive cooperation is achieved if two groups have the same goals where appropriate. In this case, we think it makes sense to have the production planners planning and the operators executing together to achieve sequence compliance.

Lot-size compliance applies to both production planners and process-center operators. Planners must release the correct lot sizes to production, and production must run the correct lot sizes when the job is received. For inventory planners, orders per period is a proxy for lot-size compliance, but a manager could measure reorder-size compliance for inventory planners also.

The list provided here is comprehensive. There may be variations on the list of measures, but these are fundamental measures because they:

1. Provide feedback on the status of the flow or stock point being controlled.
2. Tie to the natural behavior of operations and buffer control.
3. Connect actions directly to financial results.

In Chapter 8, we provide a detailed example of how the Factory Physics framework of strategy, tactics, controls, and measures is used in practice.

CHAPTER 8

Leadership, Measures, and Culture Change

We have now covered essentially all the Factory Physics concepts that a manager needs to successfully lead an organization using the Factory Physics approach. Of course, having a book with new ideas and theories is one thing. Putting them into practice is another. In this chapter we will run through an example of how the Factory Physics approach has been used by leadership of a company providing machined parts for the medical devices industry. Arc Precision, a Minnesota company, was created to take advantage of market dynamics in the machining industry. Being able to take advantage of Arc Precision's opportunity requires that Arc Precision establish very good control of operations. Arc Precision leadership has accomplished excellent control over operations through its employees' application of Factory Physics science in both operations design and daily control.

Any leadership effort requires some level of change management. Corporate leadership programs and applied behavioral science boil down to key elements of

1. Stated goals and objectives that are understood by the organization (strategies)
2. Individuals who understand their specific roles and require actions in achieving the goals (tactics)
3. Feedback loops that reinforce desired behavior and address personnel performance gaps between required and actual conduct of work (controls and measures)
4. Trust in the leaders and consistent leadership in the context of management systems

Those who fail to put these key elements into practice are much less successful in deployment. Applying these principles to ensure adherence to the organization's strategy and tactics drives success. There are many ways to lead an organization using these key elements. Function is much more important than form, which is good because it means that these elements can be applied with the Factory Physics approach in any company.

The Arc Precision approach to this blueprint is outlined here from corporate level to individual level:

1. Organizational leadership sets the vision and strategy for the company. This requires input from many different sources but ultimately is the leader's responsibility. Arc Precision's vision and strategy focus on setting its capacity and inventory buffers so that they provide response time as a competitive advantage. This design of Arc Precision's buffer portfolio then must be executed with a high degree of predictability in practice. It is also imperative that leaders set up and monitor performance measures that are aligned with the behaviors required to achieve the company's vision and strategy.

2. The vision and strategy must be turned into tactics that are updated monthly or quarterly—the sales and operations planning plus (S&OP+) process addresses this task directly. The monthly meetings monitor progress, prioritize initiatives, and ensure that resources are allocated appropriately.

3. With the monthly planning process in place and a target strategy for Arc Precision's buffer portfolio, feedback controls (e.g., CONWIP and due-date quoting) are assessed weekly:

   a. CONWIP control and throughput tracking ensure predictable output and provide a quick feedback mechanism for recognizing and reacting to problems.

   b. Due-date quoting depends on the results of CONWIP control and throughput tracking and is used to address market opportunities with existing or potential customers.

4. Daily mechanisms are instituted to address progress and issues of local and immediate concern, for example, summary e-mails and daily meetings.

5. Individual performance plans are developed so that roles and expectations are understood.

AN APPROACH TO SUSTAINABLE LEADERSHIP

Sustained, successful leadership is not easy. There are very many factors that are typically beyond a leader's control. Most managers can't say, "Jump!" and have employees ask only, "How high?" Leadership is typically not about what the leader can do; it's about what the leader can get others to do. Our experience is that the concepts provided in this book make a great platform on which to base leadership practices. The reason is that the concepts are objective, scientific, and comprehensive. Train employees in a practical, accurate understanding of the natural behavior of the business in which they work, connect those employees' efforts to the company's objectives through clearly defined goals and expectations, provide support, and stand back and watch them go. However, check them regularly to make sure that they are headed in the right direction and to provide feedback.

Whereas a clear vision is necessary for leadership, it is not sufficient. The greatest challenge of management is not how to implement the latest technology or how to listen attentively or how to set goals. The greatest challenge of operations management, or almost any management, is behavior modification. People resist change if for no other reason than it's different from what they are used to. Leadership in the context of the Factory Physics approach means helping employees to understand the natural behavior of their environment and how to use the controls at their disposal to successfully affect operations performance and help to foster effective business strategies. We've provided many examples, but it's amazing and disappointing how poorly some leaders understand or ignore the science of their own operation's behavior. Success in leadership does not require that leaders help their employees understand a science of operations. There are many leaders who it seems succeed in spite of themselves. However, leaders can provide competitive advantage for themselves and their organization by creating a common understanding of operations science that is practical, objective (usually this means that it is also scientific), comprehensive, and predictive. When leaders credibly establish and support this common understanding in their employees, the odds are greatly increased for achieving the leader's vision for the business.

Some additional thoughts on sustainable leadership include:

1. **A leader has to be empathetic.** People, for the most part, want to do a good job and are focused on the job they are doing. If there is a burning platform situation, people are more motivated to change, but otherwise lots of persistence, patience, and training are required to be successful in getting people to adapt to new practices.

2. **It's much better to focus efforts in a few key areas.** This is also the way many Lean manufacturing implementations start—focus on the high runners and establish flow. This approach often bogs down in Lean efforts after initial 5S and value-stream mapping exercises because there is not a fundamental science to establish a comprehensive approach. The Factory Physics approach is fundamentally different. Because this is a comprehensive scientific approach, *any* type of environment can be addressed regardless of complexity, for example, environments that are low volume, high mix, or make to order. The advantage of starting out simple is that the fundamental concepts and vocabulary can be worked out without the additional confusion caused by high complexity. Once the basic company framework has been designed, it can then be transferred to areas with much higher levels of complexity in processes or product mix. Further, resources are not unlimited, so it is better to focus on and execute a few initiatives than to generate a laundry list of ideas that never get done. In fact, this is entirely consistent with Little's law. By reducing the work in process (WIP; number of key initiatives), you reduce the cycle time to get them done.

3. **Limit the implementation team that owns and has accountability for initiatives to a few high-potential individuals in the organization.** The overall approach ultimately will be rolled out to everyone involved in managing the process. For example, all planners will be trained on the procedures for setting days of supply and safety stock and monitoring inventory position. That said, working out the details for everyone does not require that everyone actively participate in design of those procedures. However, it *is* important that the implementation team solicits periodic feedback from the wider organization during the design process.

4. **Control feedback must be tied directly to individuals.** Execution ultimately depends on the actions of the individual. Thus an individual must know how well she is doing versus her control limits. An example of tailoring feedback to the individual can be seen in inventory policy control described in Chapter 7. Figure 8-1 presents an *inventory-control compliance monitor* that shows the number of purchased parts that are above the control limits ("Over") and the number of purchased parts that are below the control limits ("Order") *for individual planners and buyers* (these two functions can be managed by one person, responsibility allocation varies from company to company). A manager seeing these charts once a week can very easily determine who needs attention first. The buyer and planner, seeing these charts, would quickly know where their efforts need to be focused.

5. **Training must be conducted regularly.** Training is often needed on the same topic numerous times. The progression of participant response to training is typically something like:

   a. **First session (introduction):** "Hmm. That looks interesting. I have lots of questions and here's my feedback." Afterwards—concepts quickly forgotten in the day-to-day routine.

Part ID	Planner	Buyer	Supplier No.	On Hand	On Order	$ on Order	Current BO	Reorder Point	Reorder Quantity	ROP + ROQ	Current Inventory Position	Delta	Order Status
Part9	Dax	Yeldon	Tiger Co.	15	0	$ -	12	32	12	44	3	-29	Order
Part2	Dax	Fowler	Messier Precision	11	0	$ -	0	25	10	35	11	-14	Order
Part110	Leia	Norwood	Bytheway Parts	0	0	$ -	0	12	7	19	0	-12	Order
Part96	Leia	Norwood	Bytheway Parts	0	0	$ -	0	11	6	17	0	-11	Order
Part97	Leia	Norwood	Bytheway Parts	0	0	$ -	0	4	3	7	0	-4	Order
Part112	Leia	Norwood	Aggie Inc.	0	0	$ -	0	4	4	8	0	-4	Order
Part20	Leia	Norwood	Bytheway Parts	0	0	$ -	1	2	2	4	-1	-3	Order
Part53	Leia	Lacy	Gamecock Inc.	1	0	$ -	0	4	4	8	1	-3	Order
Part11	Dax	Yeldon	Bear Mfg.	6	0	$ -	0	2	4	6	6	InRange	OK
Part13	Dax	Yeldon	Gamecock Inc.	5	0	$ -	0	3	2	5	5	InRange	OK
Part10	Leia	Lacy	Bytheway Parts	12	0	$ -	2	7	5	12	10	InRange	OK
Part15	Leia	Lacy	Wildcat Applications	4	0	$ -	0	1	3	4	4	InRange	OK
Part26	Leia	Lacy	Gamecock Inc.	0	0	$ -	0	-1	1	0	0	InRange	OK
Part39	Leia	Lacy	Wildcat Applications	2	0	$ -	0	1	2	3	2	InRange	OK
Part40	Leia	Lacy	Gamecock Inc.	4	5	$9,258	2	4	3	7	7	InRange	OK
Part22	Dax	Fowler	Einstein Mfg.	0	0	$ -	0	-1	1	0	0	InRange	OK
Part23	Dax	Fowler	Einstein Mfg.	1	3	$7,069	0	2	2	4	4	InRange	OK
Part24	Dax	Fowler	Gamecock Inc.	0	0	$ -	0	-1	1	0	0	InRange	OK
Part25	Dax	Fowler	Gamecock Inc.	0	0	$ -	0	-1	1	0	0	InRange	OK
Part36	Dax	Yeldon	Bulldog Mfg.	10	0	$ -	0	2	2	4	10	6	Over
Part38	Leia	Lacy	Wildcat Applications	5	0	$ -	0	-1	1	0	5	5	Over
Part31	Dax	Yeldon	Bytheway Parts	6	1	$2,573	0	1	2	3	7	4	Over
Part48	Dax	Fowler	Bear Mfg.	4	0	$ -	0	-1	1	0	4	4	Over
Part82	Dax	Yeldon	Bytheway Parts	1	0	$ -	0	-1	1	0	1	1	Over
Part16	Leia	Lacy	Bytheway Parts	5	0	$ -	0	1	3	4	5	1	Over
Part69	Dax	Fowler	Bear Mfg.	4	0	$ -	0	1	2	3	4	1	Over

FIGURE 8-1. Inventory-control compliance monitor

b. **Second session (prior to implementation):** "Oh yeah. I remember some of this. Now it looks like I'm actually going to have to use it. Lots of questions. A fair amount of concern that this will screw up what I've been doing."

c. **Third session (after implementation):** "I need help. I'm using this but still have questions. Give me the background again. Now that I have some experience, it'll make more sense to me. Oh, thanks for showing me those additional features. That will be helpful too. Here are some suggestions for improvement."

In the end, leaders should establish a process that connects strategy to daily execution. The measures that are used to monitor and control the process should align with the tactics created when leadership selected the business and operations strategy. Measures should provide strong motivation for working as the newly designed approach is intended. Organizational strategies and tactics that are understood and measured at an individual level help to drive culture change and execution. We turn now to the Factory Physics approach at Arc Precision.

A HIGH-LEVEL PLAN SO THAT STRATEGIES CAN BE SHARED AND UNDERSTOOD

A key tenet of this book and the Factory Physics approach is that operations strategy must support business strategy. It is helpful for people to understand the business strategy and the operational initiatives to support it. Communicating business strategy can be done in many ways and often involves multiple delivery mechanisms. Many companies have strategic plans and hold all-employee meetings. However it is done, business strategy should be communicated early and often to those involved in executing it.

The process we present as an example that has worked for us centers on a one-page strategic plan outlining vision, mission, key strategies, initiatives/tactics, and measures/controls. This outline is high level and covers overall business strategies so that it can be used beyond operations. The outline is not unique, but we find it effective. A one-page strategic plan can be given to employees and reviewed in meetings. If questions about priorities arise, all can refer to the one-page plan for guidance. To describe the planning process and provide an example, we discuss how the process is used at Arc Precision:

Vision and Mission

- **Vision.** A statement of what the organization wants to be in the long run.
- **Mission.** A statement of how the organization is going to achieve its vision.

At Arc Precision, leadership saw an underserved gap in the market space of precision machining for medical devices. Small suppliers from the traditional machining industry provided niche expertise and service but struggled to scale to support growth. Large suppliers, new to the scene after a round of industry consolidation, had scale but struggled to provide needed service for medical device companies on small and prototype volumes. These large suppliers were set up to serve the economics of scale and thus had a hunger for mostly large purchase orders. The industry needed a company that could provide small-company service with the ability to scale to support growth. Arc Precision could meet the industry need for service and scalability with International Standards Organization (ISO) 13485 precision machining backed by excellent design for manufacturing skills and the ability to scale with the Factory Physics framework.

With this as Arc Precision's business strategy, the vision and mission became pretty clear:

- **Vision.** Primary medical component supplier from prototype through midlevel production.
- **Mission.** Provide best-in-class engineering, operations, and supply-chain capabilities that deliver quality parts on time to customer request.

The vision and mission of Arc Precision have been the same since it was founded in January 2008. Arc Precision leadership developed them and continues to champion them with the organization. They are the first part of Arc Precision's one-page strategic plan. To provide an example of strategic planning at Arc Precision, we will show the buildup of a sample plan. It starts with the vision, mission, and a blank planning template for critical strategies, key initiatives, and metrics. A blank planning template is shown in Figure 8-2.

Critical Strategies					
Key Initiatives					
Metrics					

FIGURE 8-2. Planning template

Critical Strategies

Critical strategies are developed by leadership and should remain relatively consistent over time. Of course, they are specific to each company but usually involve the key areas of sales/marketing, operations, finance, and organizational development (human resources). This was the case at Arc Precision, as can be seen in the column headings of Figure 8-3.

Critical Strategies	Strategic Selling	Organization Development (scalable organization)	Operation Development (deliver on pipeline)	Capacity Planning	Financial
Key Initiatives					
Metrics					

FIGURE 8-3. Arc Precision's critical strategies

As we will discuss in the next section, deployment of the Factory Physics framework to develop and execute operational strategies, policies, and controls would be critical to support these business strategies. As the business planning process moves from high-level statements of vision, mission, and critical strategies, it becomes important to involve a broader group in developing and prioritizing key initiatives.

MONTHLY OR QUARTERLY PLANS TO ESTABLISH PRIORITIZED INITIATIVES

Key initiatives define the priorities for the next few months or quarters. These change from plan update to plan update. The development of key initiatives requires involvement from representatives of key functional areas in the company. As detailed in Chapter 6, the sales and operations planning plus (S&OP+) process is a great way to develop a monthly or quarterly plan with tactics to execute chosen strategy. A formal S&OP+ process is particularly appropriate for larger, complex companies, but the elements of S&OP+ must be performed by any company whether in a formal process or not. Tactics selected to support management strategy provide the key initiative detail for the one-page plan. Figure 8-4 shows the key initiatives in the Arc Precision example.

The Factory Physics framework provided the deployment mechanism for many of the key initiatives at Arc Precision. With the

Critical Strategies	Strategic Selling	Organization Development (scalable organization)	Operation Development (deliver on pipeline)	Capacity Planning	Financial
Key Initiatives	1. Target additional anchor customers (3 new) 4. Seek short-term revenue to fill capacity/revenue gap	5. Key hires 8. ISO and safety systems	6. Refine due-date quoting 7. Implement inventory program 9. Leverage booked orders to better load capacity	2. Implement capacity/capability initiatives in front-end process	2. Manage cost and revenue to budget

ARC
PRECISION

FIGURE 8-4. Arc Precision's key initiatives

Factory Physics framework, initiatives could be stated in terms of specific tactics for:

- Inventory optimization
- Utilization
- WIP caps
- Due-date quoting

Inventory Optimization

In support of stated business strategies, Arc Precision has implemented inventory policies which sustain the following key initiatives:

- 1. Target new anchor customers.
- 3. Manage cost and revenue to budget.
- 7. Implement inventory programs.
- 9. Leverage booked orders to better load capacity.

In terms of mechanics, Arc Precision uses inventory-optimization tactics and controls as described previously. Instead of repeating the mechanics in this section, we will provide an overview and case study of how Arc Precision uses inventory optimization across the supply chain with its customer partners. In its role as supplier of components, Arc Precision collaborates with its customers to ensure that needed components are available for assembly with the lowest possible inventories at the customer. Customers provide Arc Precision with visibility to demand. Arc Precision is able to plan component inventory levels and level load capacity. Customers pull on demand as their assembly operations require more stock.

Customers not only receive the benefit of reduced inventories, but Arc Precision is also able to provide proactive shared cost reductions because the visibility to demand allows the company to better utilize capacity. In one example, prior to partnering on supply-chain planning, the customer issued a request for quote for specific quantities and was quoted a price and lead time. After partnering on supply-chain planning, the customer provided Arc Precision with visibility to demand. Figure 8-5 shows options for lead time, cost, and inventory that Arc Precision was able to provide the customer based on the demand visibility.

	Order Quantity	Order Frequency	Lead Time	% Cost Reduction	% Inventory Reduction at Customer	Customer Agreement on Number of Units in ARC Inventory to Use Prior to Rev. Change
Initial terms	45	One P.O.	Quoted	NA	NA	NA
Partnership Scenario 1	1	As needed	Same-day pull	7%	100%	12
Partnership Scenario 2	15	Once per month	4 weeks	15%	63%	15
Partnership Scenario 3	1	As needed	Same-day pull	26%	100%	39

FIGURE 8-5. Strategic customer partnership options

When presented with these options, customers choose based on their priorities. Some prefer larger lots because of their inspection requirements. Others prefer on-demand delivery of individual units. In any case, deploying the Factory Physics framework across the supply chain provides a mechanism for Arc Precision to integrate operations strategies, tactics, and controls in support of its business strategy.

Utilization Targets

Recall the discussion from Chapter 7 about utilization targets for different industries as illustrated in Figure 8-6. Arc Precision, as a contract manufacturer, set a target machine utilization policy of 75 percent to support business strategies for needed responsiveness and establish a profitable cost structure for key initiatives as listed in the strategic planning document:

- 1. Target new anchor customers.
- 3. Manage cost and revenue to budget.
- 6. Refine due-date quoting.
- 9. Leverage booked orders to better load capacity

This tactical choice was deployed by planning and tracking throughput and utilization. Example analysis for one area of the plant

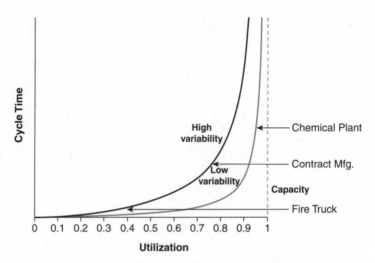

FIGURE 8-6. Utilization targets for different industries

is shown in Figures 8-7 (machines) and 8-8 (people). Figure 8-7 shows machine utilization scenarios. The machine capacity of this area was set to the utilization target of 75 percent (Scenario C) at an average projected demand of 480 hours. 100 percent machine utilization corresponds to the upper limit of expected average demand. This addresses upside demand growth. Demand fluctuations to the high side are handled with overtime to maintain responsiveness. This also allows time to add additional long term capacity should growth opportunities support the investment.

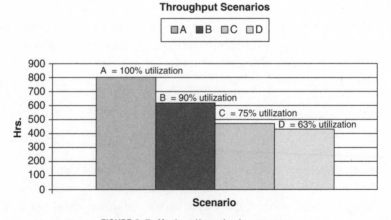

FIGURE 8-7. Machine throughput scenarios

FIGURE 8-8. Staffing scenarios

The machines require operators, and Figure 8-8 shows the staffing required for each demand level. For the target machine utilization level of 75 percent, 11 operators are required for staffing the machines. This approach is straightforward, relatively simple, and addresses a vital requirement for controlling the natural behavior of operations—feasible capacity plans.

WEEKLY SCHEDULING MEETINGS TO PLAN THE WORK

Weekly meetings can be a useful mechanism to plan work and check progress. They can help to ensure that tactics are deployed in support of strategy. The utilization target of 75 percent at Arc Precision translates into WIP caps deployed in a weekly schedule and due-date quoting policies deployed using a virtual queue. Arc Precision, as a job shop, uses a job routing software package as opposed to a traditional bill of materials based MRP/ERP. It leverages the automated data transactions in the job routing software package to provide data for its weekly schedule and due-date quoting policies. The examples presented here show how Arc Precision has created its Factory Physics DRS approach using the features in its software package combined with straightforward Excel spreadsheets to manage production scheduling in a complex environment. While Arc Precision will eventually require a more traditional MRP/ERP system as it grows, any software installation will be structured to maintain the Factory Physics DRS scheduling features. Hopefully when that time comes, traditional software vendors will offer DRS features.

We present an example of how Arc Precision uses a weekly scheduling meeting to execute WIP caps and due-date quoting.

WIP Caps

Arc Precision executes WIP caps with its weekly scheduling process. In the area we have been describing, a weekly schedule of 480 hours is the WIP cap on production in a week. The hours at each machining center combine to become the hours for the area and are capped at 480 hours per week. Individual hours at each machining center could change from week to week based on specific demands but were generally based on the average long-term load at the respective machining centers. An example of an excerpt representing 322 hours of Arc Precision's weekly schedule is shown in Figure 8-9.

Note that the scheduled amount of work at some machining centers is at the maximum. At others, space is left open for potential strategic expedites. If the open space is not needed for strategic expedites, the next job will be pulled from the virtual queue, resulting in a level load of capacity and that job being completed ahead of plan. Arc Precision holds a weekly scheduling meeting to assign jobs and personnel to finalize deployment of its WIP cap policy. The WIP caps at Arc Precision, combined with existing and projected backlog, enable Arc Precision to deploy a policy of due-date quoting.

Current Schedule Week: **November Week 3**

Miyano				03 Mazak				04 Kitamura 2xl				09 Kitamura 3XG			
Job	operation	Qty	Hrs	Job	operation	Qty	Hrs	Job	operation	Qty	Hrs	Job	operation	Qty	Hrs
10981	70	915	48	10984	100	24	9.36	Broke down				10992B	35/40	24	17
10981	80	1000	44									10992A	90	24	4.6
	james	brian													
Maximum			50	Maximum			35	Maximum			30	Maximum		60	40
Total			50	Total			9.36	Total			0	Total			21.6

Tsugami				Makino				Matsuura				07 Mazak			
Job	operation	Qty	Hrs	Job	operation	Qty	Hrs	Job	operation	Qty	Hrs	Job	operation	Qty	Hrs
10994	70	30	7	10971A	50	28	28	10992C	80	24	2.6	10992A	60	24	39
10994-1	70	600	27.4					10992C	90	24	2.13	10971A	60	28	44.33
								10992C	100	24	2.07	10970A	80	23	4.87
								10917A	63	18	5				
								10917A	65	18	3.5				
								10917A	70	18	3.5				
	james														
	brandon b	su													
													james	steve	
Maximum			35	Maximum			40	Maximum			37	Maximum		60	55
Total			34.4	Total			28	Total			18.8	Total			55

FIGURE 8-9. Weekly schedule excerpt

Due-Date Quoting

As quotes come in, the team at Arc Precision reviews the virtual queue of jobs at work centers to determine a lead time based on the routing of the job and the virtual queue at work centers in the routing. This dynamic process provides an ability to work with the customers to meet needed delivery times while quoting a lead time with high probability of on-time delivery. Figure 8-10 shows an example of virtual queues in one area of the facility.

Production Flow (Mill Indexer)		Production Flow (Mill No Indexer)	
Customer A Job 1	10	Customer B Job 1	80
Customer A Job 2	19	Customer B Job 2	73
Customer G Job 1	6	Customer B Job 3	14
Customer G Job 2	6	Customer B Job 4	3
Customer G Job 3	6	Customer B Job 5	3
Customer G Job 4	8	Customer B Job 6	42
Customer A Job 3	316	Customer B Job 7	36
Customer D Job 1	20	Customer B Job 8	8
Customer E Job 1	75	Customer B Job 9	3
Customer F Job 1	225	Customer B Job 10	3
		Customer B Job 11	153
		Customer B Job 12	38
		Customer B Job 13	83
		Customer C Job 1	162
		Customer A Job 4	48
		Customer A Job 5	110
		Customer A Job 6	280
Requires 5 axis:			
Customer G Job 5	11		
Customer G Job 6	11		
Customer G Job 7	14		
Backlog	727		1139
Capacity	100		120
LT (wks)	7.3		9.5
Includes all JB backlog	785		330
	7.9		2.8
		Reserved/Quoted	

FIGURE 8-10. Virtual-queue example

Note that average lead times in a work center are quoted using Little's law. Also, some of the backlog includes reserved/quoted jobs for anticipated orders. For any specific requests, Arc Precision reviews the routing and starts with a quote consisting of average lead time for the routing plus a time buffer to account for variability. This time buffer changes depending on the mix at a work center. Work centers with a high percentage of production work need only a small time buffer because the hours quoted will usually be close to the actual hours. Work centers with a high load of prototypes require a larger time buffer to account for the variability inherent in production of prototypes. If a shorter lead time is requested by a customer, Arc Precision can evaluate the requested job's potential for expedited lead time using one of the reserved/quoted schedule slots to move that customer to the front of the line. Use of a reserve slot is a business decision based on the current utilization load on operations, the strategic value of the customer, and the pricing power in providing the expedited service. Due-date quoting presents a microcosm of the Factory Physics framework because it provides a quantitative method to evaluate and make business choices. In contract manufacturing, the elements of price, lead time, and on-time delivery form a major piece of the value proposition. Due-date quoting provides a mechanism to account for the current status of the factory (utilization versus cycle time, variability) and the strategic importance of the order and customer. It drives alignment among strategies, tactics, and controls.

WEEKLY OPERATIONS MEETINGS TO CHECK PROGRESS

With strategy developed and tactics deployed, the organization needs established measures and feedback loops to ensure execution and continuous improvement. Measures alignment is a primary leadership responsibility. For example, Figure 8-11 shows the high-level metrics associated with Arc Precision's strategic plan.

We find that a weekly operations meeting is a useful mechanism to review results and take actions to improve them. The concept of a weekly operations meeting is not unique. Companies have been holding them for years. Chapter 6 provided some recommended guidelines for effective meetings. Any meeting that becomes the

Critical Strategies	Strategic Selling	Organization Development (scalable organization)	Operation Development (deliver on pipeline)	Capacity Planning	Financial
Key Initiatives	1. Target additional anchor customers (3 new) 4. Seek short-term revenue to fill capacity/revenue gap	5. Key hires 8. ISO and safety systems	6. Refine due-date quoting 7. Implement inventory program 9. Leverage booked orders to better load capacity	2. Implement capacity/capability initiatives in front-end process	2. Manage cost and revenue to budget
Metrics	*Number of new target customers identified and contacted. *Visible backlog (bookings at targets) *Quotes at targets *Delivery schedules	*Key position requests identified? *Programmer position filled? *Audit summary reports	*Refine measures for setup-scrap-rework *Utilization-capacity goals *On time delivery *Inventory position compliance by buyer *Production schedule adherence	*Quote logs *New part planning	*Profit managed to meet budget *$10k revenue per employee per month *Pay loan down $30K per month

FIGURE 8-11. Example of metrics at Arc Precision

"evening news," where people report but don't provide insight and propose actions, is a red flag. Typically, operations meeting agendas cover safety, quality, cost, and customer service (i.e., lead times, on-time deliveries, average days late). A weekly operations meeting can take many forms, but the meeting should include:

1. The right metrics based on tactics deployment that aligns with stated strategies.
2. Relentless follow-up to review and reinforce what is working and address what is not working.

Given the stated strategies at Arc Precision, tactics employed, and high-level metrics in the strategic plan, the weekly operations meeting focuses on predictive detailed metrics that will drive achievement of high-level metrics such as on-time delivery. Two examples include inventory compliance reports and schedule adherence. Owners of these areas should not just report the metric but instead provide insight into actions being taken to follow tactics and execute the stated business strategy.

For example, in terms of inventory tactics, the science dictates that if inventory position is between $r + 1$ and $r + Q$, then planned results will be achieved. Thus inventory position compliance monitors can proactively show whether planned tactics are being followed to achieve desired results. Here is an example of an insightful, action-oriented discussion on inventory compliance from an operations meeting: "Component compliance above target until excess inventory burns off. . . . that said, 73 percent of excess dollars are caused by 10 items. On 4 of those items, we have just way too much inventory and won't burn off for 18 months. Sales has an action to investigate and report on options for moving those 4 items faster. On the other 6 items, we have blanket orders with one supplier who keeps sending in inventory as he completes it. We are meeting with this supplier next week to explain the need to hold the inventory until we 'pull it' off their blanket order."

Figure 8-12 provides an example of schedule adherence from Arc Precision as a predictive indicator of compliance to throughput, WIP cap, and due-date quoting tactics that drive on-time delivery.

Figure 8-12 shows that electrical discharge machine (EDM) throughput fell below plan and mill throughput exceeded plan. The EDM shortfall was due to staffing issues. The plan to catch up was to run one day of overtime in the next week. Weekly operations meetings can be a useful format to check progress, reinforce tactics that are working, and take corrective actions to resolve gaps in performance.

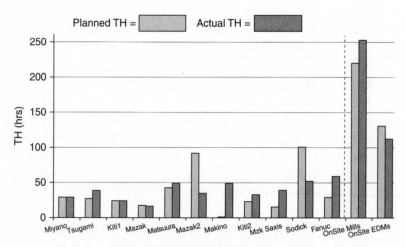

FIGURE 8-12. Schedule-adherence example

DAILY MECHANISMS FOR FEEDBACK _____

Of course, with clear tactics and real-time feedback loops, there is no reason to wait until the weekly operations meeting to take localized action. At one client, the manager reviewed inventory compliance sheets daily and sent e-mails to provide feedback. His use of the Factory Physics framework supported with timely and individual feedback was very effective in driving desired behavior. Here is a paraphrase of an actual e-mail chain between the manager and a planner:

- **Manager's e-mail:** As you know, we've been patiently waiting for our on-hand inventory to slowly burn off to the point where we'll finally be within 100 percent compliance with our established inventory policies. As we saw a couple of weeks ago, some of these inventory items were burning off so slowly that we were projecting (at the current rate of consumption) that several items wouldn't get into policy compliance for years! Despite that fact, we have been experiencing an overall inventory burn off of approximately $20,000 per week over the last 5 to 6 weeks. I am excited by our progress but was very disappointed to see on today's report (attached) that we have unexpectedly taken order action on 10 different items that had not yet hit their reorder points. On another item that had hit its reorder point we chose to ignore the reorder quantity. This order activity resulted in our overall inventory position increasing by $68,280. At our current burn rate of approximately $20,000/week, this activity has in effect set us back by at least three weeks. Please help me understand.
- **Buyer's response:** These are all are items I just put on blanket orders for cost-savings purposes.
- **Manager's response:** Can you provide a little more info. . . . I'm still struggling with the timing of this new blanket. Why did we move forward with a new blanket now, instead of waiting to reach our reorder points? Could you also provide me with what our unit costs were for each item before the blanket and after the blanket?
- **Buyer's response:** I wanted to give our vendors time to produce the increased quantities without putting other

items/POs at risk of being late. Also to make sure none of these slipped and got ordered on a nonblanket PO.

- **Manager's response:** I appreciate the intention. I know it was done in the right spirit (with cost savings in mind), but I'm still not convinced that this was the right time to include these items in any type of PO. Could you schedule a meeting with me to show me what I'm missing and why I'm not thinking about this correctly?

This e-mail exchange highlights many key benefits that can be gained from checking compliance against tactics, including:

- Visibility to individual changes or workarounds that have unintended, undesirable consequences and can take a long time to correct
- Visibility to individual changes or workarounds that have highly desirable consequence and can be standardized as a best practice
- Discussion of tradeoffs (unit cost versus inventory increase) to ensure that actions align with strategy

In this case, the manager was able to catch the change in time and take corrective action to cancel the orders so that the organization adhered to its tactics and executed its planned strategy.

Here is an Arc Precision example on the importance of monitoring daily throughput. In some cases at Arc Precision, specific WIP and throughput plans are put in place for large orders at specific machining centers to ensure that cycle time stays within range to meet the quoted lead time. The WIP level is controlled in the weekly scheduling meeting, and daily throughput is reported via e-mail with the expectation that any gaps will be addressed. Figure 8-13 shows a report that tracks daily throughput versus planned throughput.

This figure shows that the team was actually exceeding planned throughput on a regular basis, thus ensuring on-time delivery to the due date that was quoted. This was a benefit because the customer wanted parts even sooner than the quoted due date. The team was on track to meet the customer's desire for an expedited delivery and far ahead of plan to meet the quoted due date. However, on this day, throughput dropped to 68 versus a plan of 75, so the cumulative positive deviation dropped back a bit. The employee knew the plan, saw

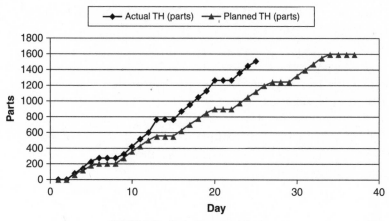

FIGURE 8-13. Daily throughput tracking

the charts, and proactively sent an e-mail stating, "All: We lost some time last night due to the bearing's going bad on the roller in bottom head. We are in the process of taking it apart and putting in new ones. Nolan and myself are working Saturday to make up for this lost time. Thanks." In this case, the use of planning and tracking in the context of the Factory Physics framework meant that the manager did not even have to ask the question about the compliance outage. The operator recognized a performance gap and took action to correct it.

Feedback loops are most powerful when they provide direction quickly so that behavior can be modified. The quantitative nature of the Factory Physics framework enables data-based and timely feedback loops to ensure policy conformance that drives strategy execution.

PERSONAL PLANS SO THAT INDIVIDUALS UNDERSTAND THEIR ROLES

A final recommendation for leaders is to restate the organization's plan and the individual's role in executing the plan on a one-page *personal plan* for the individual. A one-page plan tailored for the individual provides clear expectations for the individual and an opportunity for structured feedback from the leader. This requires some work on the leader's part. The plan does not have to be a 20-page exposition, but a manager should put thought into the plan for each employee to ensure that efforts and expectations are aligned.

Again, format is less importance than function. Factory Physics framework policy items that often show up on personal plans include:

- Inventory policy compliance for buyers
- Due-date quoting, WIP cap, and throughput policy setting for planners

Figure 8-14 provides an example from Arc Precision of a personal plan with items related to the Factory Physics framework tactics items highlighted in bold.

Clayton's Personal Plan

1. Engineering
   a. Create quotes
      i. Determine best method of production
      ii. Work with customer engineers if parts can't be made per print. (DFM)
      iii. Obtain material prices
      iv. Obtain outside service prices
      v. Calculate set up times and run rates
      vi. Determine tooling requirements
      vii. Determine fixturing requirements
      viii. Work with Mike to determine best lead time
      ix. Create tooling/fixturing sketches
      x. Create folder on EDMR and add prints to appropriate folder
      xi. Create quote audit report and work with Mike to determine the best lead times.
   b. Create jobs
      i. Review P.O.
         1. Confirm dates, revision and price match the quote
      ii. Create job
         1. Create job in Jobboss
         2. Schedule job
         3. Print traveler
         4. Print blue prints and confirm they are the correct revision
         5. Order material, special tooling, special gages
   c. Maintain quote log
2. Scheduling
   a. Create weekly schedule
      i. Print reports as needed
      ii. Support Mike as needed
   b. Do global schedule in Jobboss weekly
   c. Maintain preproduction log
3. Office staff backup
   a. Support Dawn when on vacation
      i. Throughput
      ii. Time cards
   b. Programming support-turning
4. Shop support
   a. Set up and run the required work centers as needed

FIGURE 8-14. Example of a personal plan

Clayton's plan is directly tied to the strategies, tactics, and controls of the Factory Physics framework in the areas of:

- Due-date quoting
- Using Little's law for production planning and tracking
- Using Little's law for planning and tracking the service of quoting

The personal-plan concept combined with use of the Factory Physics framework plays a key role in Clayton's employee-development process. It helps to align Clayton's daily plans and actions with company strategies, tactics, and controls. A personal plan is a simple way to provide employees with clear expectations. It also provides a useful structure for discussions on performance and development.

Hopefully, the content of this chapter provided some ideas on how to lead by using the Factory Physics framework to drive operations strategy and execution. We recognize that leadership is both situational and a matter of individual style. The Factory Physics framework of strategies, tactics, and controls provides a practical, scientific method for any leader to combine his or her personal style with the application of a predictive approach for any company.

Leadership with the Factory Physics Framework

1. Leaders should first develop the vision and strategy for the organization.
2. Leaders should work with the organization so that all members have a shared understanding of the vision, strategy, tactics, controls, and their individual role in execution.
3. Leaders should establish measures and feedback loops to ensure execution and continuous improvement.

CHAPTER 9

Examples from Industry

Avoid the precepts of those thinkers whose reasoning is not confirmed by experience.

—*Leonardo da Vinci*, Thoughts on Art and Life

We will now demonstrate use of the Factory Physics methodology in practice. This chapter contains five different examples of its use in the real world. We also include an example that takes a classic treatment from a famous book on Lean manufacturing and extends the results using Factory Physics science.

LEARNING TO SEE—FARTHER

This chapter begins with an example that is not from the real world but from an influential book, *Learning to See.*[1] In this book, Rother and Shook present simple and effective ways to illustrate flow by developing a *value-stream map* (VSM). They list a number of reasons why such maps are useful:

1. To be able to see the *flow* and not just a single process.
2. To provide a common language.
3. To see sources of waste, not just waste.
4. To make the details of flow apparent so that they can be discussed.
5. To form the basis of an implementation plan.
6. To show linkages between information and material flows.
7. A VSM is a qualitative tool to describe in detail how the facility should operate in order to create flow.

The case study is of the Michigan Steel Company, which produces two types of brackets—a right one and a left one. Other data include:

- Five process steps with process times and setup times
- Demand of 18,400 brackets per month
  - 12,000 of left
  - 6,400 of right
- Brackets moved in trays of 20
- Two shifts per day (15.33 hours)
- Twenty days per month
- Total value-added time of 3.13 minutes

The time available will be 306.667 h = 20 days × 15.33 h/day or 18,400 minutes. Because demand is 18,400 brackets per month, the *takt* time is 1 minute, or 60 seconds. Figure 9-1 provides the "current state" VSM. The various rectangles represent production processes, for example, "Stamping," "S. Weld #1," and so on, whereas the triangles indicate work-in-process (WIP) locations. The straight arrows indicate information flow, whereas the lightening arrows show electronic information flow. The thick arrows between processes indicate push material flow in the plant, and the outlined arrows represent shipments.

Table 9-1 provides the rates and setup times for each step in the flow. Note that for shipping, the statement probably should be that capacity, not process time, is unlimited. This may or may not be true, but in the context of this case, it is probably a reasonable assumption. Once the map is drawn, it is easy to determine the cycle time of the process. Interestingly, the developers of value-stream mapping process rely on Little's law to determine cycle times. The procedure is simply to count up the WIP at each station and divide by the throughput (or, equivalently, multiply by the *takt* time). This should be a much better estimate than asking the operator, "How long does it take to get through your process?" Given the pressure to keep this number low, there might be some motivation to offer an optimistic answer.

Other performance data are given in Figure 9-2. Note that there is no indication of fill rates or utilizations of the process centers.

Once the current-state map is completed, it is used to identify long cycle times and then to suggest ways to improve the process. We believe that the VSM process is extremely useful in establishing a base case and to understand the overall flow. However, a VSM is not

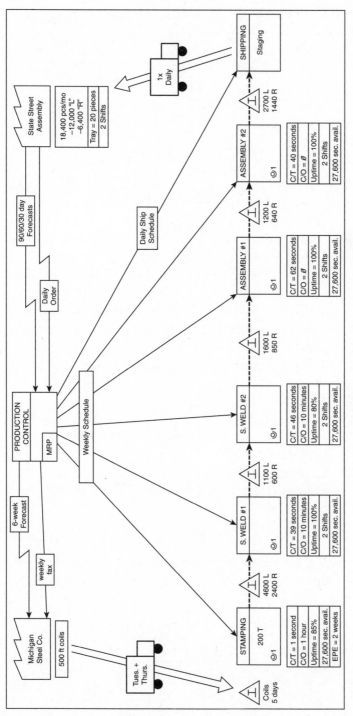

FIGURE 9-1. Example of a value-stream map (VSM)

(Used with permission, © Lean Enterprise Institute.)

TABLE 9-1. Process Rates and Setup Times for the Value-Stream Map

Process Step	Process Time (s)	Setup Time (h)
Stamping	1.0	1.000
S. Weld #1	39.0	0.167
S. Weld #2	46.0	0.167
Assembly #1	62.0	0.000
Assembly #2	40.0	0.000
Shipping	Unlimited	0.000

an input-output model, so it cannot really convey what is going to happen when changes are made to the system.

So we thought it would be interesting to take the current-state map from *Learning to See* and use it to build a Factory Physics model using the CSUITE operations analytics software and then to see how much we can reduce cycle times without spending a lot of money.

To build such as model, the following data are required for each process:

- Number of tools needed
- Number of workers needed for setup and for process
- Process rate
- Setup (changeover) time
- Availability [mean time to repair (MTTR), mean time to failure (MTTF)]
- Current WIP levels

Most of this information is available directly from the VSM. What is missing can be modeled with some simple assumptions.

Total Raw Matl. (days)	Total WIP (days)	FG (days)	Total WIP and Inv. (days)	Mfg. Cycle Time (days)	Fill Rate	Utilization
5	14.1	4.5	23.6	14.1	?	?

FIGURE 9-2. Performance data obtained from the value-stream map

☐ OEE Analysis	Product Flow	Units of Measure	Throughput (units/day)	Bottleneck Rate (units/day)	Bottleneck Type	Process Center Bottleneck	Utilization
☐ 🔍	Brackets	Bracket	920.0000	890.0598	Process Center	04 Assembly #1	103.36%

FIGURE 9-3. Initial capacity and utilization of VSM line

For instance, we can assume that one operator is required at each station (for both setup and processing). Because there is no information regarding the variability of the process times and because the case is fictional, we are free to use anything that is reasonable. Typical process times are usually low variability (i.e., CV < 0.75), but this plant appears to be run very poorly with a value-added time of only 3 minutes and a total cycle time of 23.6 days. Thus we will set the variability to be at the moderate level with an SCV of 1.0. Likewise, we are only given availability and need the MTTF and MTTR. Again, because the case is fictional, we can assume anything reasonable as long as the availabilities come out to 85 percent for stamping, 80 percent for s. weld #2, and 100 percent for all the rest. The transfer-batch size is 20 units and is given as the number of brackets per tray, whereas the process-batch size is obtained from the "each part every 2 weeks" data. This means that we make half the monthly demand every two weeks, so the process batch for left brackets is 6,000 and for right brackets is 3,200.

We put all these data into the CSUITE modeling system and run the model, finding that there is insufficient capacity. Figure 9-3 shows the calculation and that the utilization is over 103 percent. How can this be? Actually, it is obvious. Assembly 1 has a process time of 62 seconds, whereas the *takt* time is only 60 seconds. So there is no way the line can keep up with demand.

If this were a *real* factory, a manager would have to return to the factory itself and find out what is different between the model and what is really going on in the factory. Knowing some basic Factory Physics principles, however, we can determine some probable causes. One thing we know is that a plant can *never* run continuously over 100 percent utilization and probably not more than 98 percent utilization. Therefore, it is clear that there must be more time being used than the case states. Also, we are given the average WIP and cycle time of the line. Armed with these two facts, we can adjust the available time until the cycle time matches the 23.6 days given. This includes 5 days in raw material (coil storage) and 4.5 days in finished goods waiting to be shipped, so the plant cycle time is "only"

Part	Raw Matl. (days)	WIP (days)	FG (days)	Total WIP and FG (days)	Mfg. Cycle Time (days)	Total Turns	Fill Rate
Left Bracket	5.0	14.8	11.5	31.3	14.8	7.66	74.59%
Right Bracket	5.0	12.8	11.5	29.3	12.8	8.20	75.52%

Process Center	Bottleneck	Util.	Hours for One Batch	Hours in Queue
01 Stamping		3.03%	2.5	0.02
02 S. Weld #1		60.58%	50.01	14.16
03 S. Weld #2		89.21%	73.64	35.97
04 Assembly #1	BN	95.98%	79.23	116.09
05 Assembly #2		61.92%	51.11	15.23

FIGURE 9-4. Performance predictions by CSUITE

14.1 days. To achieve this result we find that the plant is running, on average, an extra 1.2 hours per day, or 24 hours per month. When we rerun the model, we get the same overall cycle time of 14.8 days for left brackets and 12.8 days for right brackets. The difference in cycle time is due to the different batch size. Figure 9-4 presents the performance data obtained from CSUITE. Note that we now have cycle time and WIP levels by part, along with fill rates and utilization levels. The bottleneck is assembly 1 with a very high utilization of 96 percent. Also, the fill rates are quite low (around 75 percent), and the finished-goods level is almost twice that reported on the VSM and is due to the variability in the cycle times causing fill rate to fall and inventories to rise.

Now that we have a feasible model that pretty well matches the performance of the real line, we would like to see how it could be improved.

First, we perform an absolute benchmarking analysis. From the VSM, we obtain a demand of 920 units per day and a WIP level of 12,990. From CSUITE, we get a raw process time of 0.93 days and a bottleneck rate of 958.57 units per day. These four pieces of data are all that we need to create the plots shown in Figure 9-5 which are quite telling. First of all, the WIP is more than 15 times the critical WIP (856). Note that the throughput is between the marginal and best cases. This tells us that the inherent variability is not the problem but that excessive WIP is.

The large WIP levels could be caused by large lot sizes—each is half a month's demand. It would appear that the large lots are to avoid the hour setups at the stamping operation. But the CSUITE analysis shows that this operation is only used 3 percent of the time,

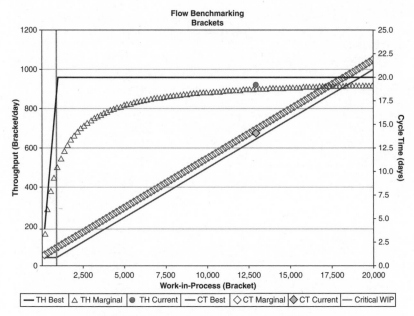

FIGURE 9-5. Initial absolute benchmark of VSM line

despite the relatively large setups. This seems impossible, so let us do a quick check to see if it is true.

The process sets up four times per month for a total setup time of 4 hours per month. The process time is only 1 second, so we use 18,400 seconds, or 5.11 hours, per month. Because the stamping operation has an availability of 85 percent, this time goes to about 6 hours per month. Thus the total time spent in setup, downtime, and processing is about 10 hours per month. Because there are 16.53 hours per day for 20 days per month, there are 330.6 hours. Consequently, the utilization will be

$$u = \frac{10}{330.6} = 0.03$$

With a utilization of only 3 percent, it would not make much difference in overall cycle time to pursue a setup-reduction project on this machine. However, if there are other products using the same stamping machine and driving a much higher utilization, then we may need to address the long setup time. We simply cannot tell from the information given.

Before addressing issues on the factory floor, we should see how much improvement we can obtain by changing parameters in the

Part	Raw Matl. (days)	WIP (days)	FG (days)	Total WIP and FG (days)	Mfg. Cycle Time (days)	Total Turns	Fill Rate
Left Bracket	5.0	1.1	0.3	6.4	1.1	19.43	93.17%
Right Bracket	5.0	1.0	0.4	6.4	1.0	19.33	94.89%

Process Center	Bottleneck	Util.	Hours for One Batch	Hours in Queue
01 Stamping		21.53%	1.09	0.21
02 S. Weld #1		63.72%	3.23	1.04
03 S. Weld #2		92.36%	4.69	4.56
04 Assembly #1	BN	95.98%	4.87	6.95
05 Assembly #2		61.92%	3.14	0.83

FIGURE 9-6. Performance predictions by CSUITE after application of the CFO

production-control systems. These include lot sizes, safety stocks, and planned lead times. Thus we use the CSUITE cash-flow optimizer (CFO) that selects lot sizes and safety stocks that minimize inventory and guarantee a given fill rate. In this case, the target fill rate is 95 percent.

After running the CFO (Figure 9-6), the cycle times drop from around 14 days to around 1 day! Moreover, even though fill rates have gone up from 75 percent to around 95 percent, finished inventory has dropped from around 11 days to less than half a day. Indeed, total turns have gone from around 8 to 19. All this was done by reconciling lot sizes, which dropped from 6,000 and 3,200 to 320 and 232. (See Figure 9-6.) No changes were made to the factory floor. The stamping machine operator might not appreciate the great benefits of the reduction in lot size because many more setups will be required, but that is one of the issues a manager has to manage.

But we can still do better if we address issues on the floor. First of all, assembly 1 is still the bottleneck, and its process time requires us to run 24 hours of overtime each month. *Learning to See* suggests reducing the maximum process time by rebalancing the weld and assembly operations. The authors also performed a *kaizen* that converted four process steps, taking a total of 187 seconds, into three process steps that each take less than 60 seconds. To accomplish this, they create a cell that does some welding and some assembly. All these changes are completely credible, especially in a place that has had little process improvement.

But we would like to see what we can do *without* reducing the total time. In fact, we will assume that changing the balance of the line actually increases the total time because of inefficiency resulting from combining the two assembly operations into one that takes 105 seconds (3 seconds more than the current configuration). Thus each operator will perform all the assembly, and it will take him a bit longer to do it. This means that we have two *parallel* operations that take 105 seconds instead of two operators in *series* taking 46 and 62 seconds, respectively.

When we run the model, cycle times go from around 1.1 and 1.0 days to 0.88 and 0.76 day. This sounds small but represents a 20 and 24 percent decrease in cycle time. This change also breaks the bottleneck at assembly 1, and now s. weld #2 becomes the new constraint at 92.36 percent utilization. It would appear that the overtime could be eliminated, but if this is done, utilization goes to 99.5 percent, with cycle times going up to around 6 days. At this extreme utilization level, cycle-time calculations are not accurate. Nonetheless, utilization calculations are accurate, and 99.5 percent is too high.

However, we notice that the new bottleneck has a fairly long MTTR of 7.2 hours. If we could have a "field-replacement part" and train the operator to install it (thereby avoiding a maintenance call), we should be able to reduce this to no more than 4 hours. This change brings the cycle times back down to nearly where they were before eliminating the overtime (0.89 and 0.76 day). Running the CFO after making these changes improves things a bit more. The utilization is now low enough that we can safely eliminate the 24 hours of overtime, a significant direct cost savings.

The VSM was an invaluable tool to see the flow and to highlight the opportunities. Combining a VSM with a fast simulation model allows us to play "what if" and, with optimization, "what's best" before making the changes in the actual plant. Figure 9-7 summarizes

Part	Mfg. Cycle Time (days)			Total Turns		
	Current	Final	% Diff.	Current	Final	% Diff.
Left Bracket	14.8	0.8	−94%	7.66	20.07	162%
Right Bracket	12.8	0.7	−94%	8.20	20.05	145%
Part	Fill Rate			Overtime per Month		
	Current	Final	% Diff.	Current	Final	% Diff.
Left Bracket	74.59%	96.25%	29%	24.00	—	−100%
Right Bracket	75.52%	97.60%	29%			

FIGURE 9-7. Summary of performance improvements

the overall improvements, which are significant. Cycle times have been reduced 94 percent, whereas turns rose by around 150 percent, and fill rates climbed by 29 percent. Finally, we went from having to schedule 24 hours of overtime per month to zero overtime in a month. All these improvements were made with inexpensive changes to the factory floor and by optimizing the production rules.

Figure 9-8 illustrates these changes graphically. Here we see an increase in capacity while minimum cycle time falls dramatically. Moreover, the variability has been greatly reduced so that it is now possible to run very close to the critical WIP (one-piece-flow).

BEYOND ABC—OPTIMAL INVENTORY POLICIES

This company is a global leader in valve monitoring and position sensing for the process industries. Its products enable plants, platforms, and pipelines to manage and control operations more intelligently and efficiently under the most demanding and extreme conditions. The process is essentially an assemble-to-order (ATO) operation, so proper management of component inventory is critical to the success of the operation.

Moreover, the components are obtained from a supply chain that, for some products, has long and variable lead times. When the lead times for the components exceed the customer-quoted lead time for the end item, the firm must forecast the demand of the components. More often than not, these forecasts have very large errors. Thus the firm has an inventory system that requires an extremely high fill rate (all the components must be available before assembly can take place) with large variability in both replenishment times and the forecasted demand.

We have discussed methods of how to deal with these issues in previous chapters. Now we would like to build on previously stated ideas on methods for configuring stock points that are more practical than the traditional ABC method.

Whereas the ABC method typically deals with demand value (part cost × demand), the natural behavior of inventory is determined by demand and replenishment times. If the supplier lead time is less than that offered for the end item to customers, then there is no need for *any* inventory. Indeed, the only inventory will be that left over from reorder quantities (ROQs) larger than immediate demand.

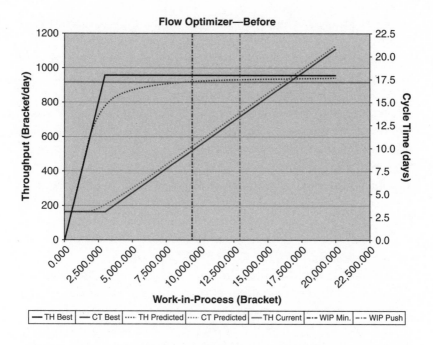

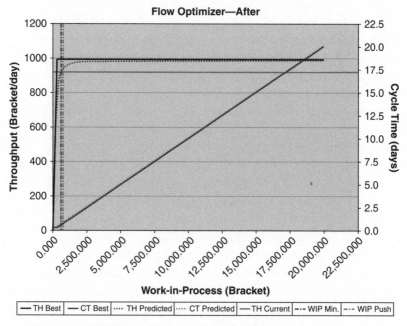

FIGURE 9-8. Before-and-after performance curves

However, when the supplier lead time (including consideration of variability in supplier performance) is greater than that offered to customers, end-item demand must be forecast and then exploded through bills of material (BOMs) to find component demand. As discussed in Chapter 4, the mean square error (MSE) of the forecast will serve as the variance in the end-item demand (as long as the forecast is unbiased). This error is then propagated through the BOM to obtain the variance of the component demand. However, if the supplier's lead time is only somewhat larger than that offered to customers, the variability in demand is effectively reduced because we need to forecast only that portion of demand for which supplier lead time is longer than the customer lead time. Thus it makes sense to divide inventories into long- and short-lead-time categories and optimize these separately.

We can further divide the inventories into two other categories—high and low demand—and create two categories of end items—standard and custom. *Standard items* are those with a large enough demand to warrant relatively large component inventories, thereby providing short lead times to customers. *Custom items*, on the other hand, are end items that are expensive and/or have low demand. It has been our experience that customers do not often expect a supplier to stock special items with low demand (the exception being large retailers and automotive original equipment manufacturers). However, if we can divide our offerings into these two categories, we can greatly reduce inventories.

Considering all these dimensions creates four categories— high demand, long lead time; high demand, short lead time; low demand, long lead time; and low demand short, short lead time. This classification *aligns a manager's inventory management practice with the natural behavior of inventory systems* as described in Chapters 3 and 4 explanations of variance of replenishment time demand. For the short-lead-time items and for the low-demand items, we can live with lower fill rates, provided that the backorder times when we are backordered are short. Thus the only category that requires a high fill rate is the long-lead-time and high-demand category. Such a strategy can greatly reduce total inventory while keeping customer service extremely high.

Because the preceding categories are quite different from the traditional and widely used ABC classification, we should comment on why it is wise to abandon a scheme that has been used for so many years. Joseph Orlicky, often considered the "father of material requirements planning (MRP)," laid out the MRP concepts in his book, *Material Requirements Planning.*[2] In that book, Orlicky cites Dickie[3] as having originated the ABC scheme and comments that the "rationale of ABC classification is the impracticality of giving an equally high degree of attention to the record of every inventory item *due to limited information-processing capacity*" (emphasis his). Thus an "A" category might be the top 5 percent of the items having the largest volume cost and would receive the bulk of the attention of the "planning and control resources." The "B" items (say, the next 15 percent) would receive less attention, but more than the "C" items, which might be ordered only once per year. Then Orlicky dismisses the need for such a system, saying, "With a computer available, this limitation disappears and the ABC concept tends to become irrelevant." However, almost 40 years later, the concept appears to be as popular as ever, and many of the large enterprise resources planning (ERP) providers (e.g., SAP and Oracle) offer software to aid in ABC analysis. Nonetheless, we submit that Orlicky's 40-year-old assessment is more true today than in 1975, given the power of modern computers and that one of the reasons for the continued existence of ABC is that software vendors tend to provide software that makes it *easier to do what is currently being done* rather than providing software that *solves the problem at hand.* Based on our experience with numerous clients, the four categories given earlier provide a much better classification than ABC.

We compared the aforementioned classification with ABC using data from our client that is a division of a Fortune 500 company with hundreds of plants worldwide. The recommended corporate inventory policy is divided into volume-cost categories (like ABC), with demand multipliers for lot size and safety stock, both in terms of days of demand. A hypothetical illustration of this client's strategy would define "A" items to be the top 50 percent of volume cost would have a lot size of 5 days and a safety stock of 7 days of demand, "B" items make up the next 30 percent and use 10 days of demand for both the lot size and the safety stock, and so on.

Figure 9-9 compares this corporate policy as implemented with the optimal policies for 1,672 items. In all cases, the inventory required was significantly lower, whereas the fill rates were either the same or slightly lower in the case of short lead times. At any rate, the expected backorder time given a backorder was not more for any of the items in the optimal cases. The total inventory investment was reduced by approximately 50 percent.

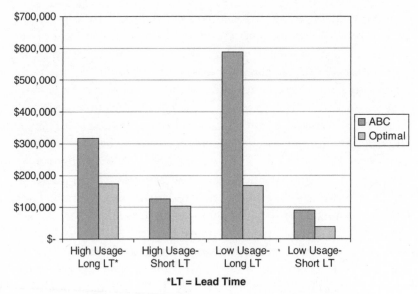

FIGURE 9-9. Comparison of ABC and usage–lead-time inventory policies

We conclude, then, that the ABC classification is a relic from the precomputer age that should be discarded for what are more practical and effective classification schemes based on the natural behavior of inventory systems.

REDUCING CYCLE TIMES IN A TRADITIONAL PHARMACEUTICAL PLANT

The plant is an attractive plant, located in a suburb of a large city in the United States. During the 1990s, the plant won an architectural award for its unobtrusive design and aesthetics. It was a medium-sized plant with around 140,000 square feet with approximately 400 employees. It produced around 40 products comprising 150 different stock-keeping units (SKUs; dosages, number of tablets, language of label, etc.). Two of the products, we will call H and C, had both the largest volumes and were the largest contributors to profit. To make things more complex, the plant had to accommodate small batches from the research and development (R&D) arm of the corporation. Traditional pharmaceutical plant logistics (as opposed to biopharmaceutical) is summarized in Figure 9-10. The steps are weigh ingredients in a clean room, blend the ingredients to make the formulation, compress into

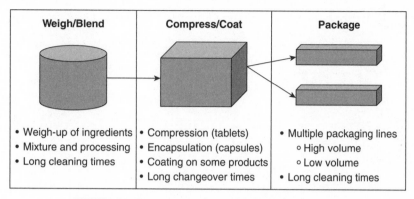

Weigh/Blend	Compress/Coat	Package
• Weigh-up of ingredients	• Compression (tablets)	• Multiple packaging lines
• Mixture and processing	• Encapsulation (capsules)	∘ High volume
• Long cleaning times	• Coating on some products	∘ Low volume
	• Long changeover times	• Long cleaning times

FIGURE 9-10. Overview of traditional pharmaceutical logistics

tablets, coat onto tablets a protective layer (optional), and package the formulation in bottles, blister packs, and so on.

Before applying Factory Physics science, the plant was fairly typical for the industry in that its organizational structure was by function, and there was very little flow. Each department maintained a "hot list" in an attempt to meet customer due dates. Most processes were batch and queue, with more than 90 percent of the cycle time made up of either queue time or extra time caused by large batches. Of course, long cycle times meant a great deal of WIP. But the excess WIP was not apparent because the batches were relatively small even though one tote was worth more than $150,000 (pharmaceutical ingredients can be precious). However, after performing an absolute benchmark study, it was clear that considerable improvement should be possible. Figure 9-11 shows the benchmarking plot. Offhand, it looks like the operation has some problems but not too bad—until we realize that the current points of WIP and throughput are reversed in order. The triangle is associated with cycle time but is closer to the throughput curve than the cycle-time curve, whereas the diamond associated with throughput has similar problems. This indicates that throughput is extremely low and cycle time is extremely high. But it also indicates great potential for improvement.

The ERP system was an old one that was used only to record financial transactions and to manage inventory (with transactions up to three weeks behind). Not surprisingly, there were spreadsheets everywhere. They were used for scheduling, hot lists, and quality and to provide a more up-to-date inventory picture. There was approximately $17 million in WIP, and cycle times were around

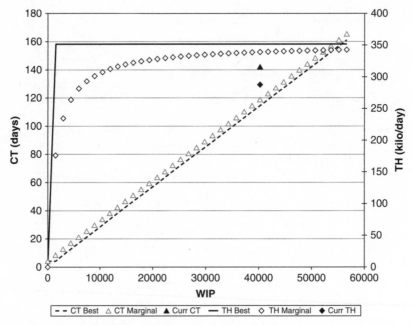

FIGURE 9-11. Absolute benchmark of main products

140 calendar days. The first step was to update the ERP system with good routings and more timely information. Bar-code readers were installed to obtain move transactions in real time. The result was an improvement in inventory accuracy from 75 percent to more than 95 percent within six months. Factory Physics science shows that WIP increases happen some time before the corresponding cycle-times increases—WIP is a leading indicator of cycle time. For predicting cycle time, the most effective approach is to track and control WIP, and this approach was incorporated into the client's practice. Next, the manufacturing organization was organized around *product flows*. Figure 9-12 provides an illustration of product flows in a pharmaceutical plant. The plant then adopted more of a matrix organization with the line management organized along the product flows and the support (engineering, maintenance, etc.) continuing to be organized by process. Although the workforce had always been somewhat cross-trained, this became formalized so that most workers in the product flow could operate any of the processes in that flow. The flow managers then became responsible for on-time delivery, WIP, cycle time, inventory, and staffing. Theirs was the job of balancing the three buffers of time, inventory, and capacity.

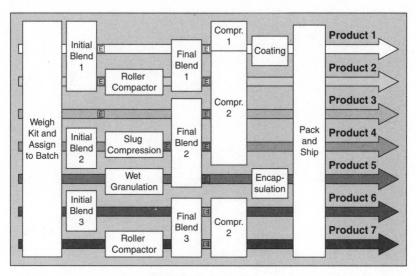

FIGURE 9-12. Product flows

Analysis showed that large batch sizes were the cause of much of the WIP. However, before batch sizes could be reduced, change-over times in the packaging area had to be reduced. Operators were trained in the methods of *single-minute exchange of dye* (SMED) and allowed to be creative in coming up with ways to reduce the change-over at packaging. After three months, the setups were reduced from 470 minutes to around 190 minutes, a 60 percent improvement. This allowed reduction of batch sizes (called *campaigns* in the phar-maceutical industry) significantly. The two large product flows for H and C were further organized using the CONWIP pull protocol (Figure 9-13). Recall that CONWIP allows the release of product only if (1) the MRP system has generated a planned work order with a release date that is today or before today and (2) the total WIP in the product flow is below a set limit. If the WIP exceeds the limit and yet there are work orders scheduled for release, the work orders are held and not released. Of course, such a situation is not sustainable. Indeed, a rising virtual queue of orders to be released is a sign of an infeasible production plan and signals the need for additional capac-ity. Nonetheless, in the short term, a manager is better off holding the release than releasing and causing cycle times to rise.

So the stage was set for a conflict between the new system, CONWIP, and the old, MRP. When this finally happened during the pilot phase of the project, the plant manager went with that which

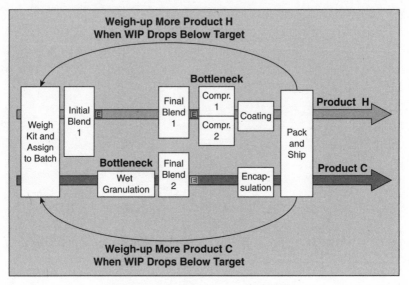

FIGURE 9-13. Work release using CONWIP

was familiar—MRP—and released a great deal of WIP. On our next visit, we noticed the increase in WIP and asked the plant manager if he realized that the almost 50 percent increase in WIP would mean a 50 percent increase in cycle time (Figure 9-14). After some convincing, he grasped the meaning of the decision and announced to his staff, "You all realize that after last week's release, cycle times are going to rise around 50 percent." It was the epiphany we were

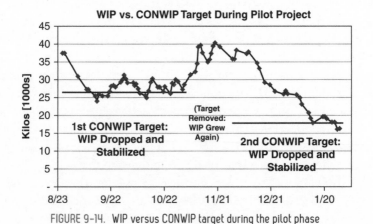

FIGURE 9-14. WIP versus CONWIP target during the pilot phase

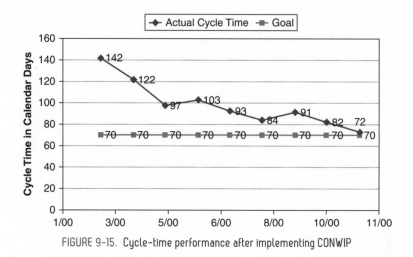

FIGURE 9-15. Cycle-time performance after implementing CONWIP

hoping for. From that point on, the plant used the CONWIP system with MRP, and cycle times steadily fell, as can be seen in Figure 9-15. The final results were:

- Cycle times cut in half for the high-value products
- A reduction of $10 million in WIP
- On-time delivery improvement from around 75 percent to almost 100 percent
- An increase in plant output of roughly 23 percent

After the project, Glenn Gerecke, the plant manager, stated, "There is no doubt that optimum WIP levels lead to a more efficient operation with less working capital exposure. Our customer delivery performance and our operational flexibility have improved dramatically by managing WIP levels throughout the operation. We are continuing to apply Factory Physics principles and are expecting further improvement."

RESTORING CUSTOMER SERVICE IN A FABRICATION AND ASSEMBLY PLANT

Moog, Inc., began more than 50 years ago as a designer and supplier of aircraft and missile components. Today Moog's motion-control technology enhances performance in a variety of markets and applications from commercial aircraft cockpits, to power-generation turbines, to Formula One racing, to medical infusion systems.

In 2002, the Industrial Controls Division of Moog, Inc., was facing a crisis. This division designed and manufactured a variety of products for industrial applications, including precision control valves, hydraulic manifold systems, and electric motors and drives. The division was having significant problems meeting customer due dates and was in danger of losing market share to its competitors. Customers were demanding price reductions as the cost of materials and production continued to rise. Manufacturing cycle times averaged 16 weeks, whereas the market was demanding 2- to 4-week lead times. The manufacturing process involved fabrication, subassembly, final assembly, and test in a configure-to-order environment.

Moog had already started a Lean manufacturing initiative with help from one of its largest customers, Boeing. The company had started a 5S housekeeping program, organized the floor into manufacturing cells, and begun working on reducing setup times. But the problem of poor customer service was not being resolved, and the number of projects (*kaizens*) needed to become truly lean was huge. More important, Moog management did not believe that it had time to wait for the benefits from its Lean initiative. The company needed better on-time delivery *now.*

George Cameron, materials manager, was one of a number of managers from Moog who had attended a Factory Physics seminar and thought that it seemed like a good tool for understanding the principles of manufacturing and assisting with improvements. He decided to call in Factory Physics Inc., to perform an assessment of the one of Moog's plants. The assessment provided a road map that would first focus on improving delivery by rearranging the existing variability buffers and then focus on reducing waste in the fabrication area.

The basic idea was to insulate fabrication from assembly and test by putting an inventory buffer between the two. To some, this sounded like heresy! Inventory is waste. Why add waste to the process?

But the rationale was simple—you do not operate on a gall bladder when the patient is bleeding to death! Stop the bleeding first. If the poor on-time delivery continued, it could have a very negative effect on revenue.

Thus the first step was to perform Pareto analysis to determine the high-volume parts. Then a supermarket stock was created that fabrication would maintain using a ROP, ROQ pull system. Assembly and test would build the final product from the components in stock based on customer orders. The effect would be reduced lead time to the customer (now only the cycle time in assembly and test) and much greater customer service. The model was first piloted in the torque motor subassembly cell. Variability in supply and demand was buffered with an inventory of about 180 part numbers in the cell that was used to create over 1,000 unique torque motors. As the process became more stable, Moog started to lower inventory levels and change to a first-in, first-out (FIFO) process. The next step was to move back to parts supply to further reduce buffers as variability was reduced. Finally, once customer service improved, focus was shifted to the problems in fabrication. To avoid adding too much inventory, Moog wanted to avoid using a traditional supermarket controlled by *kanban*. Instead, the Factory Physics, Inc., team employed an early version of the Factory Physics CSUITE inventory optimizer to set inventory policies using a ROP, ROQ model, as seen in Figure 9-16. Notice how much more effective an optimal strategy is than using

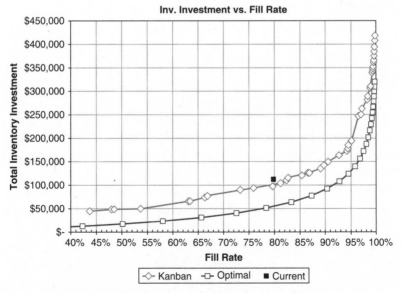

FIGURE 9-16. Inventory optimizer tradeoff plots

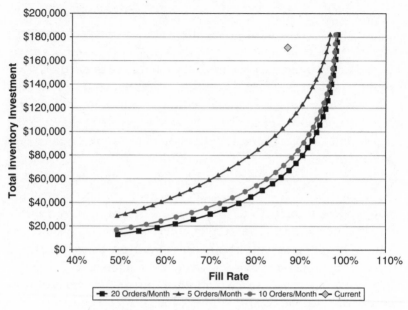

FIGURE 9-17. Inventory optimizer tradeoff plot

kanban, particularly for high fill rates. At a 98.2 percent fill rate, *kan-ban* requires more than $281,000 in inventory, whereas the optimal policy requires slightly more than $200,000 for 98.4 percent fill rate.

A slightly different version of the tool (and what became the CSUITE inventory optimizer) made it extremely easy to quantify the tradeoffs among fill rate, inventory investment, and number of setups in the cell. Figure 9-17 illustrates this tradeoff plot. Here the three different curves represent different numbers of setups (orders/month). As the number of setups increases, the inventory investment needed to achieve the same fill rate decreases. This was a great help to Moog in deciding how much setup reduction was needed. Selecting a point on the plot then generated an optimal policy, which was used to set inventory order quantities and reorder points for each part number needed for the cell.

Employees were then trained in basic Factory Physics principles and Lean manufacturing techniques during a one-week accelerated improvement workshop. One component of the workshop was the Factory Physics paper-house exercise, which was used to help supervisors and operators understand how and why a pull system works. Following the training, operators and management made changes on the shop floor to prepare the cell for a pull system.

After learning about the importance of bottlenecks, the operators changed the way they ran the cell. Formerly, an operator would perform a task on 60 parts before moving them to the next station. The operators suggested reducing this move batch significantly. They also realized that keeping the bottleneck busy was not that difficult and implemented a simple rule—keep the electrical discharge machine (EDM) busy. They quickly realized that WIP needed to move quickly through the cell and that there needed to be a queue of work before the EDM. Because the EDM was a pretty sharp bottleneck, this was not terribly difficult. Nonetheless, these simple rules increased productivity by 7 percent at a time when lot sizes were being reduced.

The results from this approach substantially improved customer service. Cycle times in the cell went from 12 to 3 days while improving on-time delivery from less than 50 percent to over 95 percent. Even better was the unexpected 7 percent boost in productivity. Although an inventory buffer had been added in the cell, the overall inventory levels dropped over 15 percent. After this initial success integrating Factory Physics science and Lean, the company moved to another subassembly cell and repeated the process. With both subassembly cells using Factory Physics WIP control and setting inventory levels using the Factory Physics inventory optimizer, cycle times to the customer went from 23 to 6 days.

George Cameron summarized the challenges and lessons learned in a presentation to management the following year:

The challenges were and are:

1. *People have memory and want to return to "the way things used to be," even in the face of a successful change.*
2. *The shop had to be convinced that working to fill a bin is just as important as filling a work order.*
3. *A system to regularly review inventory levels should be in place.*

The lessons learned:

1. *Factory Physics modeling actually works!*
2. *It is relatively easy to quantify the inventory investment/fill-rate/ setup-frequency tradeoff.*
3. *The employees understand the concepts. Streamline the process → smaller lots → shorter cycle times → FIFO → smoother consumption → less inventory.*

INCREASING THROUGHPUT IN A BIOPHARMACEUTICAL FACILITY _____

Plant Eli Lilly and Company was founded in 1876 by Colonel Eli Lilly, a chemist and veteran of the Civil War. Lilly was the first company to mass produce penicillin, the Salk polio vaccine, and insulin, including one of the first pharmaceutical companies to produce human insulin using recombinant DNA. It was the human insulin line to which we applied Factory Physics science to increase output without large capital expenditures. The details of this example are disguised and contain no proprietary information regarding process times, demand, setup times, and so on. The purpose of this case is to describe how a basic Factory Physics understanding is all that is needed to determine effective ways to increase throughput. The process involves the batch fermentation of an organism in a growth medium until a sufficient concentration is obtained. Then the medium is switched to a perfusion medium that causes the organism to excrete the desired protein into the solution. The protein is then extracted from the solution using a chromatographic process that binds the protein into a column of capture medium. The captured medium then undergoes a number of purification steps known as *downstream processing.*

The capacity of the fermentation process is established by the number of fermentation vessels that are available. The remainder of the process is tightly coupled and limits the overall capacity of the plant. The process time for the capture was 42 hours, with the remaining four processes having 20, 29, 35, and 34 hours, respectively. Thus the capture is the bottleneck. The plant works 315 days per year 24 hours per day, yielding 7,560 hours available per year. If one batch is produced every 42 hours, the theoretical output should be 180 batches per year. Currently, the plant is producing 179 batches per year—very close to the theoretical.

Currently, the capture uses a 200-L vessel in a five-cycle process. The proposal is to change to a four-cycle process using a 250-L vessel. The capture time goes from 42 to 35 hours and should result in a 20 percent increase in throughput, or 216 batches per year. However, when this was tried, it only resulted in 195 batches per year. Why? By now, you know the answer—*variability*. When the capture time was 42 hours and the next longest was 35 hours, the line had a significant (20 percent) capacity buffer to accommodate the variability. However, when the capture time was matched to the same as the downstream process, there was zero capacity buffer—both processes were bottlenecks. Thus there was nothing to buffer the variability.

However, if a small amount of interstate storage (enough for one batch) is added between each process, the throughput increases significantly from 195 to 215.6 per year, which is 20.4 percent above the current process and 10.6 percent above what was achieved without the extra storage.

It will cost around $1.5 million to modify the capture process, and each storage vessel costs around $100,000. Moreover, each batch is worth approximately $1.1 million, and there is a market for $200 million per year. So the first improvement will yield additional revenue of $17.76 million for an investment of $1.5 million, or 1,184 percent return on investment (ROI). The second is less attractive because of the market limit of $200 million per year. Nonetheless, the revenue increase from the first improvement is still $5.55 million at a cost of only $500,000, or an ROI of 1,110 percent. Clearly, both changes should be made to the line.

At the conclusion of the project, Mike Eagle, former vice president of Eli Lilly, stated, "[The Factory Physics approach] was a key ingredient in the strategy at Lilly in the 1990s. . . . It helped Lilly double production volume and sales in five years with a year-on-year reduction in new capital spending in each of those years."

DYNAMIC RISK-BASED SCHEDULING IN THE TEXTILE INDUSTRY

The Dixie Group (TDG) began in 1920 as the Dixie Mercerizing Company, headquartered in Chattanooga, Tennessee. Mercerized cotton, long popular in England because of its silklike luster, was not then widely used in the United States. In the late 1980s, the textile industry was facing its toughest times because of stiff foreign competition, changing markets, and the requirements for heavy investment in modernization of facilities. Dixie began a restructuring plan that included selling, closing, or consolidating facilities that did not fit its strategic plan for the future. In 2003, TDG sold its broadloom carpet, needlebond, and carpet recycling operations that served the factory-built housing, indoor/outdoor, and carpet-pad markets. The company became concentrated in the higher-end segments of the soft floor-covering markets, where it has been more successful and has greater growth potential. Of course, higher end means more variety and lower volumes per SKU, and it became harder and harder to manage inventories and to plan production. In 2010, TDG sought help in gaining control over the complexity of the business. At that time, it was common knowledge that traditional MRP would not work in the carpet industry for one simple reason—dye-lot integrity. Using traditional MRP, if a company had an order for 100 units of a product with two lots in stock, one having 60 units and the other having 50 units, the order would be considered covered. Not so in the textile industry. If two rolls of carpet were produced in different *dye lots*, it was unlikely they would match well enough, even though the two rolls were of exactly the same SKU. The dye technology simply was not able to match colors well enough to allow an adjacent application. Thus, when TDG called Factory Physics Inc. (FPI), it was to be a learning experience for both companies. In the end, FPI did create an MRP application that maintained dye-lot integrity. It also did something more. The textile industry MRP design enabled TDG to optimize lot-sizing and safety-stock parameters used in the MRP system and provided a production flow manager for day-to-day execution. The tufting production planning system (TPPS) is a special instance of dynamic risk-based scheduling (DRS) discussed in Chapter 7. DRS is also known as *Factory Physics planning and scheduling*. At TDG, the TPPS was used as a "bolt-on" to the existing ERP system. DRS is not simply a software application. It is a combination of software, hardware, and a set of production rules that allows a production line to run *without* detailed scheduling.

The steps of DRS are:

1. Plan capacity utilization by flow by period. Make outsourcing and overtime decisions.
2. Optimize dynamic scheduling parameters:
   a. Using customer demand and forecast, determine optimal lot sizes, safety stocks, and planned lead times.
   b. Load optimal parameters into the MRP system.
3. Create planned work orders (PWOs). Using traditional MRP operating with optimal parameters, create planned work orders but do not release.
4. Execute:
   a. Release PWOs according to CONWIP.
   b. Monitor completion times and the virtual queue.
   c. Decide whether recourse capacity is needed or not.

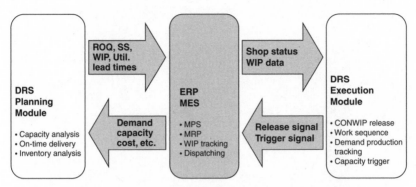

FIGURE 9-18. Schematic of dynamic risk-based scheduling

The schematic in Figure 9-18 shows how the components of DRS work with any ERP system with or without a manufacturing execution system (MES).

The TPPS developed for TDG performed these steps in the following sequence:

1. **Weekly:** Plan capacity:
   a. Compute utilization.
   b. Move demand from more highly utilized machines to other machines that are able to process the product with lower utilization.
2. **Weekly:** Optimize MRP parameters:
   a. Using the CSUITE cash-flow optimizer, determine optimal parameters for lot sizes, lead times, and safety stocks.
   b. Review and accept or reject.
   c. Load into the ERP system.
3. **Daily:** Use the TPPS system to create planned work orders: review, accept, and load into the ERP system.
4. **Daily:** Use the production flow manager for execution:
   a. Load active work orders from the ERP system.
   b. Load planned work orders from the TPPS.
   c. Prepare a report of each product flow:
      i. Timeliness of each work order
      ii. Labor requirements
   d. Print sequence of work for each production flow, and distribute to plant floor.

Figure 9-19 presents a report showing the utilization of all the process flows in the plant. Note that the highest utilization appears at

Equal To or Above Maximum Utilization   Within 10% of Maximum Utilization

Rows per Page: 20 ⌄ Page 1 of 3 Find: ____   Options ⌄

Item Details	Machine	Description	Throughput (Units/Day)	Rate (Units/Day)	Total Utilization	Utilization w/o Setups	Time Available	Time Used
☐	T48		213.141	177.011	120.41 %	9.88 %	1911.000	2301.051
☐	T07		170.133	158.049	107.65 %	6.82 %	1911.000	2057.116
☐	T20		549.150	541.371	101.44 %	36.12 %	1911.000	1938.457
☐	T22		519.248	513.762	101.07 %	35.46 %	1911.000	1931.406
☐	T62		225.217	252.680	89.13 %	10.20 %	1911.000	1703.298
☐	T53		517.640	632.713	81.81 %	26.59 %	1911.000	1563.444
☐	T13		1196.229	1465.561	81.62 %	50.49 %	1911.000	1559.808
☐	T46		2139.387	2691.224	79.49 %	77.46 %	1911.000	1519.149
☐	T05		631.579	805.115	78.45 %	60.38 %	1911.000	1499.100
☐	T24		889.913	1148.041	77.52 %	77.11 %	1911.000	1481.327
☐	T19		628.641	905.903	69.39 %	35.75 %	1911.000	1326.115
☐	T23		1055.928	1523.465	69.31 %	68.40 %	1911.000	1324.533
☐	T12		1147.935	1953.310	58.77 %	42.50 %	1911.000	1123.070
☐	T01		1065.205	2040.288	52.21 %	49.58 %	1911.000	997.706
☐	T21		399.260	793.254	50.33 %	23.62 %	1911.000	961.843
☐	T06		321.897	705.821	45.61 %	16.66 %	1911.000	871.532
☐	T40		64.858	142.639	45.47 %	5.31 %	1911.000	868.937
☐	T36		316.368	703.996	44.94 %	24.86 %	1911.000	858.782
☐	T43		548.757	1296.146	42.34 %	28.72 %	1911.000	809.071
☐	T29		468.433	1162.358	40.30 %	36.26 %	1911.000	770.137

FIGURE 9-19. Utilization report

OEE Analysis		Product Flow	Units of Measure	Throughput (units/day)	Bottleneck Rate (units/day)	Bottleneck Type	Process Center Bottleneck	Utilization
☐	🔍	T48	LF	238.0000	242.4157	Process Center	T48	98.18 %
☐	🔍	T11	LF	1992.1429	2084.5820	Process Center	T11	95.57 %
☐	🔍	T12	LF	1564.2180	1743.6760	Process Center	T12	89.71 %
☐	🔍	T43	LF	835.7669	933.5615	Process Center	T43	89.52 %
☐	🔍	E23	LF	1042.9850	1209.1414	Process Center	E23	86.26 %
☐	🔍	T58	LF	930.0376	1150.9302	Process Center	T58	80.81 %
☐	🔍	T20	LF	496.6767	653.2228	Process Center	T20	76.03 %
☐	🔍	T62	LF	258.1053	344.6340	Process Center	T62	74.89 %
☐	🔍	T22	LF	553.6466	746.7463	Process Center	T22	74.14 %
☐	🔍	E29	LF	479.7669	655.0834	Process Center	OPERATOR	73.24 %
☐	🔍	T03	LF	287.5639	392.6455	Process Center	OPERATOR	73.24 %
☐	🔍	T01	LF	435.4361	594.5532	Process Center	OPERATOR	73.24 %
☐	🔍	T21	LF	385.3759	526.2000	Process Center	OPERATOR	73.24 %
☐	🔍	T08	LF	34.9248	47.6870	Process Center	OPERATOR	73.24 %
☐	🔍	T07	LF	169.1504	230.9613	Process Center	OPERATOR	73.24 %
☐	🔍	E26	LF	303.4962	414.3999	Process Center	OPERATOR	73.24 %
☐	🔍	T14	LF	237.7820	324.6723	Process Center	OPERATOR	73.24 %
☐	🔍	T15	LF	36.0902	49.2783	Process Center	OPERATOR	73.24 %
☐	🔍	T13	LF	597.2331	815.4740	Process Center	OPERATOR	73.24 %
☐	🔍	T16	LF	23.4586	32.0309	Process Center	OPERATOR	73.24 %

FIGURE 9-20. Utilization report after rebalancing

the top of the list, with more than 120 percent. By hitting the "Item Details" icon, the planner can see which items are contributing to the utilization and whether there are alternative machines for those items. If so, the planner will move them off the over-utilized machine and onto a less-utilized machine. Once all the utilizations are below a given level, say, 100 percent, the plan is capacity feasible and ready to provide input for the parameter utilization.

Once there is a feasible capacity plan, a manager can optimize the parameters used. Figure 9-20 shows the utilizations rebalancing. Figure 9-21 highlights the performance before the optimization. The

Showing Current Values

Cycle Time and Throughput

Average Cycle Time (days)	Throughput (units per day)		Total WIP + Inv. Carrying Cost	Total Setup Cost	Total Cost
				Costs	
27.98	17,884.92		$1,807,274.29	$633,821.75	$2,441,096.04

Inventory and WIP

Total WIP Count	Total Inventory Count	Total Value of WIP	Total Value of Inventory	Total Value of WIP + Inventory
500,331.76	1,300,142.70	$6,305,125.13	$16,325,238.96	$22,630,364.09

Stock Point ID	Description	Items in Stockpoint	Demand	Predicted Value of Inventory	Avg. No. of Reorders (units)	Avg. Backorder Days (when short)
Greige MTO	Greige to Order	9	27,879.65	$81,931.11	12.84	7.60
Greige MTS	Greige to Stock	134	1,263,021.20	$13,053,933.42	304.59	7.32
FG MTS	Finished Goods to Stock	28	34,160.10	$134,317.22	84.08	8.23
FG MTO	Finished Goods to Order	594	934,699.30	$3,055,057.21	2390.96	9.72

FIGURE 9-21. Performance before optimization

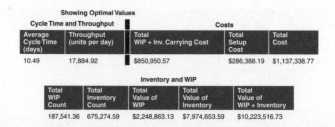

Showing Optimal Values

Average Cycle Time (days)	Throughput (units per day)		Total WIP + Inv. Carrying Cost	Total Setup Cost	Total Cost
		Cycle Time and Throughput — Costs			
10.49	17,884.92		$850,950.57	$286,388.19	$1,137,338.77

Inventory and WIP

Total WIP Count	Total Inventory Count	Total Value of WIP	Total Value of Inventory	Total Value of WIP + Inventory
187,541.36	675,274.59	$2,248,863.13	$7,974,653.59	$10,223,516.73

Stock Point ID	Description	Items in Stockpoint	Demand	Predicted Value of Inventory	Avg. No. of Reorders (units)	Avg. Backorder Days (when short)
Greige MTO	Greige to Order	9	27,879.65	$81,033.48	12.84	7.60
Greige MTS	Greige to Stock	134	1,263,021.20	$4,289,799.77	304.59	7.32
FG MTS	Finished Goods to Stock	28	34,160.10	$149,247.25	84.08	8.23
FG MTO	Finished Goods to Order	594	934,699.30	$3,454,573.09	2390.96	9.72

FIGURE 9-22. Performance after optimization

average cycle time is 28 days, whereas the total value of WIP and finished inventory is almost $23 million. The out-of-pocket cost (due to scrap loss during changeovers) is almost $634,000.

Figure 9-22 shows the performance after the optimization. Cycle times are now around 10.5 days, and the total WIP and inventory investment is just over $10 million, whereas scrap cost has come down to $286,000. Figure 9-23 shows performance curves both before and after optimization.

These parameters will now be reviewed, accepted or rejected, and then loaded into the ERP system. The example described here used real data and actual policies that had been in place. Of course, it will take a while for the effect of the new policies to be seen. Moreover, such improvements are typically only possible for systems that have never been optimized. The next week should not be very different from this week. However, with more than 100,000 SKUs, it took a long time before all the SKUs were active during optimization. In systems with fewer SKUs, this should take much less time.

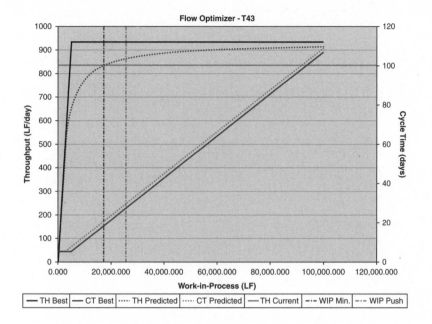

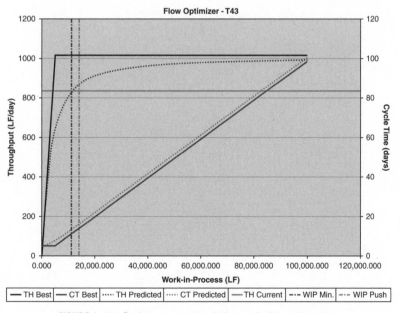

FIGURE 9-23. Performance curves before and after optimization

CHAPTER 10

Final Word on Factory Physics Science (for Now)

A truly good book teaches me better than to read it. I must soon lay it down, and commence living on its hint. What I began by reading, I must finish by acting.

—Henry David Thoreau

We wrote this book to lay out a comprehensive, practical science for managing manufacturing, service, and supply-chain operations. In Chapter 3 we referred to the idea of conjecture and refutation as a way to advance ideas by testing them in practice to see which ones hold up as predictors of performance. While Karl Popper supported the idea that good science was always trying to refute its own conclusions, a more famous author, Thomas Kuhn, suggested that "normal science" operated within the limits of a prevailing paradigm with little questioning until overwhelming new data caused the scientific community to overthrow the model in what Kuhn termed as a "paradigm shift."[1] We believe that Kuhn's is a more accurate description of the history of science, whereas Popper's is a better account of the logic of science. Indeed, a common logical mistake known as the *fallacy of affirming the consequent* goes something like this: theory A predicts observation X. Observation X is confirmed. Therefore, theory A is true. This does indeed appear to be the way "normal science" works. And it is completely invalid. Ptolemy's geocentric view of the universe is very good at predicting the movements of the planets of our solar system and, of course, is completely wrong. That incorrect theory A predicts an accurate observation does not preclude correct theory B from also predicting the same observation. The only problem is that there is no way to know that theory B is indeed the correct theory, only that we cannot refute it—yet. This fact is also reflected in the history of science, which appears to be a continual repetition of, "We used to believe A, but now we know B." Sometime later C is discovered, and the progression becomes, "We used to believe B, but now we know C." Given that we can never prove theories, we should always be trying to refute them. This is how we progress.

Actually Popper and Kuhn were not all that different. When data cause a refutation that results in a minor tweak of the current paradigm, Kuhn calls it "normal science," whereas Popper calls it a refutation. When data cause a paradigm shift, Kuhn calls this a paradigm shift, whereas Popper calls it a refutation.

It is our observation that the science of operations has been locked in the grip of two major paradigms for decades. One of the existing paradigms is the *continuous-improvement paradigm*. This is the idea that performance advances by training many people in the company on tools and techniques that have been used successfully at other companies. The other paradigm is the *manufacturing requirements planning (MRP)/advanced planning and scheduling (APS)/ information technology (IT) paradigm*, which promotes the idea that computer software can solve all problems if managers would only use the software properly. This book has provided refutations for these paradigms and conjectures for a new paradigm.

Breaking these existing paradigms depends on you, dear reader. The point is not to break the paradigms and end the use of either continuous-improvement initiatives or MRP/APS/IT systems. The point is to break through to a new paradigm of comprehensive science that accurately and practically describes the natural behavior of manufacturing, service, and supply-chain operations. In this new paradigm, science guides managers in the most appropriate use of continuous-improvement efforts and MRP/APS and other IT systems rather than the other way around. We have demonstrated the validity of these new ideas through decades of application in practice. You now have the theories (recall the Chapter 1 definition of theory) needed to form and execute the best possible business management paradigm for your unique business.

Nonetheless, if there are refutations, we want to hear them because we believe that they will only make the new paradigm stronger. The fact is that both *initiative by imitation* and *solution by software* have, in many cases, proven to be less than effective. We look forward to a community effort of advancing a more practical, comprehensive science of operations to help managers manage better.

To review that science in closing, its progression is as follows:

1. The goals of any business are sustained profit and cash flow attained by moral means and to noble ends.
2. The essence of all values streams, supply chains, processes, and so on is some form of transformation satisfying some kind of demand.
3. The structural elements of all values streams, supply chains, processes, and so on are stocks and flows. Production is a flow into a stock and demand is a flow out of a stock.
4. If there were no variability, demand and transformation could be perfectly synchronized, yielding maximum profit and cash flow—but there is *always* variability.
5. In the presence of variability, buffers are required to synchronize demand and transformation.
6. There are only three buffers—inventory, capacity, and time.
7. Increasing variability requires increases in buffers to synchronize demand and transformation. However, if the revenue generated by an increase in variability exceeds the cost of the commensurate buffering increase, increasing variability is a good thing.
8. Performance boundaries can be calculated for stocks and production flows for predictive determination of optimal performance of inventory, capacity, and time (service).
9. The ability of managers to strategically select a position within or on performance boundaries enables use of the *demand-stock-production construct* to design a buffer portfolio for most profitable variability management.
10. Further, the ability to select positions within performance boundaries translates into policies and tactics that managers can use to lead an organization to achieve desired performance. In addition, the relative position of an organization's actual performance versus desired performance provides a gap analysis that very specifically focuses continuous-improvement resources on the projects of highest value and impact.
11. Factory Physics tactics and controls ensure that the organization, down to an individual level, is performing within the ranges specified by the manager's strategic choices.

12. These tactics and controls can be standardized within an organization's existing IT system (regardless of IT vendor) to transform the IT system from a transaction-tracking system to a performance-control system.

In particular, Factory Physics science enables an organization to determine quantitatively where it is versus where it could be for the performance of its stocks and production flows—something we call *absolute benchmarking*. Once those performance boundaries are established and target performance levels (e.g., fill rate, cycle time, throughput, cost, inventory dollars, etc.) are determined, the Factory Physics approach provides the mechanics to use the existing IT system as a performance-control system rather than merely a transaction-tracking system, as is so widely the case today.

The Factory Physics framework provides executives and managers with an approach to predictably achieve high cash flow, low cost, and excellent customer service. With apologies to those in service industries, we realize the treatment of service businesses has been brief. We will address that in more detail in later books. However, the science described in Chapters 3 and 4 of this book can be put to work immediately in all types of businesses.

QUICK WINS

A key tenet of this book is that *initiative by imitation*, where one company copies another company's tactics, is not the best approach for quickly achieving results in a manager's own unique environment. We have provided the science behind operations behavior so that managers can choose the right tactics and controls for their companies. Based on our experience, we want to highlight some of the science in the Factory Physics approach that can be implemented fairly quickly so that managers can start to apply the concepts immediately in their operations. We suggest the following areas as places that can be analyzed at a basic level with immediate opportunities for action. They include:

- Operations strategy alignment with business strategy
- Absolute benchmarking
- High-level assessment of utilization
- Bottleneck analysis

- Potential for work-in-process (WIP) cap deployment
- High-level analysis of lead times
- Enterprise resources planning (ERP)/MRP mechanics

Following is a brief description of ways to get started in each of these areas.

Operations Strategy Alignment with Business Strategy

Recall the CEO from the Chapter 7 section "Utilization," whose company had a stated strategy of world-class customer responsiveness. However, when confronted with the utilization versus cycle time curve and an opportunity to cut lead times in half by dropping utilization targets to 92 percent for a small increase in the cost of capacity, the CEO stated, "I'm not going to do that until marketing can show me the benefit of responsiveness in terms of increased sales and/ or higher pricing. Perhaps responsiveness isn't really our strategy." Executives should always be checking alignment between business and operations strategies. One way to check alignment is to review metrics driving behavior and compare how these align with stated strategy. For example, if the stated strategy is focused on customer service, does a company measure on-time delivery and average days late? Does it use due-date quoting for customer lead times or have capacity triggers so that adjustments can be made based on changing status of operations? Often, poor results are not the result of poor execution, but instead the fact that operations strategy is disconnected from the stated business strategy.

Absolute Benchmarking

In Chapters 3 and 9 we described use of absolute benchmarking to provide an indication of how well a production flow is performing compared with a best and a marginal level of performance. A quick absolute benchmarking analysis requires only four pieces of data for the flow:

- Bottleneck rate
- Average raw process time
- Current throughput (which should be the demand)
- Current WIP level.

This is in contrast to a full production flow absolute benchmark completed by modeling all the performance data of a flow (individual process times, setup times for each product at each process center, etc). The first two data for a quick absolute benchmark allow one to create a best-case curve and a marginal-case curve of throughput versus WIP and, using Little's law, cycle time versus WIP. The last two data provide a point on these curves for comparison of current performance to performance boundaries. For such a small amount of data, a great deal can be learned:

- If the WIP is near or below the critical WIP, then throughput can be significantly increased by increasing WIP. However, this will also result in an increase in cycle time. But, if the cycle times are short, this may be a better alternative than adding extra capacity.
- If WIP is well into the flat part of the marginal performance throughput curve, then cycle time can be reduced by simply reducing and capping WIP (see below) without much loss of throughput.
- A point lying below the marginal throughput curve indicates high variability or very large batches. An investigation will quickly reveal which, if not both, are the causes. Once identified, the appropriate action to remedy the problem will usually be apparent.

High-Level Assessment of Utilization

Capacity is a first-order effect. If a company has too much open capacity, the business won't make money. If it has too little capacity, the business won't be responsive enough or will be forced to carry a lot of inventory to be responsive. Without enough capacity in the supply chain, a company won't even be able to generate enough inventory to be responsive with inventory. A quick hitter for executives is to think about the level of utilization in their own facility and across their supply chains to ensure that they are on the "right spot" on the curve shown in Figure 10-1 to support the chosen business strategy.

Bottleneck Analysis

Because the science of operations shows that the output of a facility is limited by the effective capacity of a fully utilized bottleneck,

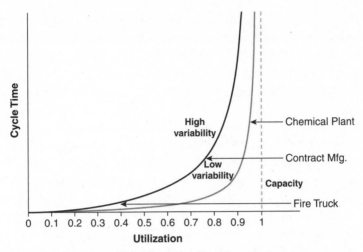

FIGURE 10-1. Utilization targets for different businesses

executives should check to see that bottlenecks are not unintentionally starved. This is easy to do. For example, we once walked through a facility where immediately prior to the bottleneck, batching was done in the name of labor efficiency. The bottleneck was a testing operation. Parts waited to form a batch before the bottleneck until, once a day, an operator moved the batch into the testing operation. Thus the testing operation was sometimes starved, and output declined. Managers should continually check the process flow into and utilization of bottlenecks to ensure that output is not unintentionally constrained. Again, this is easy. Determine what the bottleneck operation is. This is sometimes easier said than done with varying product mixes, but a manager should be determining the long-term bottleneck (for instance, based on monthly demand), *not* reacting to today's (temporary) problem work center. Walk out on the floor a couple or three times a week to see if the specified constraint operation is actually running. If it is not, either the manager has not specified the right constraint or there is poor management of the constraint. Simple remedies, such as having a floating worker spell bottleneck workers over breaks and lunches, can greatly increase throughput with little expense.

There is one caveat to this. If a manager is working in an industry where low utilization is common, then the bottleneck will not be running all the time. For instance, it's not unusual in the electronics manufacturing services industry (EMS) for companies to have

50 percent capacity utilization. In this case, an executive would expect to see the constraint operation running only on half the visits to the shop floor. Still, if the constraint is running only 30 percent of the visits, problems remain with either understanding of constraints or constraint management.

Potential for WIP Cap Deployment

Little's law reveals that cycle time is directly correlated with WIP. Lean manufacturing "pull" systems work because they constrain WIP. There are many ways to limit WIP. Sometimes the most effective solution is not the most complex solution. For example, CONWIP is a simple, robust way to implement a WIP cap. Executives who have not implemented Lean should consider whether or not predictive and reduced cycle times would advance their business strategy. If so, those executives should look for places to limit WIP with one of the forms of WIP caps discussed in this book. Executives already deploying Lean should consider the complexity of their existing implementation and current results. Are they unintentionally starving the bottleneck with a *kanban* system that is too restrictive on WIP? Do they carry too much inventory in the *kanban* supermarkets? Is the environment a low-volume, high-mix one where it is difficult to maintain a *kanban* supermarket? If the answer to any of these questions is yes, then the use of a simple CONWIP strategy should greatly improve operations.

High-Level Analysis of Lead Times

We often find that companies have somewhat arbitrary lead times. This is often true with "standard" lead times. This can lead to poor service or excess cost depending on the operating environment at a given company. Executives should consider options for adjusting lead times in view of the characteristics of their company's market and their internal operations capability. Using the time buffer where possible will reduce the cost of the inventory and capacity buffer. On this note, we find it useful to look at the demand profile for various products that are offered. Some products are standard in the market and require quick lead times. Other products are considered custom, and customers are often willing to wait. Executives should segment product lead times based on market requirements. The "one size fits all" approach to lead time leaves money on the table.

Finally, make sure that measures and targets align with chosen market segments. We see many companies that segment lead times but then use one, arbitrary measure and target to assess performance. For example, same-day quick-ship programs for spare parts may require 99+ percent on-time delivery. However, such a high service level is probably not appropriate for delivery of custom products, nor would it be appropriate for projects or prototypes.

Moreover, targets based on percent on-time delivery alone are often not appropriate. For instance, for business-to-business customers, it might be better to have a target of 90 percent fill rate with an average days late of one day than a 99+ percent fill rate with an average days late of two weeks. Of course, in retail, if the product is not there when the customer wants it, it is usually a lost sale. So it is very important to have the right performance measure for a given situation.

ERP/MRP Mechanics

Chapter 7 discussed the mechanics behind ERP/MRP planning. Executives should check to see how inputs to the ERP/MRP system were determined and how often they are refreshed. This can be accomplished by picking a few items and following their planning and transaction history in the ERP/MRP system. If existing polices aren't aligned with strategy or seem outdated, it might be worthwhile to consider an initiative to perform regular updating of these inputs.

In conclusion, executives should quickly review their current strategies and initiatives in the areas discussed here. Doing so will provide a quick assessment of potential opportunities to use the Factory Physics science of operations to improve their business.

MORE COMPLEX IMPLEMENTATIONS

Some areas require more detailed analysis to develop effective strategy, tactics, and controls. These areas require the use of the math behind the science to develop quantified tactics and controls. They include:

- Utilization targets and cycle times
- Inventory optimization

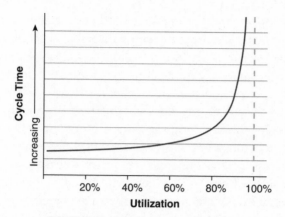

FIGURE 10-2. Utilization versus cycle time

- Optimal batch sizing
- Dynamic risk-based scheduling parameters

A common characteristic of each of these decisions is that the environment, as well as the policies used to deploy tactics, can be characterized by the curves shown in Figures 10-2 through 10-4.

We find that, for many people, the understanding these curves convey is not intuitive, particularly the curves governing cycle time

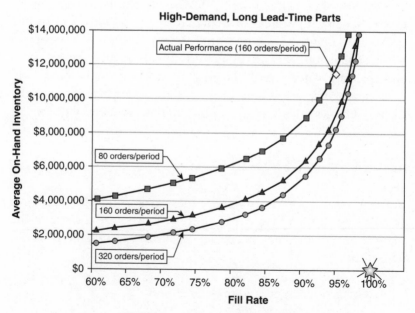

FIGURE 10-3. Inventory versus fill rate

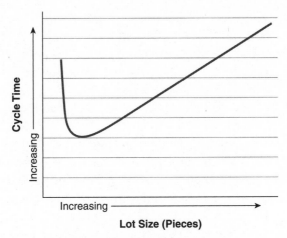

FIGURE 10-4. Lot size versus cycle time

and inventory as utilization and fill rates approach 100 percent. To better inform decision making, mathematical analysis based on Factory Physics science should be performed in these areas. As stated, intuitive knowledge of the dynamics of the Factory Physics performance curves can lead to better decision making, but in complex situations, it may be necessary to have a good model. Executives have options for this type of analysis. For more mathematical detail on the contents of this book, they can consult the *Factory Physics* textbook, and to perform the analysis, they will need to hire consultants or employees trained in operations research and industrial engineering. Alternatively, one can use software packages such as CSUITE to perform the modeling. Of course, all these alternatives require an investment, but there are great dividends to be had when achieving the best-possible performance from resources deployed in capacity, inventory, and ERP/MRP systems. To put it bluntly, if an executive spends millions of dollars on an ERP/MRP system, he or she should invest a little money making sure that it works as planned.

A LARGE COMPANY IMPLEMENTATION

The discussion in Chapter 8 provided extensive detail on implementation in a fairly small company, Arc Precision. Before closing, we provide a short description of an implementation at a large company for that segment of the audience involved in such organizations.

The vice president of manufacturing for a division of a leading multibillion-dollar medical equipment company was looking for a way to take his organization to the next level of performance. This case study describes the path the company took to deploy Factory Physics methods and software that resulted in in over 70 million dollars of savings in three years and an improved competitive position.

The vice president's division was recognized within the company for being at the leading edge of performance improvement, and the company is widely known for having a competitive edge in operations. This division had absorbed many productivity-improvement initiatives over the years, such as Theory of Constraints, Lean manufacturing, and Six Sigma. The problem that the company now faced was that there were too many gaps between how all the initiatives fit together and no coherent structure for understanding which method was appropriate for a given situation. A major benefit of the Factory Physics approach is the excellent clarity it provides in prioritizing where to improve. In addition, the Factory Physics approach provides predictive capability, allowing the company to quantitatively determine what benefits would be gained through implementation of improvements.

Factory Physics Inc. (FPI), engaged with the division in 2004 for an initial assessment for a plant in Spain. The vice president and one of his directors attended the initial assessment and, through intense questioning and observation, determined that the Factory Physics principles and implementation methods should indeed provide a competitive advantage for their operations. The results of the initial assessment were then presented at the division-wide operations management review in January 2005. Also in attendance at the management review was the vice president of manufacturing strategy for the entire company. The upshot was that the approach detailed through the initial assessment resulted in a global effort to train personnel and implement the Factory Physics approach.

Five target projects were chosen in Europe and two in the United States to serve as high-potential projects for training personnel. Additionally, other less mission-critical sites were selected, and over 20 candidates were chosen to become factory physicists. The title *factory physicist* is an FPI certification for operations professionals who have shown mastery of Factory Physics principles and have demonstrated significant results through application of the Factory Physics tools and techniques to company operations.

With plant visits to the high-potential sites by FPI personnel and quarterly review sessions with the remainder of the candidate factory physicists, the company has incorporated the Factory Physics approach into its culture. The initiative has provided a massive return on investment, with many of the improvements being realized within the first six months. Examples of results provided include:

- Increased throughput of 30 percent
- Major avoidance of capital expenditures through increased throughput from high-demand facilities
- Reduction in inventory investment
- Clarification of best applications for Lean and Six Sigma projects

In summary, the Factory Physics implementation provided a framework and the tools to enable the company's operations professionals to build on their years of experience and advance the control, optimization, and profitability of their processes to the highest levels possible.

ALTERNATIVE HISTORIES

In our attempt to compare and contrast the Factory Physics approach to Lean and other methods, it might appear that we have been overly critical of those companies that have led in these efforts. It may not have been possible to avoid such criticism, but we were certainly not suggesting that these previous methodologies were somehow rash or absurd. The creators of these systems, particularly the Toyota Production system and, thereby, Lean, had an incredibly deep understanding and intuition of the way production systems behave and of the effects of variability on such systems. Our primary criticism is that they did not communicate that understanding effectively. Ohno and Shingo wrote very short books and provided no scientific description and very little details.

The plethora of books that followed focused mostly on details but with, again, little scientific description. These defects made the methods difficult to transplant into different business environments except by inserting a literal copy of the system into the new situation which may or may not have been appropriate.

Let's consider what might have happened if first, Toyota had employed Factory Physics science and then if Boeing had done the same. We believe that if Ohno had had the basic understanding offered by Factory Physics science, he would have developed essentially the same Toyota Production System but would have done it in several years instead of 25. We believe Ohno would have made two fundamental changes. He already knew that Toyota could not compete with the large lot sizes used by his American competitors. But instead of developing a *kanban* "supermarket," Ohno would have implemented CONWIP because it is simpler and accomplishes the same objective of controlling WIP. Instead of rigorously setting aside 2 hours for every 12 hours, he would have made use of recourse capacity only when it was needed. Making these two changes would have reduced costs by avoiding wasted capacity set aside for problems that may or may not happen. He would have also reduced inventory since CONWIP does not maintain a stock of every part but only what is needed in WIP.

If Boeing had followed this version of the Toyota production system, it would have realized that the secret of profitable production did not require a moving assembly line. It would have more profitably employed the three buffers of inventory, time, and capacity and focused on increasing capacity to realize the most revenue with the highest possible return on investment. This would involve a focus on process improvements such as systems to drill holes more accurately and by externalizing other processes such as prebundling wiring harnesses so that these could be done in parallel. They would have focused on coordinating the sequence of subassembly production with optimal investments in inventory and capacity rather than trying to set a takt for the entire factory. By doing these things, they would have increased the output of the plant by reducing the takt time without ever talking about a takt time. If the output goes up while the WIP stays constant, the overall cycle time will come down. Consequently, Boeing would have been able to increase output during the peak of demand *and* improve on-time delivery. This would have avoided the $250 million investment in a moving assembly line while moving as quickly as was possible to achieve the objectives of highest possible cash flow and profit.

THE FUTURE

We have presented the Factory Physics approach based on the science of operations and characterized by five fundamental steps:

1. Understand the environment.
2. Visualize and choose strategy.
3. Develop and quantify tactics.
4. Execute using feedback controls and SPC-type control limits.
5. Monitor using measures aligned with strategy.

This approach, graphically illustrated in Figure 10-5, offers executives a mechanism to understand their business environments so that they can choose strategy, develop tactics, and execute with controls connecting performance with strategy. As discussed much earlier, a strategy is a plan of action designed to achieve a specific end. Executive strategy typically involves long-term, large-investment decisions such as: "What are our markets?" and "What is our technology?" and "How much installed capacity do we need?" Tactics are policies or actions implemented to accomplish a task or objective.

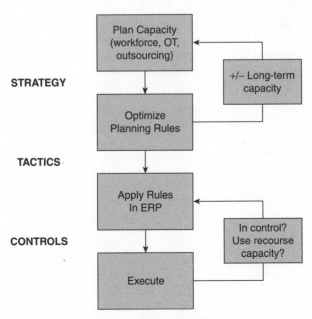

FIGURE 10-5. The Factory Physics approach

Management tactics typically involve medium-term decisions such as "What do we need to make or buy?" "When do we need to make or buy it?" and "Do we need recourse capacity?" Tactics are often deployed with planning rules the organization follows and often puts into its ERP systems. Controls in an operations world are methods or systems used to implement tactics for achieving desired performance. Controls manage such things as, "Is demand within planned limits?" "Is inventory within limits?" and "Is WIP below its maximum limit?"

Before the development of Factory Physics science, there really was no way to directly link strategy to tactics and controls. In the past, executives set strategy, and lower-level managers tried to implement it—sometimes with success and sometimes not. In the past, there was no way to determine whether a given strategy was even feasible, not to mention profitable. But now that Factory Physics science is not only a proven theory but also a proven practice, it is time to move past the *innovation by imitation* and *software solves all* approaches that have dominated the landscape for the past 25 years or longer to provide strategies, tactics, and controls that are suited to each particular company and each particular division within the company.

As Winston Churchill once said, "Success is not final, failure is not fatal: it is the courage to continue that counts." We look forward to your continuing work to improve manufacturing, service, and supply-chain operations performance. Operations performance improvement has been a large part of civilization's advancement over the last 200 hundred years. It is a noble effort.

For more information on Factory Physics science and resources to help in your application of the concepts, visit the Factory Physics website at www.factoryphysics.com.

Notes

Chapter 1

1. http://www.nas.edu/evolution/TheoryOrFact.html.

2. Henry Ford and Samuel Crowther, *My Life and Work*, New York: Doubleday, Page, 1922.

3. W. J. Hopp and M. L. Spearman, *Factory Physics*, 3rd ed., Long Grove IL: Waveland Press, 2008.

4. http://www.epa.gov/lean/environment/studies/gm.htm.

5. "Bulletproof Quality Came Only After a Long Struggle." *Automotive News*, October 2007; available at http://www.autonews.com/apps/pbcs.dll/article?AID=/20071029/ANA03/710290347#axzz2dYX6Cw9F.

6. Alan Robinson,*Modern Approaches to Manufacturing Improvement: The Shingo System*, New York: Productivity Press, 1990, p. 54.

7. From Roberta Russell and Bernard Taylor, *Operations Management*, 3rd ed. For website, see http://www.prenhall.com/divisions/bp/app/russellcd/PROTECT/CHAPTERS/CHAP15/HEAD01.HTM.

8. S. S. Chakravorty, "Where Process-Improvement Projects Go Wrong," *Wall Street Journal*, June 14, 2012.

9. "Why Lean Programs Fail—Where Toyota Succeeds: A New Culture of Learning," *Forbes*, February 5, 2011.

10. *APICS Dictionary*, 13th ed., Chicago: Association for Operations Management; available at: http://www.apics.org/dictionary/dictionary-information?ID=3286.

11. Boeing Annual Reports for 2003–2009; available at: www.boeing.com.

12. http://www.boeing.com/boeing/commercial/777family/777movingline.page.

13. http://www.youtube.com/watch?v=huDo9138ncg.

14. Bill Vogt, "What You Can Do When You Have To." *Target* 15(1st Quarter): 6–8, 1999; Bill Vogt, "The Production Runs of the Century: A Comparison of Plant II and Willow Run," *Target* 15(1st Quarter): 9–21, 1999.

Chapter 2

1. PW 2013 Presentation, "Process Excellence at Jabil: Intelligent BPM and Real-Time Lean Six Sigma," available at http://www.pega.com/resources/pw-2013-presentation-process-excellence-at-jabil-intelligent-bpm-and-real-time-lean-six.

2. Ibid.

Chapter 3

1. A. E. Jinha, "Article 50 Million: An Estimate of the Number of Scholarly Articles in Existence," Learned Publishing, 23(3):258–263, 2010. doi:10.1087/20100308.

2. Readers may be familiar with the debate between Thomas Kuhn and Karl Popper concerning the nature of science. We discuss this in more detail in Chapter 10.

3. M. George, *Lean Six Sigma: Combining Six Sigma Quality with Lean Production Speed,* New York: McGraw-Hill, 2002, p. 43.

4. Ibid.

5. Sir Isaac Newton and John Machin, *The Mathematical Principles of Natural Philosophy*, Vol. 1, p. 19, translated by Andrew Motte, (1729), available as Google eBook, http://books.google.com/books?id=Tm0FAAAAQAAJ&source=gbs_navlinks_s.

6. http://www.merriam-webster.com/dictionary/intuition.

7. Larry Bossidy and Ram Charan, *Execution: The Discipline of Getting Things Done,* Houston, TX: Crown Business, 2002.

8. J. D. C. Little, "A Proof for the Queuing Formula: $L = \lambda W$," *Operations Research* 9(3):383–320, 1961.

9. M. L. Spearman, D. L. Woodruff, and W. J. Hopp, "CONWIP: A Pull Alternative to Kanban," *International Journal of Production Research* 28(5):879–894, 1990.

Chapter 4

1. *Close* is relative and is further away when dealing with variances than when dealing with means. In other words, the variance is a less accurate measure than the mean. This should not be surprising because the variance is measuring how *variable* the data are—a measurement that is inherently variable itself.

2. Although we are making a distinction between *lead time* and *replenishment time*, many authors call both *lead time*.

Chapter 6

1. Wikipeida, http://en.wikipedia.org/wiki/Policy.

Chapter 9

1. M. Rother and J. Shook, *Learning to See: Value-Stream Mapping to Create Value and Eliminate Muda,* Version 1.3, Cambridge, MA: Lean Enterprise Institute, June 2003.

2. J. Orlicky, *Material Requirements Planning: The New Way of Life in Production and Inventory Management,* New York: McGraw-Hill, 1975.

3. H. F. Dickie, "ABC Inventory Analysis Shoots for Dollars," *Factory Management and Maintenance,* July 1951.

Chapter 10

1. Massimo Pigliucci, "Popper vs. Kuhn: The Battle for Understanding How Science Works," *Skeptical Inquirer* 35(4):23–24, 2011.

Acknowledgments

We would like to acknowledge and thank Wally Hopp for his influence on all of us. We acknowledge some of the key leaders featured, perhaps not by name, in the book. These include Jim Blumenschein, Larry Doerr, Bill Fierle, Kennedy Frierson, Jeffrey Korman, Matt Levatich, Jim Lind, Andrew Lux, Giulio Noccioli, Gus Pagonis, Zane Rakes, Vance Scott, Chandra Sekhar, Mike Severson, Eric Stebbins, Clayton Steffensen, Joan Tafoya, Bill Vansant. We acknowledge the contributions of all the individuals and companies deploying the Factory Physics framework. We thank Jeffrey Krames for his role in guiding us through the publishing process.

Index

About the Authors

Edward S. Pound is chief operations officer at Factory Physics Inc.

Jeffrey H. Bell is a managing partner of Arc Precision, a supplier of precision-engineered components to the medical device industry. He also serves on the advisory board of Factory Physics Inc.

Mark L. Spearman, Ph.D., is the founder, president, and CEO of Factory Physics Inc. and coauthor of the previously published textbook *Factory Physics*.